# MYP Life Sciences

**A concept-based approach**

Andrew Allott

OXFORD
UNIVERSITY PRESS

OXFORD
UNIVERSITY PRESS

Great Clarendon Street, Oxford, OX2 6DP, United Kingdom

Oxford University Press is a department of the University of Oxford. It furthers the University's objective of excellence in research, scholarship, and education by publishing worldwide. Oxford is a registered trade mark of Oxford University Press in the UK and in certain other countries



First published in 2019



British Library Cataloguing in Publication Data
Data available

978-0-19-836997-4

10 9 8 7 6 5 4 3 2 1

Paper used in the production of this book is a natural, recyclable product made from wood grown in sustainable forests. The manufacturing process conforms to the environmental regulations of the country of origin.

Printed in China by Golden Cup

**Acknowledgements**

The author would like to thank David Mindorff for the valuable contributions that he made to this book. The author would also like to thank the editor, Ben Rout, for his diligent and highly professional work.

The authors and publisher are grateful for permission to reprint the following copyright material:

**Earthwatch Institute**: excerpt from 'Climate Change in Wytham Woods 2017', reprinted by permission of Earthwatch Institute (Europe)

**Dr Yaniv Erlich**: two quotations from article 'How DNA could store all the world's data in a semi-trailer' by Chloe Cornish, 5 February 2018, *Financial Times*, reprinted by permission of the *Financial Times* and Dr Yaniv Erlich.

**Martin T. G., Chadès I., Arcese P., Marra P. P., Possingham H. P., Norris D. R.**: excerpt from article 'Optimal Conservation of Migratory Species', 15 August 2007, copyright © 2007 Martin et al., this is an open-access article distributed under the terms of the Creative Commons Attribution License.

**Jim Lovell**: quotation by Jim Lovell, crew member of the Apollo 8 spacecraft, from the transcript of audiotapes of the Apollo 8 telecast, December 24, 1968, page 277/1, National Archives, Records of the National Aeronautics and Space Administration.

The publishers would like to thank the following for permissions to use their photographs:

**Cover**: Sarah Peters/Getty Images; **p2(tl)**: Inspirestock Inc./Alamy Stock Photo; **p2(br)**: Ian Dagnall/Alamy Stock Photo; **p3(t)**: Courtesy of the author; **p3(bl)**: Bodom/Shutterstock; **p4**: Mikael Damkier/Shutterstock; **p5(l)**: SCOTT CAMAZINE / SCIENCE PHOTO LIBRARY; **p5(r)**: MOLEKUUL / SCIENCE PHOTO LIBRARY; **p5(b)**: Photo courtesy of 3D Molecular Designs.; **p7(t)**: VOLKER STEGER / SCIENCE PHOTO LIBRARY; **p7(c)**: tornadoflight/Shutterstock; **p7(bl)**: Science History Images/Alamy Stock Photo; **p9(t)**: Jason Winter/Shutterstock; **p9(c)**: Rhey T. Snodgrass and Victor F. Camp/Wikimedia; **p9(b)**: World History Archive/Alamy Stock Photo; **p10(tl)**: Isak55/Shutterstock; **p10(cl)**: Benjamin Albiach Galan/Shutterstock; **p10(cr)**: Viacheslav shpenyk/Shutterstock; **p11(tr)**: DR GOPAL MURTI / SCIENCE PHOTO LIBRARY; **p11(br)**: Agarianna76/Shutterstock; **p11(bl)**: Courtesy of the author; **p12**: Illustration by David S. Goodsell, RCSB Protein Data Bank.; **p13(t)**: Illustration by David S. Goodsell, RCSB Protein Data Bank.; **p13(c)**: Jacek Chabraszewski/Shutterstock; **p14(cl)**: ALFRED PASIEKA / SCIENCE PHOTO LIBRARY; **p14(cr)**: Jose Luis Calvo/Shutterstock; **p15(t)**: AB Forces News Collection/Alamy Stock Photo; **p16(tl)**: Chadsikan Tawanthaisong/Shutterstock; **p16(tr)**: LDprod/Shutterstock; **p16(cl)**: wavebreakmedia/Shutterstock; **p16(cr)**: Sergey Dubrov/Shutterstock; **p16(bl)**: B-D-S Piotr Marcinski/Shutterstock; **p16(br)**: Mykola Churpita/Shutterstock; **p17(c)**: PhotoAlto/Alamy Stock Photo; **p17(bt)**: Gregory F. Maxwell <gmaxwell@gmail.com> PGP:0xB0413BFA/Wikimedia Commons; **p17(bc)**: FDBB2AMedStockPhotos/Alamy Stock Photo; **p17(bb)**: Cultura Creative (RF)/Alamy Stock Photo; **p19(t, c)**: Courtesy of the author; **p20(t)**: Wavebreakmedia/Shutterstock; **p20(b)**: EQUINOX GRAPHICS/SCIENCE PHOTO LIBRARY; **p22**: Andre Blais/Shutterstock; **p24(tl)**: Ron Yue/Alamy Stock Photo; **p24(br)**: Nnigel Westwood/Alamy Stock Photo; **p25(t)**: Edmund Sumner-VIEW/Alamy Stock Photo; **p25(b)**: Lisa F. Young/Shutterstock; **p27(t)**: MarcelClemens/Shutterstock; **p27(cr)**: Getty Images; **p27(cl)**: Blickwinkel/Alamy Stock Photo; **p28(t)**: The Granger Collection/Alamy Stock Photo; **p28(b)**: Martin Shields/Alamy Stock Photo; **p29(t)**: Granger Historical Picture Archive/Alamy Stock Photo; **p29(c)**: IngridHS/Shutterstock; **p31**: Telia/Shutterstock; **p33(t)**: BIOPHOTO ASSOCIATES/SCIENCE PHOTO LIBRARY; **p32(t)**: Komsan Loonprom/Shutterstock; **p32(b)**: Courtesy of the author; **p34**: J.C. REVY, ISM/SCIENCE PHOTO LIBRARY; **p36(t, b ), 37(t, c)**: Bill and Nancy Malcolm, nancym@clear.net.nz; **p37(b)**: DR GOPAL MURTI/SCIENCE PHOTO LIBRARY; **p38**: Image courtesy of William Bourland ; **p39(t)**: WIM VAN EGMOND/SCIENCE PHOTO LIBRARY; **p39(b)**: Lebendkulturen.de/Shutterstock; **p40**: Courtesy of the author; **p43**: Stocktrek Images, Inc./Alamy Stock Photo; **p45(t)**: MARILYN SCHALLER/SCIENCE PHOTO LIBRARY; **p45(b)**: Artem Povarov/Alamy Stock Photo; **p46(t)**: Ian Patrick/Alamy Stock Photo; **p46(b)**: Milsamil/Shutterstock; **p47(t)**: Sergey Uryadnikov/Shutterstock; **p47(b)**: Nigel McCall; **p48(bl)**: Tish1/Shutterstock; **p48(br)**: Max Herman/Shutterstock; **p49(t)**: KARL H. SWITAK/SCIENCE PHOTO LIBRARY; **p49(b)**: Thieury/Shutterstock; **p51**: Bon Appetit/Alamy; **p52**: Shutterstock; **p53, 54**: Courtesy of the author; **p55**: Action Plus Sports Images/Alamy Stock Photo; **p56(c)**: Monkey Business Images/Shutterstock; **p56(bc)**: Leo Mason/Corbis; **p56(bl)**: Maxisport/Shutterstock; **p56(br)**: Stocksnapper/Alamy Stock Photo; **p57(t)**: LAGUNA DESIGN/SCIENCE PHOTO LIBRARY; **p57(c)**: Ibreakstock/Shutterstock; **p57(b)**: Christi Tolbert/Shutterstock; **p58**: OUP; **p59**: Aleksander Gamme; **p60(t)**: Bill Malcolm; **p60(c)**: Studiomode/Alamy Stock Photo; **p61**: Alice-photo/Shutterstock; **p62(tl)**: Getty Photodisc; **p62(c)**: Divedog/Shutterstock; **p62(b)**: Bertl123/Shutterstock; **p63(tr)**: DPL/Alamy Stock Photo; **p63(tl)**: Marcelo Casimiro Cavalcante; **p63(br)**: Bolbras/Wikimedia; **p63(bl)**: HT-Pix/Shutterstock; **p66(t)**: Blickwinkel/Alamy Stock Photo; **p66(b)**: Juniors Bildarchiv GmbH/Alamy Stock Photo; **p67(t)**: Marco Maggesi/Shutterstock; **p67(b)**: Jason Bazzano/Alamy Stock Photo; **p69(t)**: 6 editions of 'The Origin of Species' by C. Darwin,. Credit: Wellcome Collection. CC BY; **p69(b)**: National Geographic Image Collection/Alamy Stock Photo; **p71(t)**: Stephen Barlow; **p70(b)**: Shinichi Nakahara/Florida Museum; **p70(t)**: Boaz Rottem/Alamy Stock Photo; **p71(c)**: Robert Wyatt/Alamy Stock Photo; **p71(b)**: Anthony Wallbank/Alamy Stock Photo; **p72(tr)**: Shutterstock; **p72(c)**: David Osborn/Alamy Stock Photo; **p72(tl)**: CrispyPork/Shutterstock; **p73(l)**: NOAA; **p73(r)**: MIA TEGNER/SCIENCE PHOTO LIBRARY; **p74(tl, tr)**: Renee Lopez; **p74(cl)**: DR T E THOMPSON/SCIENCE PHOTO LIBRARY; **p74(cr)**: PHILIPPE PSAILA/SCIENCE PHOTO LIBRARY; **p74(bl)**: CAROLINA BIOLOGICAL SUPPLY CO, VISUALS UNLIMITED/SCIENCE PHOTO LIBRARY; **p74(br)**: HERVE CONGE, ISM/SCIENCE PHOTO LIBRARY; **p75**: Les Hickok; **p77(l)**: Science Photo Library/Alamy Stock Photo; **p77(r)**: Cultura RM/Alamy Stock Photo; **p79(bl)**: Minden Pictures/Alamy Stock Photo; **p79(br)**: Buiten-Beeld/Alamy Stock Photo; **p80(t)**: Aurora Photos/Alamy Stock Photo; **p80(c)**: BIOSPHOTO/Alamy Stock Photo; **p80(b)**: Stephen Barlow; **p81(t)**: HHelene/Shutterstock; **p81(c)**: Tim Gainey/Alamy Stock Photo; **p81(b, t)**: Courtesy of the author; **p82**: Radharc Images/Alamy Stock Photo; **p83(cl)**: Arco Images GmbH/Alamy Stock Photo; **p83(cr)**: RICHARD G. RAWLINS, CUSTOM MEDICAL STOCK PHOTO/SCIENCE PHOTO LIBRARY; **p87(tl)**: Courtesy of the author; **p87(tr)**: Jane Gould/Alamy Stock Photo; **p87(cl)**: Science Photo Library/Alamy Stock Photo; **p87(c)**: Courtesy of the author; **p87(cr)**: Juliet Blankespoor; **p87(bl)**: Stephen Barlow; **p88(bl)**: Susan & Allan Parker/Alamy Stock Photo; **p88(br)**: Blickwinkel/Alamy Stock Photo; **p92(t)**: Eco2drew/iStockphoto; **p92(b)**: Molekuul_be/Shutterstock; **p93(b)**: Mkant/Shutterstock; **p94**: Seyms Brugger/Shutterstock; **p95(tl)**: Brian A Jackson/Shutterstock; **p95(tr)**: Blickwinkel/Alamy Stock Photo; **p95(cl)**: Stanislav Fosenbauer/Shutterstock; **p95(cr)**: Marta Jonina/Shutterstock; **p95(bl)**: MJTH/Shutterstock; **p95(br)**: IreneuszB/Shutterstock; **p96(t)**: BioMedical/Shutterstock; **p96(bl)**: DON W. FAWCETT/SCIENCE PHOTO LIBRARY; **p96(br)**: DR. ALVIN TELSER, VISUALS UNLIMITED/SCIENCE PHOTO LIBRARY; **p97**: Six Red Marbles/Oxford University Press; **p98(t)**: Fir Mamat/Alamy Stock Photo; **p98(bl)**: STEVE GSCHMEISSNER/SCIENCE PHOTO LIBRARY; **p98(br)**: EDWARD KINSMAN/SCIENCE PHOTO LIBRARY; **p99**: Puwadol Jaturawutthichai/Shutterstock; **p100(t)**: PATRICK LANDMANN/SCIENCE PHOTO LIBRARY; **p100(b)**: Sebastien bonaime/Alamy Stock Photo; **p102(t)**: THOMAS DEERINCK, NCMIR/SCIENCE PHOTO LIBRARY; **p102(b)**: Allison Herreid/Shutterstock; **p103**: OpenStax College/Anatomy & Physiology, Connexions Web site. http://cnx.org/content/col11496/1.6/, Jun 19, 2013./Wikimedia; **p104**: Goodluz/Shutterstock; **p105**: BruceBlaus/Wikimedia; **p108(b)**: NASA Goddard Space Flight Center; **p108(t)**: Lloyd Homer, GNS Science; **p109**: Courtesy of the author; **p110**: AfriPics.com/Alamy Stock Photo; **p111(b)**: Ori Fragman-Sapir; **p111(t)**: Courtesy of the author; **p112**: BMJ/Shutterstock; **p113(tl)**: Granger Historical Picture Archive / Alamy Stock Photo; **p113(tr)**: Nature Photographers Ltd/Alamy Stock Photo; **p113(c)**: PhotoStock-Israel/Alamy Stock Photo; **p114**: Dpa picture alliance archive/Alamy Stock Photo; **p115**: Award-winning online butcher farmison.com; **p116(t)**: Max Planck Institute for Ornithology; **p116(bl)**: Arto Hakola/Shutterstock; **p117(tl)**: WILDLIFE GmbH/Alamy Stock Photo; **p117(cl)**: Dinodia Photos / Alamy Stock Photo; **p116(br)**: McPhoto/Trunk/Alamy Stock Photo; **p117(tr)**: Minden Pictures/Alamy Stock Photo; **p117(cr)**: Scooperdigital/Shutterstock; **p117(b)**: Keith Douglas/Alamy Stock Photo; **p118**: Ryan M. Bolton/Alamy Stock Photo; **p119**: Courtesy of the author; **p120**: Jonathan Knopp; **p122(t)**: Photo courtesy of Robert Wallis <who has given his permission>; **p122(b)**: Rehman Asad/Alamy Stock Photo; **p124(t)**: UlyssePixel/Alamy Stock Photo; **p123(t)**: KGPA Ltd/Alamy Stock Photo; **p123(b)**: Alexander Turnbull Library, Wellington, New Zealand.; **p124(b)**: Christopher Reed/Alamy Stock Photo; **p125(bl)**: Cephas/Wikimedia; **p125(br)**: Copyright Carnegie Institute, Carnegie Museum of Natural History; **p128(t)**: Eye35/Alamy Stock Photo; **p128(b)**: © 2019 Calder Foundation, New York / Artists Rights Society (ARS), New York; p129(t): Wikimedia Commons; **p129(b)**: Carlos Mora / Alamy Stock Photo; **p130**: Nature Picture Library/Alamy Stock Photo; **p131(c)**: Teresa Otto/Shutterstock; **p131(b)**: imageBROKER/Alamy Stock Photo; **p131(t)**: Mark Miller Photos/Getty Images; **p132**: Daniel Mayer/Wikimedia; **p135(t)**: Robin Runck/Alamy Stock Photo; **p135(c)**: Francesco Veronesi, https://www.flickr.com/photos/francesco_veronesi/25288199298/Wikimedia Commons; **p135(b)**: Courtesy of the author; **p136(t)**: Soru Epotok/Shutterstock; **p136(b)**: Chris2766/Shutterstock; **p136**: Data from Wytham Woods: Oxford Ecological Laboratory, Oxford University Press, 2011; **p137(c)**: Dancestrokes/Shutterstock; **p137(br)**: Judy Gallagher; https://www.flickr.com/photos/52450054@N04/8505045055//Wikimedia; **p137(bl)**: TTphoto/Shutterstock; **p137(bc)**: Shutterstock; **p138(tr)**: Giancarlo Liguori/Shutterstock; **p138(cr)**: Geoff Gallice/Wikimedia; **p138(cl)**: Amazon-Images/Alamy Stock Photo; **p138(tl)**: © Corel Corporation 1994; **p140(tl)**: CENTRE FOR INFECTIONS/PUBLIC HEALTH ENGLAND/SCIENCE PHOTO LIBRARY; **p140(tr)**: Cosmin Manci/Shutterstock; **p140(cl)**: Stephen Barlow; **p140(cr)**: Sergey Uryadnikov/Shutterstock; **p144**: Getty Images; **p145(c, b)**: Colin Munro; **p146(t)**: Kate Bronner; **p146(b)**: Velela/Wikimedia; **p147(t)**: NASA/Johns Hopkins APL/Steve Gribben; **p147(b)**: NASA; **p148**: Gregory Johnston/Shutterstock; **p149**: Rich Carey/Shutterstock; **p150(t)**: DR KEN MACDONALD/SCIENCE PHOTO LIBRARY; **p150(b)**: SINCLAIR STAMMERS/SCIENCE PHOTO LIBRARY; **p152**: D. Kucharski K. Kucharska/Shutterstock; **p153**: North American Forests. Produced by Canadian Forest Service (CFS), US Forest Service (USFS) and the Comisión Nacional Forestal (CONAFOR). Published by the North American Forestry Commission (NAFC) Inventory and Monitoring Working Group in partnership with the Commission on Environmental Cooperation (CEC), 2011. < http://www.cec.org/tools-and-resources/map-files/north-american-forests-2011; **p154(t)**: Picturepartners/Shutterstock; **p154(b)**: Artit Wongpradu/Shutterstock; p155: Photographee.eu/Shutterstock; **p156(t)**: Courtesy of the author; **p156(c)**: Tamara Potter; **p156(b)**: J.M. Sarneel, Umeå 2014; **p157**: Ibreakstock/Shutterstock; **p160**: CHRISTIAN JEGOU PUBLIPHOTO DIFFUSION/SCIENCE PHOTO LIBRARY; **p162**: FloridaStock/Shutterstock; **p164, 165**: University of Birmingham, BIFoR; **p166(t)**: Cactus.man/Wikimedia; **p166(b)**: The Schøyen Collection, Oslo and London/MS 5328; **p167(t)**: World History Archive/Alamy Stock Photo; **p167(b)**: ClassicStock/Alamy Stock Photo; **p168**: René & Peter van der Krogt, http://statues.vanderkrogt.net; **p170(tl)**: Rita Kochmarjova/Shutterstock; **p170(tr)**: Arterra Picture Library/Alamy Stock Photo; **p170(cl)**: Tierfotoagentur/Alamy Stock Photo; **p170(cr)**: Bob Langrish/Alamy Stock Photo; **p171(t)**: Ivonne Wierink/Shutterstock; **p171(b)**: Sebastian Kaulitzki/Shutterstock; **p172(a-h)**: Courtesy of the author; **p173(t)**: WaterFrame/Alamy Stock Photo; **p173(b)**: Tom Roche/Shutterstock; **p174(t)**: Friedrich Stark/Alamy Stock Photo; **p174(b)**: ERIC LAFFORGUE/Alamy Stock Photo; **p175(t)**: ARCTIC IMAGES/Alamy Stock Photo; **p175(b)**: Nigel Cattlin/Alamy Stock Photo; **p176(t)**: Stephen Barlow; **p176(b)**: Norma Jean Gargasz/Alamy Stock Photo; **p178(tl)**: Stephen Barlow; **p178(tr)**: Ggw1962/Shutterstock; **p178(b)**: Minden Pictures/Alamy Stock Photo; **p179**: Classic Image / Alamy Stock Photo; **p180**: Wikimedia Commons; **p182**: © Dr Mark Hill 2019, UNSW Embryology ISBN: 978 0 7334 2609 4 - UNSW CRICOS Provider Code No. 00098G; **p183**: Archive PL/Alamy Stock Photo; **p184**: Catmando/Shutterstock; **p185(b)**: Nicolas Primola/Shutterstock; **p185(t)**: Tayfun Sertan Yaman/Alamy Stock Photo; **p186(t)**: FLPA/Alamy Stock Photo; **p186(c)**: Dinoton/Shutterstock; **p186(bl)**: Ann Baldwin/Shutterstock; **p186(br)**: Steffen Foerster/123rf; p189: Photographer's Choice/Getty Images.

Artwork by QBS Media Services Inc.

Every effort has been made to contact copyright holders of material reproduced in this book. Any omissions will be rectified in subsequent printings if notice is given to the publisher.

# Contents

# Introduction

The MYP Life Sciences course, like all MYP Sciences, is inquiry based. To promote conceptual understanding, the MYP uses key concepts and related concepts. Key concepts represent big ideas that are relevant across disciplines. The key concepts used in MYP Sciences are change, relationships and systems. Related concepts are more specific to each subject and help to promote more detailed exploration. Each chapter is focused on a topic area in Life Sciences, one key concept and two or three of the 12 related concepts.

The nine chapters in this book do not form a fixed linear sequence. They form a 3×3 matrix, organized by key concept:

| Relationships | Systems | Change |
|---|---|---|
| Genes | Cells | Food |
| Reproduction | Organisms | Migration |
| Communities | Ecosystems | Evolution |

There are many different ways of navigating through this matrix. The ideal route will depend on students' ages and any additional requirements from the local science curriculum.

The objectives of MYP Science are categorized into four criteria, which contain descriptions of specific targets that are accomplished as a result of studying MYP Science:

**A.** Knowing and understanding

**B.** Inquiring and designing

**C.** Processing and evaluating

**D.** Reflecting on the impacts of science

Within each chapter, we have included activities designed to promote achievement of these objectives, such as experiments and data-based questions. We have also included activities designed to promote development of approaches to learning skills. The summative assessment found at the end of each chapter is framed by a statement of inquiry relating the concepts addressed to one of the six global contexts and features both multiple-choice questions and questions that require longer answers.

Overall, this book is meant to guide a student's exploration of Life Sciences and aid development of specific skills that are essential for academic success and getting the most out of this educational experience.

# How to use this book

To help you get the most out of your book, here is an overview of its features.

## Concepts, global context and statement of inquiry

The key and related concepts, the global context and the statement of inquiry used in each chapter are clearly listed on the introduction page.

 ## Activities

A range of activities that encourage you to think further about the topics you studied, research these topics and build connections between life sciences and other disciplines.

 Vocabulary features are designed to introduce and familiarize you with the key terms you will need to know when studying the life sciences.

## Experiments

Practical activities that help you develop skills for assessment criteria B & C.

 ## Data-based questions

These questions allow you to test your factual understanding of life sciences, as well as study and analyse data. Data-based questions help you prepare for assessment criteria A, B & C.

## ATL Skills

These approaches to learning sections introduce new skills or give you the opportunity to reflect on skills you might already have. They are mapped to the MYP skills clusters and are aimed at supporting you become an independent learner.

 ## Community project feature

Community project features show how you can apply your understanding of science to make a positive impact on the community and collaborate with others through community service.

## Summative assessment

There is a summative assessment at the end of each chapter; this covers all four MYP assessment criteria.

# Mapping grid

This table shows you which key concept, related concepts, global context and statement of inquiry guide the learning in each chapter.

| Chapter | Key concept | Related concepts | Global context | Statement of inquiry | ATL skills |
|---|---|---|---|---|---|
| **1 Genes** | Relationships | Consequences Models Patterns | Identities and relationships | Patterns in human identity that we see around the world are a consequence of both ancestral relationships and environment influences. | **Communication skills:** Organize and depict information logically <br><br> **Communication skills:** Negotiating skills |
| **2 Cells** | Systems | Function Balance Models | Scientific and technical innovation | Discoveries made using new techniques can change our understanding of the natural world. | **Creativity and innovation:** Making guesses |
| **3 Food** | Change | Energy Transformation | Globalization and sustainability | We will need to change how we transform materials and energy to achieve sustainable production and equitable distribution of food in the 21st century. | **Information literacy skills:** Present information in a variety of formats <br> **Media literacy skills:** Evaluating websites <br> **Communication skills:** Interpreting discipline-specific terms |
| **4 Reproduction** | Relationships | Consequences Form Patterns | Personal and cultural expression | The relationships between specific organisms are affected by their form of reproduction. | **Information literacy skills:** Present information in a variety of formats and platforms |
| **5 Organisms** | Systems | Form Function | Identities and relationships | Human identity includes the impulse to help family members and also those we are not closely related to. | **Collaboration skills:** Working effectively with others |

| Chapter | Key concept | Related concepts | Global context | Statement of inquiry | ATL skills |
|---|---|---|---|---|---|
| **6 Migration** | Change | Energy Evidence Movement | Orientation in space and time | Evidence can be used to detect changes in the spatial patterns of migrating birds. | **Critical thinking skills**: Evaluating evidence |
| **7 Communities** | Relationships | Interaction Balance | Fairness and development | To achieve fairness, development must balance the needs of current communities with the needs of future communities. | **Collaboration skills**: Use social media networks appropriately to build and develop relationships |
| **8 Ecosystems** | Systems | Environment Interaction Movement | Globalization and sustainability | The Earth will become uninhabitable for humans and many other organisms if we continue to damage the environment. | **Reflection skills**: Consider ethical, cultural and environmental implications |
| **9 Evolution** | Change | Environment Evidence Transformation | Orientation in time and space | Evidence of past changes helps us to understand life today and how it might be transformed in the future. | **Affective skills**: Analyzing and attributing causes of failure |

A summary of how these chapters can be used to support Life Science Progression of disciplinary core ideas for Grades 6 to 8 (Middle School) in the Next Generation Science Standards is available on the support website (www.oxfordsecondary.com/myp-science-support).

# 1 Genes

> " O wad some Power the giftie gie us
> To see ourselves as others see us! "

◁ This is from Robert Burns' poem 'To a Louse'. Burns wrote this poem in his native Scottish dialect, which was an important part of his identity.
What are some typical thoughts we have when we see our image in the mirror?

▷ Artists give an answer to the question "Who am I?" in self-portraits. Rembrandt painted himself over 50 times during his long career. This self-portrait dates from the 1660s. What is Rembrandt telling us about himself?

▶ Cloud Gate in Chicago is a public sculpture by Anish Kapoor. Its outer mirrored surface reflects the city and the navel-like underside gives distorted reflections of those who venture there. Why do people find this so fascinating?

**Statement of inquiry:**

Patterns in human identity that we see around the world are a consequence of both ancestral relationships and environmental influences.

◀ Identity cards must be carried in some countries. These voter ID cards are used in India to prove who a person is, for example when voting in an election. ID cards usually include the person's name, passport photo, date and place of birth. Biometric data such as face, hand or iris measurements are increasingly included. What other information about our identity might be included in the future?

**Statement of inquiry:**

Patterns in human identity that we see around the world are a consequence of both ancestral relationships and environmental influences.

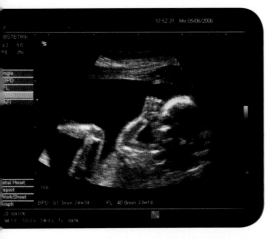

▲ A fetus in the uterus is largely shielded from the outside environment so development is mostly influenced by genes inherited from the baby's mother and father. There are some environmental influences—for example, babies whose mothers eat garlic during pregnancy are more likely to enjoy the taste of it in their childhood!

## Introduction

The question "Who am I?" does not usually concern young children much, but teenagers often become interested in it. It's a question of identity. The answer is all of the unchanging qualities that we have—things that don't vary depending on the time of day or our mood. Identity is both our similarities with other people and our distinctiveness. The life sciences help us to understand our identity by revealing how relatedness and differences are developed.

Genes influence how an organism looks and how it functions. No two organisms produced by sexual reproduction are likely to have exactly the same genes. Because of this, and also because of differences in the environment, organisms vary. We see this pattern of variation in animals, plants and any other sexually reproducing organism.

Genes are passed on from parent to offspring. They are located on chromosomes in the nucleus of cells. A chromosome has many genes on it. Individuals have two of each type of chromosome, one inherited from their mother and one from their father. These pairs of chromosomes carry the same genes but have different variants of some of the genes. Most genes control the production of a specific protein. The consequence of gene variants is differences in our proteins, which in turn affect the traits of an individual.

A human child inherits half of its genes from the mother and half from the father. When children grow up and reproduce, they pass on half their genes to each of their children. The half that they pass on is a random selection. For every gene where an individual has two different variants, either of them could be passed on, with a probability of 50%. There is therefore a strong element of chance in which of our traits we share with each of our parents.

Genes are made of DNA. Because of its small size, the structure and functioning of DNA has been investigated using models. Only identical twins have exactly the same DNA. Millions of people have had their DNA tested to find out more about their identity. From DNA we can learn about our ancestral origins, helping to answer the question "Who am I?".

## What is DNA?

The full name of DNA is deoxyribonucleic acid. It is a helical molecule and is composed of carbon, hydrogen, oxygen, nitrogen and phosphorus. It has two strands so is described as a double helix. Each strand has a chain of alternating sugar and phosphate units that we can think of as a backbone. A base is linked to each sugar in the backbone. The two strands are linked by their bases.

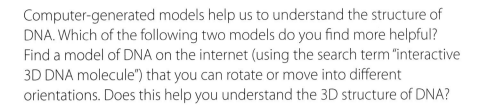

Computer-generated models help us to understand the structure of DNA. Which of the following two models do you find more helpful? Find a model of DNA on the internet (using the search term "interactive 3D DNA molecule") that you can rotate or move into different orientations. Does this help you understand the 3D structure of DNA?

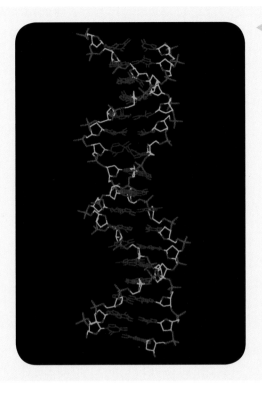

◄ In this model, bonds are shown but not atoms. Sugars are green, phosphates pink and bases are blue

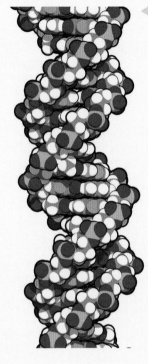

◄ In this model, atoms are shown but not bonds. Carbon is grey, hydrogen white, oxygen red, nitrogen blue and phosphorus yellow

 **Making models of DNA**

Model-making helped Crick and Watson to discover the structure of DNA. There are many ways to make physical models of the double helix.

- Go to http://pdb101.rcsb.org/learn/paper-models/dna and download the instructions for making a paper model.

- Buy a kit for making a plastic or Styrofoam model—there are many versions available.

- Make an edible model, for example from liquorice, mini marshmallows or fruit and toothpicks—instructions can be found on the internet.

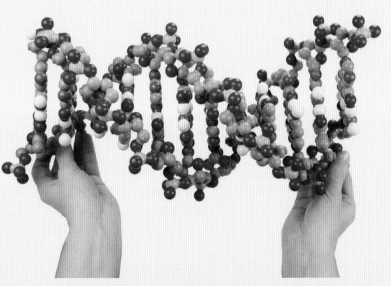

▲ This model was designed by the MSOE Center for BioMolecular Modeling in Milwaukee. Magnets inside the subunits allow the model to be assembled and disassembled easily

## How do we get samples of DNA?

Every living organism has DNA in its cells and there are simple methods that can be used to extract it. These are the stages in the extraction process:

1. The cells are burst open with a detergent, releasing the DNA.

2. Enzymes digest the proteins that are linked to the DNA.

3. A salt solution clumps together cell components apart from DNA.

4. The clumped cell components are separated from the DNA by spinning in a centrifuge.

5. Ice-cold ethanol is used to make the DNA precipitate.

Strands of DNA should then appear.

Any tissue from the human body can be used to get a DNA sample; however, the most convenient way is to scrape the inside of your mouth with a cotton swab. A single hair can also provide a sample as there are cells in the root of the hair. There are cells and therefore DNA in bodily fluids such as blood and urine. Anything that we have touched such as clothing and toothbrushes is likely to have some of our cells and therefore our DNA stuck on it. DNA can be obtained from long-dead material such as dodo remains in natural history museums or woolly mammoths buried in Siberian ice.

Tiny samples of DNA can be copied to produce enough DNA for analysis. This can be done using a process called PCR (polymerase chain reaction). PCR machines use a cycle of stages to double the amount of DNA. By carrying out 30–40 cycles, one copy of DNA can be increased to more than a billion and this only takes a few hours.

## What can we do with DNA?

Apart from identical twins, every person's DNA is different so it provides powerful evidence of identity. It also contains the instructions for how to make an organism. Here are some of the ways that DNA can be used.

### 1. Paternity

DNA is sometimes analyzed to test who the parents of a child are. Swabs are taken from the inside of a child's cheek and the possible parents. Genetic fingerprinting is then done on the DNA samples. Usually it is obvious who the mother is because she gave birth to the baby, but it may not be certain whose sperm fertilized the mother's egg, and therefore who the biological father is. There are also rare cases of babies becoming mixed up in hospital soon after birth. In cases like this, evidence is needed to show who both parents are.

> " A virus, a cucumber, an elephant, Donald Trump, whatever, you store the most important information in your life in your DNA. "
>
> *Yaniv Erlich, Associate Professor of Computer Science at Columbia University. (Source: Financial Times Ltd.)*

## 2. Forensics

Analysis can show whether or not two DNA samples came from the same person. This is useful in criminal investigations where it could show, for example, whether blood on a suspect's clothing is from the person who has been murdered. DNA from one hair found at a crime scene gives evidence that a suspect was there. Sometimes mass screening of DNA in a community is carried out to try to identify the perpetrator of a crime.

## 3. Ancestry

Analysis of DNA samples can test how closely related two people are, so it can help us construct a family tree to display our ancestors. As more and more people have their DNA tested and the results stored on databases, it is becoming increasingly possible to find out about our ethnic origins. DNA evidence can also be used to trace migration of populations.

## 4. De-extinction

Although it has yet to be done, it may be possible in the future to get DNA from an extinct species and use it to generate living members of this species again. This is most likely to be successful with recently extinct species such as the thylacine, Carolina parakeet and the woolly mammoth.

Are there any extinct animals that you would like to see alive again? If everyone in your class chooses a different animal, you could debate which animal is most worthy of de-extinction.

Samples of DNA have been obtained from bones of long-dead animals and from close relatives of humans. This bone of a Neanderthal from the Altai Mountains, more than 50,000 years old, is being prepared for DNA extraction. The biologist in the photo is wearing protective clothing to prevent contamination. What sort of contamination must be prevented?

Richard III of England was killed at the Battle of Bosworth in 1485. Until recently it was not known where he was buried, but in 2012 archaeologists discovered some remains under a car park in Leicester. DNA was obtained from the bones. There is one piece of DNA in humans that is always inherited from the mother. This type of DNA was found to be identical to a living person, who could trace their ancestry back many generations to Richard's mother. This is powerful evidence that these bones are Richard's—they are now placed in a tomb in Leicester Cathedral

The giant moa was 3.6 metres tall and lived in New Zealand until about 750 years ago when the Maoris arrived. Soon afterwards the giant moa and the other eight moa species became extinct

**Crime scene detective**

Detectives investigating crimes can get powerful evidence from **DNA fingerprinting**. This procedure is also called DNA profiling. It uses small pieces of DNA that are very variable between different people. The pieces of DNA are extracted from samples and are then separated in a sheet of gel. DNA from different samples moves in parallel strips across the gel and can then be compared. Each type of DNA appears as a dark band. If there is the same type of DNA in two samples, they will form bands at the same distance across the gel. The pattern of bands is the DNA fingerprint. This term is used because it is very unlikely that two people will have exactly the same pattern of bands unless they are identical twins.

The gel shown below is from the first crime investigation that was solved using DNA fingerprinting. Lanes **a–e** show DNA taken from the two victims of the crime. The two lanes labelled **s** show DNA from the blood of the prime suspect.

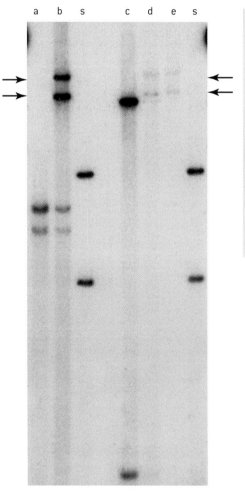

**a** = hair roots from victim 1

**b** = mixed bodily fluids from victim 1

**c** = blood of victim 2

**d** = swab taken from victim 2

**e** = bodily fluid stain from victim 2

**s** = blood of suspect

1. Do the DNA samples from the hair roots of victim 1 and the blood of victim 2 have any of the same bands?

2. Two bands are indicated by arrows on the gel. What is the origin of this DNA? Explain the evidence.

3. Was the suspect the person who committed the crime? Explain the evidence.

4. What would you have done next if you were investigating this crime?

**ABC** To find which person a sample of DNA came from, a method called **genetic fingerprinting** or **DNA fingerprinting** is used.

A **codon** is a sequence of three bases in the genetic code.

The **genetic code** is the meaning of the 64 different codons, which determines the sequence of amino acids in proteins.

**Cryptology**

Information is stored by DNA using a **genetic code**. Four bases, A, C, G and T, can be arranged in any sequence. Groups of three bases form codewords, called **codons**.

ATGGCCCTGTGGATGCGCCTCCTGCCCCTGCTGGCGCTGCTGGCCCTCT
GGGGACCTGACCCAGCCGCAGCCTTTGTGAACCAACACCTGTGCGGCT
CACACCTGGTGGAAGCTCTCTCCTAGTGTGCGGGGAACGAGGCTTCTTCT
ACACACCCAAGACCCGCCGGGAGGCAGAGGACCTGCAGGTGGGGCAGG
TGGAGCTGGGCGGGGGCCCTGGTGCAGGCAGCCTGCAGCCCTTGGCCCT
GGAGGGGTCCCTGCAGAAGCGTGGCATTGTGGAACAATGCTGTACCAGCA
TCTGCTCCCTCTACCAGCTGGAGAACTACTGCAAC

▲ Part of a binary file is shown here. A computer would read it as a series of bytes

▲ This base sequence contains information needed for making insulin in humans. ATG is the start codon and the code is read in groups of three bases from there onwards

1. How many different possible codons are there in the genetic code?

Computers use binary code where the codewords are combinations of ones and zeros.

2. a) How many possible codewords would there be if computers used groups of 3 ones or zeros?

   b) Computers use bytes, which are groups of 8 ones or zeros. How many different bytes are there?

3. Compare and contrast Morse code (right) with the genetic code and computer code.

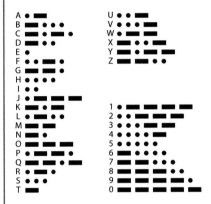

▲ Morse code was used for many years to transmit telegraph and other text messages

In the late 19th and early 20th century, archaeologists discovered large numbers of clay tablets in Crete inscribed with a script that came to be known as Linear B. There are about 87 signs that represent syllables and more than 100 signs that represent things such as honey or a sheep. The tablets are about 3,400 years old and from the Minoan civilization. Linear B proved very hard to decipher and success only came in the 1950s. Another script, Linear A, has still not been decoded. By contrast, the structure of DNA was discovered in 1953 and the genetic code had been cracked 13 years later in 1966.

4. Suggest some reasons for the genetic code being cracked much faster than Linear B.

▲ Part of a tablet from Crete, dating from 1400 BC, inscribed with Linear B script

 **Communication skills**

## Organize and depict information logically

1. What qualities should a code have?

2. Think of a situation where a new code would be useful.

3. Design a suitable code for it.

4. Compose a message using your code.

9

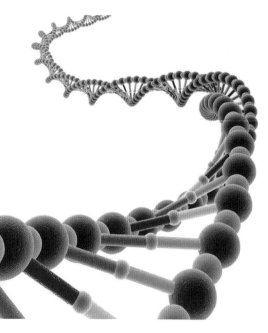

Part of the base sequence of a gene is shown here. A typical gene has over a thousand bases

In this model of DNA, the bases are shown as colored bars. Small blue blobs linking the bases represent chemical bonds

# What makes DNA so good at storing information?

These features of DNA make it ideal for storing information:

1.  DNA contains a sequence of bases. There are four possible bases and they can be arranged in any order, so the number of different sequences is almost infinite.

2.  The structure of DNA makes it possible to copy the base sequence very accurately. There is no limit to how many times it can be copied, so each cell in the body can be given a full set of our genes. Exact copies can also be made to pass on to our offspring.

3.  DNA is a very stable substance, so it can store information robustly and reliably throughout our lifetime and sometimes far longer than that. None of the artificial digital data storage media so far invented has lasted that long. For example, the estimated lifespan of recorded CDs and DVDs is 2–5 years, and most hard drives last approximately 3–5 years.

This 2 terabyte hard drive weighs over half a kilogram. Data on it may not last longer than five years. Half a million of them would be needed to store as much data as the DNA that can be dissolved in one milliliter of water

4.  DNA is a very small molecule—it is just 2 nanometres wide and the length of 1 millimetre has a sequence of 2.93 million bases. Vast amounts of data can be stored by DNA in a very small space. The data storage is even more compact because of the coding. In computers binary code, with the symbols 0 and 1, is used. In DNA, the genetic code is quaternary as there are four different bases—A, C, G and T. Because there are more symbols, the codewords can be shorter, so DNA can store information in a very compressed form.

5. DNA is stored in water, which can be moved without damaging the DNA. This is useful when a cell divides, or when cells or organisms change shape. It also means that DNA can be poured into a bottle or any other container. Solid data storage systems such as printed paper, magnetic tape or silicon chips are much less versatile.

6. Living organisms have used DNA as an information store for over 3 billion years. Apart from some viruses, all organisms have genes made of DNA. All species use the same coding system, so transfer of information between species is possible. Unlike IT devices invented by humans, it is highly unlikely that DNA will ever become obsolete.

> "
> We need about 10 tons of DNA to store all the world's data. That's something you could fit on a semi-trailer.
> "

*Yaniv Erlich (Source: Financial Times Ltd.)*

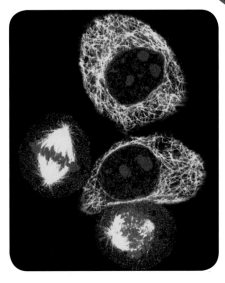
▲ The DNA in these human cells is stained pink. In two of the cells the DNA is in the nucleus. In the other two, the DNA has been copied and the copies are being separated, prior to cell division. The nucleus is only a hundredth of a millimetre across and yet it can hold all of the 25,000 human genes. The total mass of DNA in a human cell is just 7 picograms (0.000,000,000,007 grams)

 **Modeling DNA replication with zippers**

Models can help us to understand a structure or a process. The following colored zippers have been used to model copying of DNA. The two strands of DNA unzip. A new strand is then assembled on each of the single strands. This process could be repeated any number of times, doubling the number of copies each time.

1. In what ways is a zipper similar to DNA?

2. Zippers do not model the arrangement of bases in DNA very well. How are they different?

3. Can you think of a better way of modeling the copying of DNA?

▲ Coconut octopuses (*Amphioctopus marginatus*) collect shells from coconuts or shellfish and squeeze inside to hide from danger, without damage to their DNA. They sometimes even get into bottles that litter the seabed

## What information does DNA store?

DNA stores information in units called **genes**. A gene is like a set of instructions. It is similar to a recipe that we use when cooking. Even the simplest bacterium has hundreds of genes, because the bacterium has to do many different things. In a human there are about 25,000 genes, each of which has the instructions for something that cells might need to do during our life.

Most genes contain instructions for making one particular protein. There are 20 different **amino acids** and an average protein has over a hundred linked together in a chain and then folded up into a precise shape. Every amino acid in the chain must be the correct one, or the wrong shape of protein will form. The information needed to make a protein is therefore the sequence of amino acids that should be linked up.

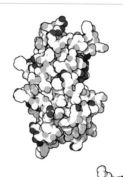

These models show the structure of two of the 20,000 or so proteins that are made in human cells. On the left is GH (growth hormone) and on the right is IGF (insulin-like growth factor)

GH and IGF are two examples of proteins made by human cells. They both act as messengers in the body. GH has 191 amino acids and IGF has 70. A gland in the brain makes GH. It travels through the blood to the liver and tells the cells there to make IGF.

In children, IGF stimulates growth in the ends of the long bones in the arms and legs. If either GH or IGF is not made in a child's body, they will not grow as tall as they might have done. Extra GH is sometimes given to children who do not naturally make enough.

**ABC** A **gene** is a piece of DNA inherited from a parent that has the instructions for one task, usually production of a particular protein.

**Amino acids** are the subunits that are linked together to produce a protein.

An **enzyme** is a protein that speeds up a particular chemical reaction.

Of the 25,000 genes in humans, about 20,000 of them contain instructions for making proteins. Our cells can therefore make a huge range of proteins. Many of these proteins are **enzymes**, which cause chemical reactions to occur in cells. Other proteins have a structural role in the body or act as messengers. Proteins do a huge range of jobs in the body and this is one reason why so many genes are needed.

5,000 or so genes in humans do not contain instructions for making a protein. They have two other types of role. Some genes are regulators and help to control when the various types of protein are made. This is very important as it decides how a cell will develop and what activities it will perform. A small number of genes contain the instructions for making RNA, which is a substance rather like DNA that plays some key roles within the cell.

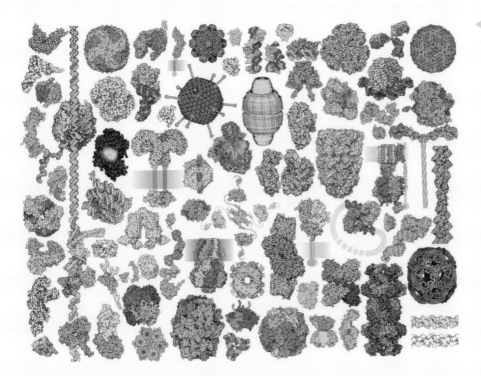

Proteins come in a huge range of shapes and sizes because they do many different jobs. Most, but not all, of the proteins shown here are human

## How are genes stored and used?

Plants and animals store nearly all their genes in the cell nucleus. The nuclear membrane protects the genes and reduces the chance of them being damaged. When the information in a gene is needed to make a protein, a copy of the gene is made and is sent out to the cytoplasm, where proteins are produced.

As genes are made of DNA and there are about 25,000 genes in a human nucleus, we might expect there to be this number of DNA molecules. In fact, there are far fewer, because genes are part of much longer molecules. These long DNA molecules are called chromosomes. Humans have 46 chromosomes in the nucleus. Other species have a different number of chromosomes. Some examples are shown in the margin.

The number of chromosomes in organisms that reproduce sexually is even, rather than odd. This is because the male gamete (sperm) and female gamete (egg) both contain one of each of the types of chromosome. When the male and female gametes fuse together to produce a zygote, there are therefore two of each type of chromosome, so the total must be an even number of chromosomes.

In humans for example, the sperm and egg each contain 23 chromosomes—one of each of types 1 to 22 plus one sex chromosome. The zygote therefore has 46 chromosomes. Each time cell division occurs, all of these 46 chromosomes are copied, so body cells also have 46.

In a library it is important to have the books arranged in a logical sequence, so that they can be found easily. We might expect something similar with genes in a nucleus

### Chromosome numbers

| Garlic | 16 |
| --- | --- |
| Chimpanzee | 48 |
| Dog | 78 |
| Carp | 100 |

Think of an even number and see if you can find a species with that number of chromosomes.

## Gene locations

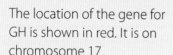

The location of the gene for GH is shown in red. It is on chromosome 17.

Can you find the locations of genes that code for the following proteins?

1. Insulin—a hormone that helps to regulate blood glucose
2. Myoglobin—a protein that stores oxygen in muscles
3. Rhodopsin—a protein that absorbs light in the retina of the eye
4. Factor VIII—a protein that helps with the clotting of blood

In a human cell there are two each of chromosomes 1 to 22, plus two sex chromosomes. Males have one large X chromosome and one small Y. Females have two X chromosomes. In this diagram, blue indicates a chromosome inherited from the mother and pink from the father

# How are genes arranged on the chromosomes?

Each of our 25,000 genes is found on one particular type of chromosome. For example, the gene that codes for growth hormone is always located on chromosome 17. In humans there are 22 types of chromosome, numbered 1 to 22, plus two sex chromosomes (X and Y).

The genes on a particular chromosome type are always arranged in the same sequence. Rather like a book that is kept in the same position on a particular shelf in a library, a gene is stored at the same point along one particular type of chromosome. The Human Genome Project (HGP) revealed the sequences of genes on all of our chromosomes.

## Looking at chromosomes

We can see the chromosomes of a cell when it is dividing. The long DNA molecule of each chromosome is coiled up, so it is short and fat. It would be difficult to get dividing cells from your own body—they are in regions such as bone marrow, the growing ends of bones and healing wounds. It is much easier to find dividing cells in plants such as garlic or onion.

1. Get a garlic or onion bulb to grow roots by placing its base in water.
2. Cut off the tip of the growing roots. These roots will contain dividing cells.
3. Carry out an internet search for a method to fix, soften and stain the root tip.
4. Squash the root tip on a microscope slide to get a single layer of cells.
5. Examine the root squash with your microscope.

   Alternatively, your teacher may provide you with a microscope slide that has already been prepared.

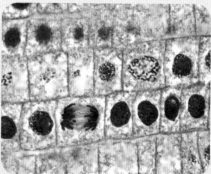

Garlic and onions both have 16 large chromosomes, which are easier to see than the 46 smaller chromosomes of humans

# Why do we have pairs of genes?

We have two copies of most of our genes. There are several reasons for this.

1. We have two copies of each type of chromosome. Each of our genes is kept in a particular position on one type of chromosome. We therefore have two copies of each gene. For example, the ABO

gene which determines our blood group (A, B, AB or O) is located on chromosome 9. We have two copies of chromosome 9 and therefore two copies of the ABO gene.

There is a slight complication over the sex chromosomes. Girls have two X chromosomes, so have two copies of all the genes that are on it. Boys have one X and one Y chromosome, so have only one copy of genes that are located on those chromosomes. There are very few genes on the Y chromosome and girls do not have any copies of them. An example of a gene on the Y chromosome is TDF. It causes testis development, so is not needed in girls.

2. There are advantages in having two copies of most genes. Sometimes one copy of the gene is faulty and cannot be used to produce the right protein. As long as the second copy of the gene is normal, the protein can still be produced and there should be no harmful effects.

3. We have two copies of most genes because of sexual reproduction. A new life starts with the fusion of a male and female gamete (sperm and egg). Gametes are living cells so need a full set of genes. When a sperm and egg join together, the cell that is produced, which is a zygote, has two full sets of genes and therefore two copies of each gene (apart from genes on sex chromosomes in boys).

▲ The President of the United States travels on a plane called Air Force One. There are actually two identical planes (SAM28000 and SAM29000) so one is always available if a fault is being repaired in the other

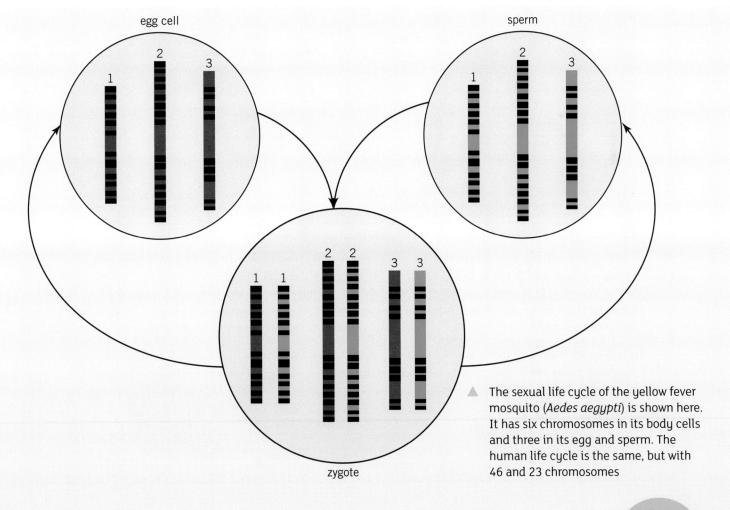

egg cell

sperm

zygote

▲ The sexual life cycle of the yellow fever mosquito (*Aedes aegypti*) is shown here. It has six chromosomes in its body cells and three in its egg and sperm. The human life cycle is the same, but with 46 and 23 chromosomes

**Testing blood groups and other traits**

Many things make up our identity, from the base sequences of our DNA to personality traits such as how extravert we are. If we test one or two of these, we may find that we are the same as others, but if enough traits are examined, differences are found between all humans. No two people have the same identity. Some tests that you can carry out are suggested here, but there are many more.

### ABO blood group

You can find out whether you are group A, B, AB or O, and also if you are rhesus-positive or rhesus-negative, using a simple test kit. Your teacher may be able to provide one.

### Left or right handedness

You will know whether you work faster and more precisely with your left or right hand. About 10% of humans are left-handed but the percentage is higher in some occupations, for example architecture.

### Curly or straight hair

The shape of our hair follicles influences whether our hair is straight, wavy, curly or tightly coiled. Look carefully at some of the hair on your scalp. Which word describes your hair best?

### Eye color

Which description matches your eyes?

1 Light blue 2 Darker blue 3 Blue with brown pupil ring

4 Green 5 Green with brown iris ring 6 Green outer brown centre

7 Brown with some peripheral green 8 Brown 9 Dark brown

### Ear wax

The two types of ear wax are sticky orange–brown and dry flaky grey. Ask a friend to look in your ear to see which type you have. Don't stick anything inside your ear to get a sample.

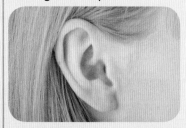

### Navels

A navel is the scar left where our umbilical cord was. An 'innie' is concave and an 'outie' is convex. There are various shapes of innie—round, vertical, oval, T-shaped. Most navels become outies during pregnancy.

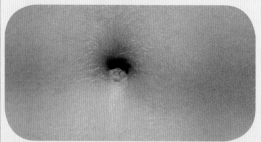

**Citizen science**

Students can often get involved in data collection efforts by scientists in research institutions. For example, the Royal Society for Chemistry created an online survey asking students to compare their sense of smell with that of their parents, to help understand the genetics of smell perception.

The small cabbage white (*Pieris rapae*) is one of the most common butterflies worldwide. In another project, people were asked to gather samples from their area and send them to the researchers. The researchers could then investigate DNA differences to determine how the species has successfully spread and adapted to many different environments.

Research online using the search terms "citizen science" and "DNA" to find citizen science opportunities related to DNA studies.

> **ABC** An **allele** is an alternative form of a particular gene.

## What makes us different from our siblings?

A sibling is a brother or sister. We might expect siblings to be very similar to each other because they have the same parents, but there can be big differences. Many of these differences are explained by variation in genes.

There are alternative variants of most genes. The official name for variants of a gene is **allele**. The alleles of a gene usually only differ slightly—sometimes just one base is different in the base sequence. Even if this alters just one amino acid in the protein product of the gene, the protein may not work properly and there may be major consequences for a person with the allele. Some examples of genes with more than one allele are shown in the table.

▲ If you have any siblings, how are you similar to them?

| Gene | Alleles of the gene | Consequences | |
| --- | --- | --- | --- |
| ABCC11 | Two alleles are known, *G* and *A*, which have just one base difference in their base sequence. | The *G* allele gives sticky orange–brown ear wax (right) and the *A* allele gives dry, flaky grey colored ear wax. |  |
| ABO | Three alleles were originally found, *A*, *B* and *O*, but more variants of the *A* and *O* alleles are now known. There are other blood group genes including the MN gene. | These alleles determine whether a person is in blood group A, B, AB or O. Knowing which blood group a person has is important in blood transfusions. | |
| CFTR | Most humans have the normal allele but over 1,500 other alleles have been documented, one of which (ΔF508) is the most common. | ΔF508 and other variant alleles cause the genetic disease cystic fibrosis, affecting the lungs (right), pancreas and other organs. | |

**Parent's Blood Group: O**

Parent's alleles *OO*
Alleles in gametes: *O*

**Parent's Blood Group: AB**

Parent's alleles *AB*
Alleles in gametes: *A* or *B*

**Parent's Blood Group: MN**

Parent's alleles *MN*
Alleles in gametes: *M* or *N*

**Parent's Blood Group: AB and MN**

Parent's alleles *AB MN*
Alleles in gametes: *AM, AN, BM* or *BN*

We have two copies of most of our genes. One copy is from our mother and one from our father. Our parents also have two copies of most genes. If a parent has two of the same allele of a gene, they will pass on that allele to all of their children in their gametes (egg or sperm). If they have two different alleles, they will pass on just one of them to their children. Therefore, there is a 50% chance of each of the alleles being passed on.

If the parent also has different alleles of a second gene, the number of possible combinations of alleles in the sperm or egg rises to $2 \times 2 = 4$. An example is shown in the margin. With each extra gene where a parent has different alleles, there are twice as many possible combinations of alleles in their eggs or sperm. If there are two different alleles in just 10% of a parent's 25,000 genes, the number of possible combinations of alleles that they could pass on to their children is a vast number ($2^{2500}$). Both parents can pass on an almost limitless number of combinations of alleles in their gametes, so it is no surprise that siblings are different.

## How much of our identity do we inherit from our parents?

"What makes me who I am?" is an important question about our identity. We **inherit** many characteristics totally from our parents. These traits are influenced only by our genes. Here are some examples:

- Blood groups
- Type of ear wax
- Color blindness and other genetic conditions

Some of our traits are nothing to do with our genes. They are due to factors around us, including chance events such as accidents that cause disability and deliberate actions. Biologists call these influences **environment**. Here are examples of traits that develop because of our environment:

- Changes to our body such as ear piercing
- The language that we speak
- Religion and other features of our culture

There is a third group of traits that are due both to the genes that we inherit and our environment. Here are some examples:

- Skin color
- Height
- Tumors such as those of breast cancer

1. Can you find another example of a trait in each of the three groups?

2. Identical twins can be used to investigate whether a trait is due to genes, environment or both. Identical twins that have been adopted

**ABC** **Inheritance** is the passing on of genes that affect characteristics from parent to offspring.

The **environment** is all of the external conditions that affect an organism or a community.

and raised in different families are particularly useful. What makes identical twins reared apart especially useful for this research?

3. It's rare for identical twins to be adopted by different families, so researchers often compare identical and non-identical twins. What can be discovered with these comparisons?

 **Experiment**

**The effect of light on plant growth**

Local conditions affect the growth of plants. You can investigate this by germinating seeds in different conditions.

These are some conditions you could test:

- Bright light with the light coming from above.
- Total darkness.
- Light from one side only, for example inside a box with a hole cut in one side.
- Blue light, either from blue LEDs or from white light passed through a filter.
- Red light, from red LEDs or a filter.
- Green light, from green LEDs or a filter.

Sow as many pots of seeds as you need, using mung beans or some other type that will germinate and grow quickly. What factors should be kept the same for each pot of seeds?

When plants have grown from the seeds you can assess these traits:

- Height of plant
- Direction of stem growth
- Size of leaves
- Color of leaves
- Plus any other traits that you can observe

How much is plant growth affected by the quantity, direction and color of light?

▲ Traits in plants are also influenced by both inheritance and environment. Flower structure in these *Hydrangea* flowers is due to genes, but flower color is affected by soil conditions. In acid soils, the flowers are blue, whereas in alkaline soils, they are pink

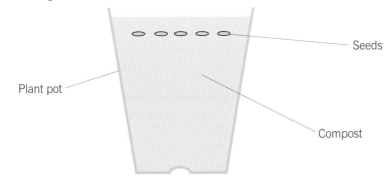

Seeds

Plant pot

Compost

Should parents be allowed to select any of the features of their baby? Gene editing technology has made this a possibility

## What is a designer baby?

There has been talk in recent years of "designer babies". This makes it sound as though all of the genes for a new baby will be designed and made artificially, but even making one useful new gene would be very challenging.

A more likely option is modifying existing genes. It is already possible to make small changes in the base sequence of a gene. This is called gene editing. A new method called the CRISPR/Cas9 system has made gene editing much easier and more accurate. It could be used to alter a specific gene in a targeted way in a human embryo. An obvious reason for doing this would be to change a faulty gene that causes a **genetic disease**. More controversially, it might be possible to make changes to features such as eye color or height.

1. Should parents be able to change genes that would cause a genetic disease in their children? Explain your answer.

2. Is it acceptable to change features other than genetic disease by gene editing? Explain your answer.

3. How do we decide what features are desirable in our children?

4. Is gene editing acceptable for improving crop plants or farm livestock? Explain your answer.

5. What might be the effects on the identity of a person if they knew that they had been a designer baby?

### ATL Communication skills

## Negotiating ideas

When considering controversial issues, it is often the case that different perspectives on the issue can exist among your peers. Classroom discussion is most productive when we are open to new ideas. Start with the position that your own view is not the only possibility. Take a genuine interest in what the other possibilities are. This involves seeking and actively encouraging others to share their views. This also involves taking a risk to share your viewpoint. Finally, it is not enough to just be aware of all of the various perspectives. You must evaluate them in order to come to a more informed viewpoint.

This computer-generated image shows DNA (grey) being edited by a CRISPR/Cas9 complex. The red part of the complex finds the base sequence in the DNA that is to be edited

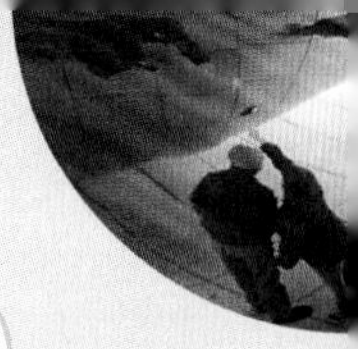

# Summative assessment

**Statement of inquiry:**

Patterns in human identity that we see around the world are a consequence of both ancestral relationships and environmental influences.

ABC **Genetic diseases** are caused by faulty genes, which can be passed on to future generations.

**Mutations** are changes to the base sequence of a gene.

## Genes in humans and tobacco plants

**1.** What are the genes of a tobacco plant made of?

**A.** chromosomes
**B.** DNA
**C.** nicotine
**D.** protein

**2.** The tobacco plant has 48 chromosomes in each of its leaf cells. How many chromosomes does it have in each of its root cells?

**A.** 0
**B.** 24
**C.** 48
**D.** 96

**3.** The male gametes of a tobacco plant are inside its pollen grains. How many chromosomes are there in the male gamete of a tobacco plant?

**A.** 0
**B.** 24
**C.** 48
**D.** 96

**4.** Some chemicals in cigarette smoke react with bases in DNA. Errors are then made when the DNA is copied, so DNA is produced with an altered base sequence. What is a likely consequence of this?

**A.** Proteins are produced in lung cells with an altered amino acid sequence.
**B.** The smoker becomes addicted to cigarettes.
**C.** Tobacco plants develop tumors.
**D.** The genetic code has to be modified.

**5.** On chromosome 17 in humans there is a gene called BRCA1, which helps to prevent breast cancer. How many copies of this gene are there in men's body cells?

**A.** 0
**B.** 1
**C.** 2
**D.** 17

## Does smoking cause visible changes to our skin?

Smokers absorb thousands of different chemicals from tobacco smoke, with many adverse consequences. There are claims that smoking causes visible changes to the skin. Wrinkles and sagging would be a consequence of damage to collagen and elastin proteins in skin. Liver spots and hyperpigmentation would be a consequence of **mutations** in skin cells.

To investigate whether smoking causes visible changes to our skin, researchers from Case Western Reserve University recruited pairs of identical twins during the Twins Days Festival in Twinsburg, Ohio. In each of the 45 pairs recruited, only one twin smoked and the other had never smoked. Professional photographers took size-matched photos of these twins. Using suitable search terms, such as "smoker and non-smoker twins", find these pairs of photos on the internet. Can you identify the smoker in each pair of photos?

6. Design a procedure for testing the hypothesis that smoking causes visible changes to our skin. [10]

Our skin inevitably ages, but does smoking hasten this process?

## Is smoking behavior influenced more by genes or environment?

The Netherlands Twin Register (NTR) collects data on physical and mental health, lifestyle and personality. Surveys in 1993–95 and 2009–10 recorded how many young adult twins had been cigarette smokers or had never smoked (apart from a few cigarettes to try them).

| | 18–25 year old twins in 1993–1995 | | | 18–25 year old twins in 2009–2010 | | |
|---|---|---|---|---|---|---|
| | Total number of twins | Number who had smoked | % who had smoked | Total number of twins | Number who had smoked | % who had smoked |
| men | 1162 | 592 | | 768 | 175 | |
| women | 1505 | 595 | | 1573 | 352 | |

**Source of data:** https://bmcpublichealth.biomedcentral.com/articles/10.1186/ 1471-2458-11-316

7. Complete the table by calculating the percentages who had smoked. [2]

8. Display the data in a graph or chart. Only display the numbers that you think are significant and choose a format that you consider most suitable. [2]

9. **a)** What changes in smoking behavior took place in the Netherlands between 1993–95 and 2009–10? [2]

   **b)** Is this change likely to be a consequence of a change in genes or environment? Explain your answer. [2]

   **c)** How could the data collected by the NTR be used to investigate whether genes influence smoking behavior? [1]

The Swedish Twin Register collected data on smoking behavior for identical twins and non-identical twins who had been reared in the same or in different families. Data for twin boys are shown in the table.

| Twin type | Both twins or neither of them are smokers | One twin is a smoker but the other is not |
|---|---|---|
| identical reared together | 78.2% | 21.8% |
| identical reared apart | 79.5% | 20.5% |
| non-identical reared together | 70.6% | 29.4% |
| non-identical reared apart | 60.0% | 40.0% |

Source of data: https://jamanetwork.com/journals/jamapsychiatry/fullarticle/205750

10. a) (i) Which are more similar in their smoking behavior—identical twins or non-identical twins? [1]

   (ii) What conclusion can you draw from this? [1]

   b) (i) Which are more similar in their smoking behavior—twins reared together or twins reared apart? [1]

   (ii) What conclusion can you draw from this? [1]

   c) Based on this data, explain whether smoking behavior is more influenced by genes or by the environment? [2]

## How does smoking cause bladder cancer?

Smoking increases the risk of at least 17 classes of cancer. It is easy to understand how smoking could cause lung cancer, but less obvious how bladder cancer could be a consequence of smoking.

11. Research the link between smoking and bladder cancer. Identify each stage in the process from smoke inhalation to a tumor developing in the bladder.

   a) How does smoking cause bladder cancer? Write a concise answer to this question using scientific language effectively. [6]

   b) List the sources that you used during your research. [2]

   c) Write a very brief health statement for printing on cigarette packs to warn smokers about the risk of bladder cancer. [2]

# 2 Cells

◀ Most homes are dependent on supplies of electricity, natural gas, drinking water and food and they also require removal of sewage and other wastes. Earthships are designed to allow "off-grid" living by avoiding the need for any of these services. The aim is to develop truly sustainable systems for human life, with minimal impacts on the environment. What features does an earthship need to have?

▶ Houses can be constructed from components such as lumber and bricks. Within months a new home can stand where there was none before. New cells cannot be constructed in the same way—they are only produced when an existing cell divides in two. What are the consequences of the different ways of making houses and cells?

▲ Unite d'Habitation is a block of 337 apartments designed by French architect Le Corbusier and built in Marseille. It opened in 1952. The apartments were equipped with built-in furniture and specially designed storage walls containing various cupboards with sliding doors. Many of the apartments still have their original design in place today due to their efficient use of space. Is this apartment block a useful analogy for a multicellular organism?

◀ Motorhomes have been in production for over a hundred years. Initially they were small and simple, but the size and range of features has increased. Some actors insist on the largest and most luxurious motorhomes while on set. What factors should be considered when deciding how large a motorhome should be? Are these factors similar to those that influence how large cells grow before dividing?

25

**Key concept:** Systems

**Related concepts:** Function, Balance, Models

**Global context:** Scientific and technical innovation

**Statement of inquiry:**

Discoveries made using new techniques can change our understanding of the natural world.

# Introduction

All living things are made up of cells. Biologists say that cells are the fundamental unit of living organisms.

A cell has many components, which cannot survive without each other. For this reason, a cell is the smallest unit that is considered to be alive. Some organisms consist of a single cell—they are unicellular. Larger organisms are multicellular—they consist of many cells and many different types of cell.

A cell is an example of a system, because of these features:

- it has different types of component

- each component has a different function (role)

- the components work together so the cell as a whole can carry out its tasks.

A cell is an example of an open system, because materials and energy can pass in and out. A cell membrane is the frontier that controls what enters and leaves the cell. It therefore helps regulate the inside of a cell and keep things in balance.

Most cells are too small to see unless they are magnified. Over hundreds of years techniques for magnification have improved enormously. Simple lenses were used initially, followed by increasingly sophisticated microscopes. Each innovation in the design and construction of microscopes has allowed new discoveries to be made.

▼ In this simulation of membrane channels, green particles were able to diffuse across the membrane but blue particles were not

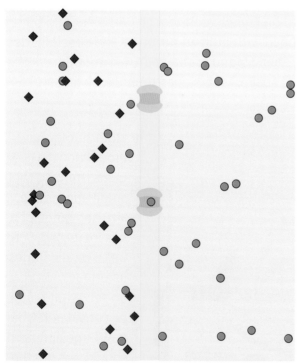

Membrane

It is often impossible to watch processes as they actually occur in a cell, because they are too fast, too complex or happen on too small a scale. Even with the most powerful electron microscopes, the tiniest structures within cells cannot be seen. For example, it isn't possible to see particles moving across membranes or proteins being assembled from smaller subunits.

Research into cells is therefore often done by modeling. Sometimes a physical model is made to represent key features of a cell and can be used in experiments.

Another approach is to use computers to do simulations of cell processes. Increasing computer power allows more and more sophisticated modeling of cell processes.

# What is a cell?

Lumps of pure gold called nuggets are sometimes discovered. If we cut a gold nugget in half, we would have two smaller pieces of gold. If we took one of them and cut it in half again, we'd have even smaller pieces of gold. We could repeat this process again and again, but would eventually end up with just one atom of gold. This is the smallest possible amount of gold that there can be, because if we managed to split it up further, the parts wouldn't have the properties of gold.

We can do a similar thought experiment with living tissue. Think of a peeled banana. As we cut the banana in half, we get smaller and smaller pieces of living tissue. But eventually we have a piece about a quarter of a millimeter long that contains just one banana cell. It is alive, but if we cut it in half it will die. A cell is the smallest unit that can be said to be alive.

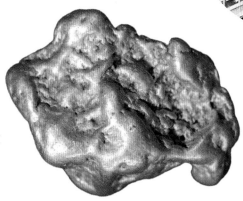

▲ A gold nugget is small, but it is in fact made up of even smaller atoms of gold

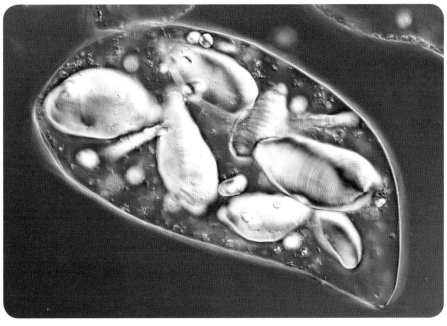

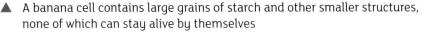

▲ A banana cell contains large grains of starch and other smaller structures, none of which can stay alive by themselves

**Creativity and innovation**

## Making guesses

What is the difference between a guess and an estimate?

Guess how many cells there are in a banana. Compare your guess with other students in your class.

The volume of one typical banana cell is 0.002 cubic millimeters. Measure the volume of one peeled banana using water displacement. You can use a measuring cylinder or jug to do this. You can now work out an estimate of the number of cells in the banana. Compare your estimate with estimates from other students.

When you compared your results with your classmates, which were closer together—your guesses or your estimates? How can we evaluate the quality of an estimate?

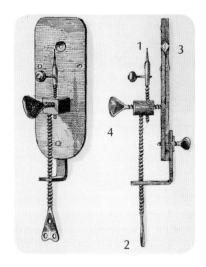

▲ In this diagram of van Leeuwenhoek's microscope, 1 is a pin where the specimen is mounted, 2 is a screw to adjust the position of the specimen, 3 is the lens and 4 is a screw used for focusing

▼ Robert Hooke's compound microscope

# How were cells discovered?

Most cells are too small for the naked human eye to see, unless we use a lens or a microscope. A convex lens makes a small object look larger than it really is. This is called magnification.

The lenses that we use today usually only give a magnification of ×10, but in the 17th century Antonie van Leeuwenhoek developed a method of making spherical glass lenses that gave much higher magnification. He built simple microscopes containing his lenses that allowed him to focus on very small living things. For example, van Leeuwenhoek discovered single-celled organisms in drops of pond water and a few of the larger structures inside cells. He could even see some large types of bacteria.

1.  What does the word magnification mean?

2.  Using the ray diagram, explain how a convex lens produces a magnified image.

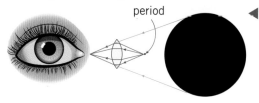

period

◀ A period or full stop in a newspaper or other printed page is about 0.5 mm in diameter. With a hand lens it appears much larger. To check this out, view the period at the end of this sentence with a ×10 hand lens.

3.  Compared with a lens that you hold in your hand, what are the advantages of van Leeuwenhoek's simple microscope?

4.  Van Leeuwenhoek kept his method of producing lenses secret. Do you think he was right to do this? Explain your answer.

Van Leeuwenhoek's devices were simple microscopes because they only had one lens. As the magnification of a lens increases, the image it produces becomes less and less clear. This problem can be overcome by using compound microscopes with two lenses, which were invented in the 17th century.

The scientist Robert Hooke obtained a beautiful compound microscope ornamented with leather and gold. Using his microscope he made an important discovery. He cut "an exceedingly thin piece" of cork and examined it "very diligently with a microscope". He saw "a great many little Boxes" which he called cells. Hooke added:

> **"**
>
> **...nor is this kind of Texture peculiar to cork only: for upon examination with my Microscope, I have found that pith of the hollow stalks of other Vegetables [...]. have much such kind of Schematisme, as I have lately shewn that of Cork.**
>
> **"**

Hooke had just discovered that plants are made of many small cells.

 **"A thing almost incredible"**

The title of this activity was Robert Hooke's comment when he calculated how many cells there must be in a piece of cork. "I counted threescore (60) of these small cells placed endways in the eighteenth part of an inch in length whence I concluded that there must be near eleven hundred of them in the length of an inch."

Using Hooke's measurements calculate the diameter of a cork cell in millimeters. (1 inch is 25.4 mm.) Assuming that cork cells are cubic in shape, calculate how many cells are there in a cylindrical cork with a diameter of 20 mm and length of 40 mm. (Volume of a cylinder = $\pi r^2 h$)

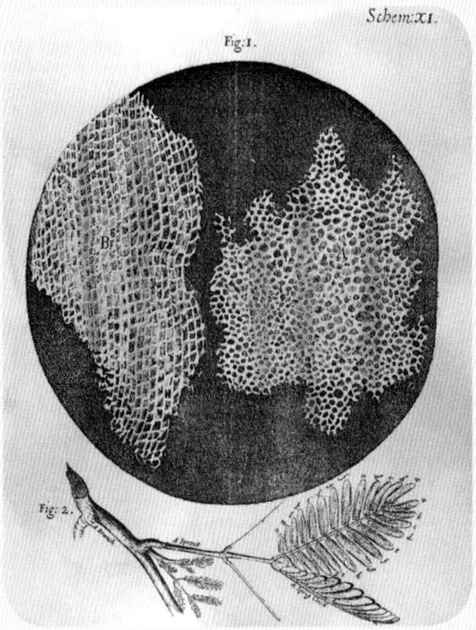

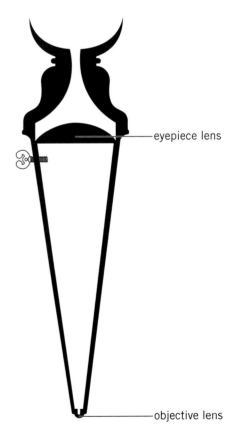

▶ Hooke's drawing of cork cells, sectioned horizontally and vertically

 **Poppy seeds**

1. Look at some poppy seeds using each of these methods. In each case describe what you can see:

- Method X: Use just your eye with no microscope lens to help you (unless you normally wear glasses/contact lenses).

- Method Y: Lick the end of your finger and use the moisture to pick up a few poppy seeds. Hold a hand lens near your eye and move the finger carrying the seeds closer to the lens until the seeds are in focus.

- Method Z: Put some seeds under the microscope. Shine light onto the upper surface of the seeds. Focus on them using the low power lens of the microscope.

2. Work out a method for measuring the diameter of poppy seeds. Can you measure them more accurately with a microscope, hand lens or the naked eye?

3. Sow the poppy seeds on some damp paper towel or seed-sowing compost. Poppy seeds are very long-lasting so unless they have been killed, they should germinate.

▲ Poppy seeds are dispersed through small holes at the top of the seed capsule

eyepiece lens

objective lens

▲ This diagram shows the two lenses in the microscope used by Robert Hooke

**Experiment**

### Researching the structure of carrots

Use the flowchart below to see if you can obtain a clear image of the structure of carrots. You will need a carrot and apparatus for cutting sections, staining and imaging.

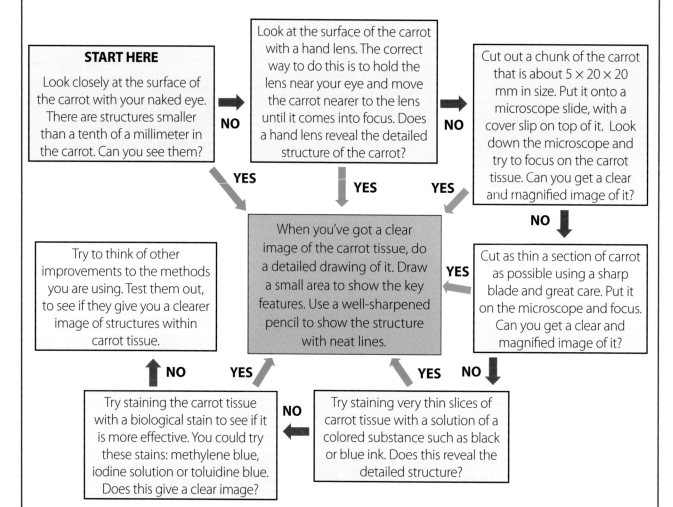

1. Explain how the following techniques can help when researching the structure of carrots:

   a) using a microscope rather than a hand lens or the naked eye

   b) cutting thin slices—biologists call them *sections*

   c) staining the carrot.

2. The carrot that you were using was living tissue—it could have continued to grow under suitable conditions.

   a) What are the reasons for looking at living carrot tissue rather carrot that has been killed by cooking?

   b) Are there any ethical objections to using living carrot tissue in your research? Explain your answer.

3. The magnification of a compound microscope is calculated by multiplying the magnification of the two lenses together. For example, if the objective lens (nearer the sample) is ×40 and the eyepiece lens (nearer the eye) is ×10, the image produced will be ×400.

   Some compound microscopes can give magnifications above ×400 but it becomes more and more difficult to get sharply focused images. Can you explain why this is?

4. By the middle of the 19th century, the compound microscopes that were being produced gave very clear images, with magnification up to at least ×400. These allowed many more discoveries to be made of the structure of plants, animals and other organisms. Carry out some research into another discovery that was made using a microscope.

## Which living organisms are made up of cells?

When microscopes were first used to reveal the structure of living organisms, this is what was discovered:

- Smaller organisms consist of a single cell—they are unicellular.
- Larger organisms contain many cells—they are multicellular.
- In multicellular organisms, the different tissues and organs are composed of different types of cell.

In conclusion, living things are made of cells.

In some living organisms there are cells which grow to a large size without dividing up into smaller cells. There are also some organisms where groups of small cells fuse together to form much larger structures. Because of this, we cannot say that all parts of all living things are made up of small cells, but most living organisms show a cellular structure. Also, most cells are small—less than 0.1 mm in diameter.

1. What are the advantages of having many small cells rather than a few large ones?

2. What is the advantage of having:

   a) muscle fibers that are much longer than normal cells?

   b) long hyphae in a fungus that are not divided up into individual cells?

▲ Some bread molds (Mucor) have thread-like hyphae that grow very long without dividing up into small cells

You can test the claim that living organisms are made of cells by looking at plant and animal tissues with your own microscope, or by looking at microscope photos of tissues online. Can you find any tissues that are not made of cells?

Cells and the structures inside them are very small. If their size is given in **millimeters**, there are lots of zeros after the decimal point. To avoid this, biologists usually convert millimeters into **micrometers**. The symbol for micrometers is μm. One micrometer is a thousandth of a millimeter (1000 μm = 1 mm) so 0.2 μm is 0.0002 mm.

## What were the first structures to be discovered inside cells?

The first structure discovered inside cells was the **nucleus**. In 1833, Scottish botanist Robert Brown wrote that "a circular area somewhat more opaque is observable". He saw one such structure in each **epidermis** cell of an orchid flower and in cells from elsewhere in the orchid. He saw nuclei in other plants: "In *Tradescantia virginica* and several nearly related species, it is uncommonly distinct, not only in the epidermis and jointed hairs of the filaments but in the tissue of the ovule."

Other structures in cells were discovered in the 19th century, including **chloroplasts**, vacuoles and **cell walls**. The magnification of microscopes is enough for us to see any structure that is 0.2 micrometers (0.2 μm) or more across. **Cell membranes** were also discovered even though they are much thinner than 0.2 μm—this is because they form a complete layer around the cytoplasm of a cell and are therefore clearly present.

### Observing, interpreting and recording cell structure using a light microscope

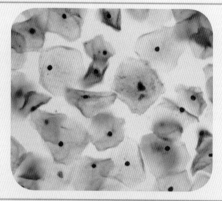

1. The photograph on the left was taken through a microscope. It shows the results of a cervical smear test. In this procedure, cells are taken from a woman's cervix to check for cancer cells. In this case the cells are all normal. Cervix cells are naturally transparent, but a stain has been used to make them show up. The nucleus of each cell is stained purple and the cytoplasm pink.

Draw one of the cells carefully. Label the cell membrane, cytoplasm and nucleus. There are instructions for how to do biological drawings on page 34.

2. The cells in the microscope image on the left are part of the leaf of a hornwort plant. Each cell has a cell wall, a cell membrane, a large central vacuole, one large chloroplast in the cytoplasm and a nucleus. No stain has been used, so the cytoplasm, vacuole and nuclei are hard to see.

Draw one of the cells carefully. Label all the cell components that you have included.

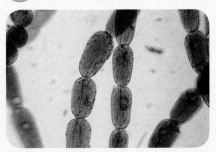

▲ Stamen hair cells in Tradescantia

*Tradescantia* has hairs on its stamens consisting of a series of ovoid cells. Robert Brown commented that they are "one of the most interesting microscopic objects with which I am acquainted". The nuclei are clearly visible and on the outside of the cells there are evenly spaced parallel lines that are about 1.5 μm apart. Also, the fluid inside the cells, now known as cytoplasm, can often be seen to circulate. If you look at these cells yourself with a microscope, or watch a video on the internet, you will see why Brown found them so fascinating.

## What is the correct way to use a microscope?

To look at the structure of a wide range of cell types you will need to use a microscope. Knowing how to use a microscope correctly is an essential skill to learn in the life sciences.

Find all the parts in your microscope and then follow these instructions.

1. Connect your microscope to the electricity supply and switch on the light.

2. Put the slide that you want to look at on the stage in the middle of area of light.

3. Select the low-power objective lens (the shortest lens).

4. Use the coarse focus to move the lens as close to the slide as possible, without them touching.

5. Look down the eyepiece.

6. Use the coarse focus to move the slide further from the objective lens until the cells come into focus.

7. Use the fine focus to sharpen the focus as much as possible.

8. Move the slide on the stage to search for the best area of cells.

9. Position the slide so the best area is exactly in the middle of the area of light.

10. Refocus with the high-power lens, using instructions 4–7.

There are many types of cell that you could study with your microscope. Here are some examples.

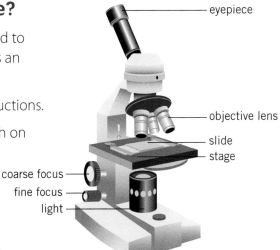

- Animals:
  - o cells scraped from the lining of your mouth
  - o cells smeared off a piece of fresh liver
  - o cells on a prepared slide of kidney tissue.

- Plants:
  - o epidermis taken from inside an onion
  - o cells from a leafy liverwort
  - o cells in leaves of a pondweed such as *Elodea*.

**ABC** The **cell membrane** is a thin layer surrounding the cytoplasm of a cell.

The **cell wall** is a rigid outer wall of plant cells.

**Chloroplasts** are tiny components of plant cells that contain chlorophyll.

The **nucleus** holds a cell's genes inside a nuclear membrane.

The **epidermis** is the layer of cells covering the top and bottom of a leaf.

## How do we draw cells?

An obvious way to record the structure of a cell seen using a microscope is to take a photograph. You may be able to do this using your cell phone. Cameras can be attached to microscopes where the eyepiece is positioned.

An alternative approach is to draw what you see. A drawing shows less detail than a photograph. It is an interpretation of what is visible. The aim is to show structure as clearly as possible without any unimportant or misleading detail.

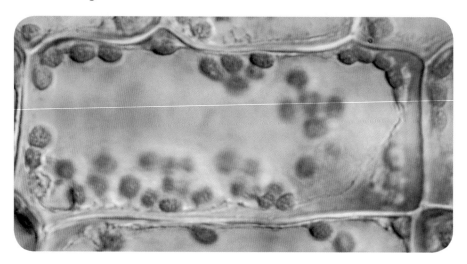

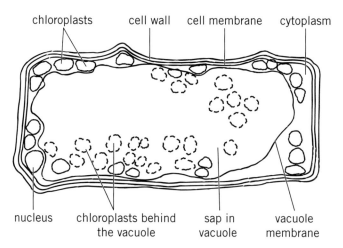

chloroplasts    cell wall    cell membrane    cytoplasm

nucleus    chloroplasts behind the vacuole    sap in vacuole    vacuole membrane

▲ In a scientific drawing, important aspects of the structure are emphasized and unimportant detail is omitted. The cell that has been drawn here is from a pondweed leaf. There is a large vacuole in the centre of the cell. In the micrograph, some out-of-focus chloroplasts are visible behind the vacuole. These could be shown with dotted lines in a drawing to indicate that they are not inside the vacuole, or they could be omitted entirely

1. Are photographs or drawings a better way of recording cell structure?

Here are some instructions for drawing cells and other biological structures.

- Make your drawing as large as possible because it is easier to get the details correct.

- Use a sharp 2H graphite pencil. Do not use felt tip or ball point pens.

- Draw single continuous lines to show the edges of structures.

- Press hard enough with the pencil to draw clear lines that are easily visible.

- Try to get the drawing right first time—if you use an eraser it will almost always show.

- Colored shading of areas on the drawing can be effective, but it should be pale and even.

- Add labels to your diagram, with a gap between the labels and the drawing.

- Lines connecting a component to its label don't need arrow heads and should be drawn with a ruler.

- Consider using ink for labels and labeling lines, so it is clear that they aren't part of the drawing.

- When drawing labeling lines, make sure that these don't overlap.

## What are the components of a cell?

The following four cell components are all separated from the rest of the cytoplasm by membranes:

- The nucleus is a component of plant and animal cells. It holds over 99% of the cell's genes and produces copies of these genes when they are needed.

- Mitochondria are present in plant and animal cells. They release energy from foods by the process of aerobic respiration.

- Chloroplasts are a component of plant cells. They are green in color because they contain chlorophyll, allowing them to absorb light and make foods by photosynthesis.

- Vacuoles are sacs of water containing salts and other dissolved substances. Small ones may be used for digesting food or collecting excess water from the cytoplasm. Large ones may store chemicals, or simply pump the cell up to a larger size.

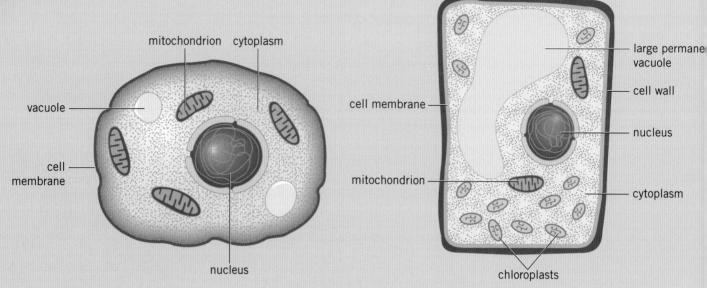

mitochondrion   cytoplasm

vacuole

cell membrane

nucleus

▲ An animal cell with a nucleus, mitochondria and small vacuoles

large permane vacuole

cell wall

nucleus

mitochondrion

cytoplasm

chloroplasts

▲ A plant cell with a cell wall and chloroplasts

1. For each of the four cell components discussed on page 35, there are some cells that lack them. Can you find examples?

2. Find and name an example of an animal cell that lacks both a nucleus and mitochondria.

Some cells, including plants, have an extra layer outside the cell membrane.

The cell wall is much thicker than the cell membrane and can resist much higher pressures in the cytoplasm without bursting. It is porous, so water, sugars and other chemical substances can easily pass through it.

3. Which type of cell do you expect to have cytoplasm at higher pressures—plant or animal? Explain your reasoning.

There are other cell components that you can research if you want to know more about cell structure.

## 📊 Identifying cell components

1. Look at the photo on the right.

a) Look at the photo of moss leaf cells on the right. What are the green cell components?

b) What other cell components do you expect these cells to have?

c) Suggest some possible reasons for some cell components not being visible in this photograph.

▶ Leaf cells in a moss (Atrichum androgynum)

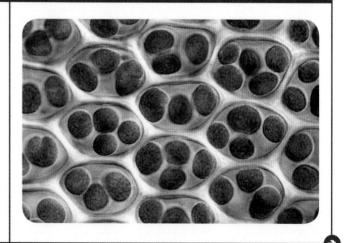

2. Look at the photo of the fern cells on the right.

   a) There are no chloroplasts in these cells. Suggest a possible reason.

   b) Look carefully. Does each cell have its own cell wall, or do adjacent cells share a wall?

   c) Each cell contains one rounded component, either in a corner or along the side of the cell. What is it?

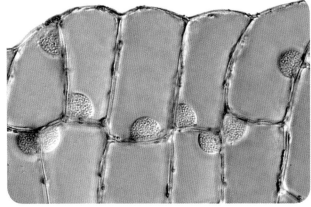

▲ Cells in the covering that protect a fern's spores on the underside of the leaf (Lastreopsis hispida)

3. Look at the photo of liverwort leaf cells on the right.

   a) The central area of these cells looks empty but it is not. What is in the center and what is the reason for it looking like a gap rather than a structure?

   b) There are spherical yellow or orange-colored structures near the margin of each cell that contain droplets of oils. The oils are toxic and do not taste good at all. What function might they have in a liverwort plant?

   c) What other cell components can you see and what are their functions?

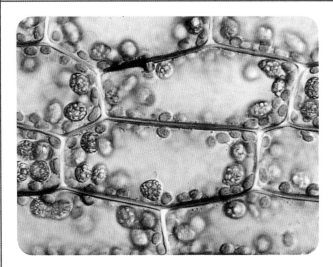

▲ Leaf cells in a liverwort (Balantiopsis montana)

4. Look at the photo on the right.

   a) What shape are these cancer cells? You could answer this question by drawing the shape.

   b) What are the differences in number and size of nuclei and mitochondria in these cells?

   c) From the location of the mitochondria, where is most energy likely to be needed?

   ▶ Fluorescent markers have been used in these two cervical cancer cells to make some of the cell components visible: nuclei (yellow), mitochondria (red or pink) and actin filaments (green), which are proteins close to the cell membrane that maintain the cell's shape

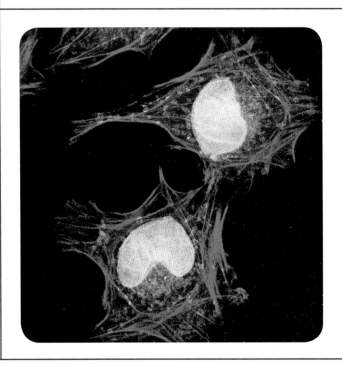

## How do organisms with only one cell live?

Plants and animals are large and complex organisms with many cells—they are multicellular. The vital functions that keep a plant or animal alive are shared out among different types of cell, with each type of cell carrying out a different task. If one cell becomes damaged or worn out, it can usually be replaced, so many plants and animals can live for a very long time.

Unicellular organisms (unicells) only have one cell that must perform all vital functions. If any of its components stop working properly then the organism as a whole will die. However, unicells can reproduce very rapidly by dividing their cell in two. This can happen quickly, generating clones of cells that are unlikely all to die.

Lakes, rivers and oceans are teeming with unicellular organisms. Some are bacteria, which have a cell membrane and cytoplasm but no nucleus. Almost all of their genes can be found in a single chromosome in the cytoplasm. Other unicells have nuclei and mitochondria, in addition to the cell membrane and cytoplasm that all cells possess. These more complex unicells vary in structure, because of differences in their life style. Each type has structural features to suit its activities—this is called adaptation. Three examples are featured here. All can very easily be viewed using a microscope. Video clips of their activities are widely available on the internet. There are also many other types of unicell that you could research.

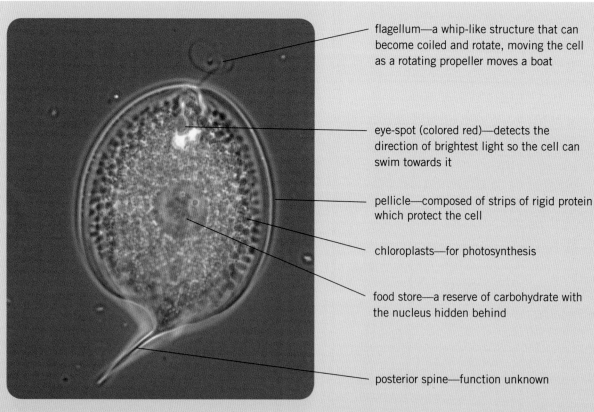

flagellum—a whip-like structure that can become coiled and rotate, moving the cell as a rotating propeller moves a boat

eye-spot (colored red)—detects the direction of brightest light so the cell can swim towards it

pellicle—composed of strips of rigid protein which protect the cell

chloroplasts—for photosynthesis

food store—a reserve of carbohydrate with the nucleus hidden behind

posterior spine—function unknown

▲ *Phacus*—a flagellate

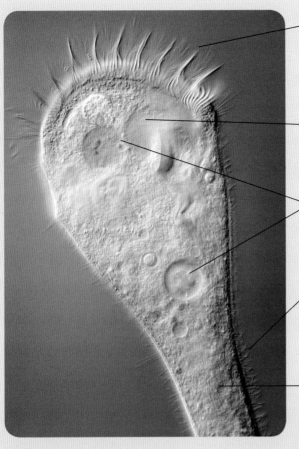

cilia—whip-like structures that create a current of water when they beat. These long cilia draw food particles into a funnel at the end of the cell, where they can be taken in

contractile vacuole—fills up with excess water from the cytoplasm and then expels it through the cell membrane

food vacuoles—digest food that has been taken in and absorb sugars and other useful products of digestion

cilia—these short cilia allow the cell to swim through the water to a new location

narrow base of cell containing contractile fibres— attaches the cell to a surface and holds the feeding structures up in the water

▲ *Stentor*—a ciliate

pseudopodia—where an amoeba is pushing cytoplasm out, to move into a new area. At the same time the amoeba withdraws cytoplasm from other parts of the cell, so the cell as a whole moves

food vacuoles—digest food that has been taken in and absorb sugars and other useful products of digestion. This amoeba has been feeding on bacteria and green ciliates

contractile vacuole—fills up with excess water from the cytoplasm and then expels it through the cell membrane

nucleus—contains most of the cell's genes

mitochondrion—releases energy for use inside the cell. Although too small to be clear, some of these cell structures will be mitochondria

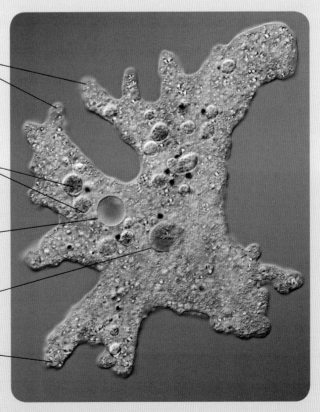

▲ *Chaos*—an amoeba

**Access to clean water and sanitation**

1. A number of diseases are caused by organisms that are only visible through a microscope. Carry out some research to identify diseases caused by single-celled organisms.

2. Disease-causing organisms are called pathogens. Pathogens can enter the body through the consumption of unsafe drinking water. Research the types of pathogens that are ingested in unsafe drinking water.

3. The UN has identified 17 global goals for promoting sustainable development—see www.globalgoals.org. For each goal, there is a section called "Take Action". Goal 6, for example, refers to improving access to clean water and sanitation. The site suggests that you could run a campaign on hygiene-related issues. Raise awareness about the hygiene issues in your community through social media, a school/university campaign or even a campaign in the neighborhood you live in. Alternatively, you could undertake a campaign to support a charity providing safe toilet facilities in impoverished areas.

 A **hypothesis** is a proposed explanation based on limited evidence as a starting point for further investigation.

A **particle** is an extremely small portion of matter, such as an atom or molecule.

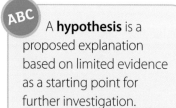 **Experiment**

**How fast is diffusion?**

**Method**

- Fold a tea bag in half and then roll it up to form a cylindrical shape. Put the rolled tea bag in the bottom of a test tube or specimen tube, with the folded part of the bag facing upwards and the thin edges downwards. Choose a tube that gives a snug fit.

- Pour water over the tea bag until the tube is nearly full. The water that you use should be at room temperature and during the experiment the water should not be heated or cooled, because this can cause currents in the water. After pouring the water into the tube, try to ensure that it doesn't move again, so don't pick up the tube or stir its contents.

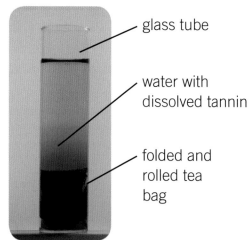

glass tube

water with dissolved tannin

folded and rolled tea bag

- Examine the water in the beaker continuously for a few minutes and then at intervals. It may help to put a white surface behind the tube, such as a piece of paper. You will need to check the results over as long a period as possible, for example once a day for a week.

- Observe any color changes in the water near the tea bag and further away.

## Questions

1. **a)** What changes do you see gradually happening in the water?

   **b)** What explanation can you give for your observations?

2. The color that you observe in this experiment is due to the presence of tannin. There was a high concentration of tannin in the tea leaves inside the tea bag.

   **a)** What state was the tannin inside the dry tea bag in: solid, liquid or gas?

   **b)** Were the **particles** of tannin able to move when they were in this state?

3. When you added water, the tannin dissolved. Were the tannin particles able to move when they dissolved?

4. Was the paper of the tea bag permeable to: **a)** water; **b)** tannin?

5. In a liquid, particles move in random directions. Choose which of the four possible statements about the movement of tannin particles is correct **a)** at the start of the experiment and **b)** a few minutes after the start.

   **A.** They only moved out of the tea bag.

   **B.** They only moved into the tea bag.

   **C.** More moved into the tea bag than out of it.

   **D.** More moved out of the tea bag than into it.

The process that you have observed is diffusion. It can only happen in liquids and gases, because it is due to the random movements of particles. Diffusion happens when the particles are more concentrated in one region than another. It causes particles to spread from the higher to the lower concentration, causing the concentration to even out. This happens because the particles can move randomly in any direction, but inevitably more particles move from the higher to the lower concentration than from the lower to the higher. This gives us a definition: diffusion is a net movement of particles from a higher to a lower concentration.

6. Describe the speed of diffusion in this experiment. Explain your answer.

7. To observe the diffusion of bromine, your teacher might be able to show you an experiment in which a drop of bromine is placed at the bottom of a tube.

   **a)** Was the diffusion of bromine faster or slower than the diffusion of tannin?

   **b)** What are the reasons for the difference?

8. Tannin is not a single substance—it is a group of related chemical compounds, all of which have large particles. The formula of a typical tannin compound is $C_{76}H_{52}O_{46}$ whereas glucose is $C_6H_{12}O_6$ and water is $H_2O$. Do you expect tannin or glucose to diffuse faster in water? Give reasons for your answer.

9. The bark of trees, especially oaks, contains high concentrations of tannin. Find out about the properties of tannin and what its function in tree bark might be. Design an experiment to test your **hypothesis**.

You could carry out further diffusion experiments using living cells. For example, you could investigate the factors that affect diffusion of red pigments from colored tissues such as beetroot.

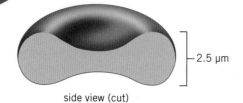

side view (cut)

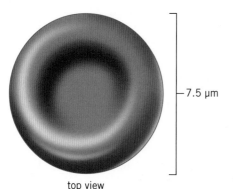

7.5 µm

top view

▲ Red blood cells have a cell membrane and cytoplasm inside it containing hemoglobin, which is red in color. Up to 1 billion oxygen molecules diffuse into a red blood cell through its cell membrane during the few seconds it spends passing through the lungs!

## What is the function of the cell membrane?

Cell membranes are a feature of all living cells. They are the boundary between the internal environment of a cell and its external environment. The internal environment of cells is very carefully regulated—this is an example of balance. The cell membrane plays a vital part in achieving this balance.

- Membranes are continuous structures—they neither begin nor end. They can therefore prevent cytoplasm leaking out and unwanted materials from leaking into the cell. Can you think of other structures that have no beginning or end?

- Membranes are selectively permeable, meaning that they allow certain substances to pass through by diffusion. They therefore control what can enter or leave a cell. Do you know of any other structures that are selectively permeable?

- Membranes are extremely thin—about a hundred thousandth of a millimeter thick. This allows substances to pass through quickly, but other substances can still be prevented from crossing the membrane. How thick is a cell membrane in nanometers?

- Membranes have an inner surface next to the cytoplasm and an outer surface that is in contact with the outside environment. These surfaces are different in structure and function. What other things have an inner and outer surface?

- Membranes contain many tiny proteins that actively pump substances across the membrane in one specific direction. This is useful when large amounts of a substance are needed, or when a substance must be moved from a lower to a higher concentration. Membrane pumps allow concentrations of substances inside the cell to be regulated. What happens when something is pumped?

## What enters and leaves cells?

Cells are examples of open systems because materials and energy can enter or leave. Only energy can pass in and out of closed systems. The cell membrane forms a boundary that prevents entry of most materials that are either toxic or not needed by the cell. It allows entry of useful substances.

All cells allow gases to diffuse in and out. Usually one gas enters and another gas leaves—this movement is called gas exchange. For example, plant cells that are carrying out photosynthesis absorb carbon dioxide and release oxygen.

1. What gases enter and leave human cells?

2. Under what conditions do you expect liver cells to **a)** absorb glucose from the blood and **b)** release glucose into the blood?

3. Do you expect human muscle cells to absorb or release glucose? Give reasons for your answer.

Energy in different forms enters and leaves cells. Heat energy can cross the cell membrane freely. Heat either enters or leaves cells, depending on whether a cell or its surroundings are at a higher temperature. All cells produce some heat, so the predominant movement of heat is outwards from cells. Foods contain chemical energy, so when glucose, fats and other foods enter or leave cells there is also a movement of energy. Cells that are carrying out photosynthesis absorb light energy. Some cells that are **phosphorescent** or **fluorescent** release it.

4. Suggest conditions in which human cells will gain heat from their surroundings.

5. Suggest types of plant cells that **a)** take in foods and **b)** release foods.

6. Which parts of the human body have cells that absorb light?

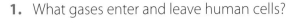**ABC** **Fluorescent** cells give out light immediately after absorbing it.

**Phosphorescent** cells give out light for a long time after absorbing the light or by generating it within the cytoplasm.

▼ Phosphorescent cells such as these algae in the sea allow light out through their cell membranes

# Summative assessment

**Statement of inquiry:**

Discoveries made using new techniques can change our understanding of the natural world.

 ## Cell structure

For questions 1–4, select your answer from these options:

**A.** nucleus **C.** mitochondrion

**B.** cell membrane **D.** chloroplast

**1.** Which cell component contains nearly all of a cell's DNA?

**2.** Which cell component can regulate the concentration of substances such as sodium ions in the cytoplasm?

**3.** Which cell component releases energy by aerobic respiration?

**4.** Which cell component produces oxygen?

**5.** Which organisms are made of cells?

**A.** All organisms

**B.** All organisms apart from bacteria

**C.** All organisms apart from bacteria and fungi

**D.** Plants and animals only

**6.** What is most likely to happen if a living cell was cut in half?

**A.** Both halves would die.

**B.** One half would survive and the other half would die.

**C.** Both halves would survive if they contained mitochondria.

**D.** Both halves would survive if they contained half the nucleus.

**7.** Which of these parts of the human body are made of cells? Put a tick or cross next to your answer(s). [2]

- muscle
- skin
- nerve
- bone

**8.** Which of these organisms are made of cells? Put a tick or cross next to your answer(s). [2]

- chimpanzees
- jellyfish
- redwood trees
- yeast

 ## Hypotheses and evidence

**9. a)** Imagine that a new disease appears which destroys anything made of cells. Which of the following will be destroyed by this disease? Put a tick or cross next to your answer(s). [4]

- humans
- bacteria
- clouds
- rivers
- air
- meat
- plastic
- dead bodies
- fire
- trees
- crops

**b)** How did you decide what would be destroyed by the disease? [2]

**10. a)** Which number is closest to the total number of cells in the human body? [1]

**A.** 50

**C.** 50,000,000 (50 million)

**B.** 50,000 (50 thousand)

**D.** 50,000,000,000,000 (50 million million)

**b)** Did you guess or did you use evidence to get your answer? Which is the best approach? [1]

**c)** How can you tell if your evidence is reliable or not? [1]

## Using electron microscopes to research cells

The photograph on the right was taken using an electron microscope and shows a small part of a plant cell.

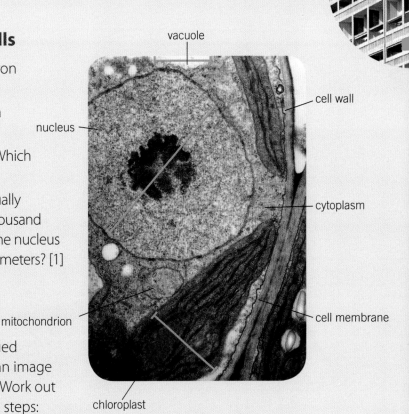

11. Could this type of cell be part of a petal, a root or a leaf? Give reasons for your answer. [1]

12. a) Seven cell components are shown in the photo. Which is the thinnest? [1]

b) Because cell components are small, biologists usually measure their sizes in micrometers. There are a thousand micrometers in one millimeter. The diameter of the nucleus is 0.0033 millimeters. What is its diameter in micrometers? [1]

c) The chloroplast and the mitochondrion have smaller diameters than the nucleus. Work out their diameters in millimeters. [1]

13. Electron microscopes are used to produce magnified images of cell components. The magnification of an image is how much larger it is than the actual structures. Work out the magnification of this photo by following these steps:

a) Use a ruler to measure the diameter of the nucleus in the photo. Do this in millimeters, not centimeters. [1]

b) Convert the diameter in millimeters to micrometers. [1]

c) Divide the diameter of the nucleus in the photo by its actual diameter, which you worked out in 12.b). Be sure that both diameters are in micrometers. The value that you have calculated is the magnification of the photo. [1]

14. From your answers to previous questions, what are the reasons for using electron microscopes to study the structure of cell components? [3]

## Blood cells and anemia

This is the appearance of human blood, viewed with a microscope at a magnification of ×400. Red blood cells are visible. In normal blood about 50% of the volume is cells (approximately 4 million cells per cubic millimeter of blood) and the other 50% is a pale yellow fluid called blood plasma. If someone is anemic, they have fewer red blood cells than normal and a smaller percentage of the volume is cells.

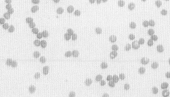

15. Design a method for testing a person's blood to find out whether they are anemic. [5]

16. Look at the statements A and B below.

A. After looking at blood using a microscope, people sometimes misunderstand the structure of living organisms and think that they **contain cells**.

B. By looking at many different parts of animals and plants we can see that living organisms are **made of cells**.

Using scientific language effectively, explain why conclusion A is misleading and how conclusion B is supported by evidence. [5]

# 3 Food

◄ In 2003, illusionist David Blaine spent 44 days suspended in a transparent case with water to drink but no food. During this time his body mass decreased by 25% and his body mass index (BMI) dropped from 29.0 (overweight) to 21.6 (ideal weight). What are the dangers of fasting for this length of time? Would the consequences have been different if Blaine's weight at the start of the experiment was the "ideal" weight? Under what circumstances might a human experience conditions similar to these? Carry out some research to determine the strategies the human body uses to survive starvation

◄ Have you ever heard the saying "You are what you eat"? Is this true? If so, could you identify someone as a meat-eater or a vegan, by just looking at them?

We will need to change how we transform materials and energy to achieve sustainable production and equitable distribution of food in the 21st century.

▲ To survive on Earth, humans need to compete with other species for air, water, food and space. For example, orangutans in South-East Asia have lost much of the forest habitat that used to feed them because the land has been cleared for palm oil production

How much of the food produced on Earth do humans need and how much should be available to all the other organisms? Through research, find out what fraction of food produced by agriculture is actually consumed and how much is wasted

▶ How do plants such as these lilies (*Cardiocrinum giganteum*) grow over two meters tall in just a few weeks without us having to feed them any carbohydrates, fats, protein or vitamins?

# Introduction

<table>
</table>

**Key concepts:** Change

**Related concept:** Energy, Transformation

**Global context:** Globalization and sustainability

**Statement of inquiry:**

We will need to change how we transform materials and energy to achieve sustainable production and equitable distribution of food in the 21st century.

- Food is the variety of chemicals that we need to sustain life.
- Food is both a building material and a fuel.
- Some organisms, including animals, get food by consuming other organisms.
- Other organisms, including plants, make their own food using photosynthesis.
- Energy from the Sun is used in photosynthesis to change simple chemicals, such as carbon dioxide and water, into foods by a sequence of chemical reactions.
- To use food as a fuel, we release its energy in a chemical process called respiration.
- Every cell has to carry out respiration to supply the energy that is needed to sustain life.
- Respiration is a series of chemical reactions, each of which changes food.
- Certain key stages in respiration release energy in a usable form.
- Respiration can occur either with oxygen (aerobic) or without oxygen (anaerobic).
- Two examples of the use of energy are maintaining body warmth and motion (movement).

▼ Photosynthesis in corn plants is particularly efficient in hot and dry conditions. Global production of corn is now greater than any other crop. It is used as a food for both humans and livestock and is also used to produce ethanol, which is a renewable fuel for vehicles. How is a corn crop changed into ethanol?

▼ On average, a person will use 11,000 kilojoules (kJ) of energy to run a marathon. Glucose (the sugar carried in blood) contains 16 kJ per gram, so nearly 700 g of glucose would be needed to supply this energy. The body stores glucose in the form of glycogen in the liver and muscles. Unfortunately, only about 500 g can be stored. What are the consequences of this for marathon runners?

- To use food as a building material in our bodies, it has to be in the form of small subunits.
- Digestion involves breaking down large complex chemicals in our food into small subunits.
- Our cells then use the small subunits to build large and complex chemicals that are key components of our bodies.
- Cells produce these complex chemicals when they are growing and also when repairs are needed.
- Without food neither growth nor cell repair is possible.

Photosynthesis produces vast quantities of food. In his book *Harvesting the Biosphere*, Vaclav Smil assesses how much of this is taken and used by humans. The amount is currently estimated to be between 17% and 25%. It is used in four ways: food for humans, food for livestock, fuel that is burned to provide energy, and material for making things such as buildings and paper.

Is it acceptable for one species to take up to a quarter of all the food produced on Earth, when there are millions of other species that also need food to survive?

The UN has projected the global human population to reach 11.2 billion by 2100. What percentage of food produced by photosynthesis would be needed for that population? What would the effect of this human population rise be on other species?

Biologist EO Wilson believes that half of the Earth's land surface should be designated a human-free natural reserve to preserve biodiversity. Do you agree? Research his Pulitzer prize-winning book *Half-Earth* on the internet.

▲ A snake may only feed once a month, or even less, but it is very effective at digesting the prey that it has swallowed. Only the tough protein keratin, which makes up hair and feathers, remains undigested.

 **Hens' eggs**

Laying hens produce about 330 eggs per year. To produce a typical egg weighing 55 g (not including the egg shell), a hen needs to eat 132 g of food containing about 1,560 kJ of energy. The egg contains 610 kJ.

Use pie charts to display this data. What happens to the energy in the hen's food that does not end up in the egg?

**ATL** **Information literacy skills**

## Present information in a variety of formats

Pie charts are used to represent information in the form of proportions or percentages.

1. Looking at the data in the question on hens' eggs, what other formats could be used to display it?

2. How does the purpose of the data affect the choice of display format? For example, if the information were meant to indicate a food chain, why is the preferred format of data display usually a pyramid shape rather than a pie chart?

## What nutrients are needed in the human diet?

Humans need five types of chemicals in their food: carbohydrates, lipids (fats and oils), proteins, minerals and vitamins. These dietary chemicals are known as nutrients. Water is also needed in the diet but is not usually thought of as a food or a nutrient.

Study the information in the table below and then answer the questions that follow.

**Carbohydrates and lipids** are both mainly used to provide energy, though they are also used in smaller quantities for constructing parts of cells. For example, omega-3 fatty acids, found in some lipids, are needed for making cell membranes, especially in brain cells.

| **Carbohydrates** | **Lipids** are high-energy |
|---|---|
| are sweet-tasting sugars and chemicals such as starch that are made by linking sugars up to form larger molecules.<br><br>Sugars and starch only contain carbon, hydrogen and oxygen, in a CHO ratio at or close to 1:2:1. | carbon compounds that do not dissolve in water. They contain only carbon, hydrogen and oxygen, but there is less oxygen than in carbohydrates. Two important types are fats and oils. Both are liquid at human body temperature (37°C) but at room temperature (20°C) fats are solid and oils are liquid. |

**Proteins** can be used as an energy source, but more importantly they supply the building blocks for making the cell's own proteins. These building blocks are called amino acids. A protein molecule consists of a string of amino acids, often hundreds, and sometimes even thousands, of amino acids long.

There are 20 different amino acids in proteins. We need all of these, but some amino acids can be converted in our cells into other ones. There are 12 amino acids that we cannot make in this way, so they are called essential amino acids. These must be in our diet or we suffer a deficiency disease and cannot make enough protein in our cells.

Protein deficiency has various names around the world, including kwashiorkor, but the signs are always the same: restricted growth and fluid retention that makes the abdomen swollen.

**Minerals and vitamins** are needed in relatively small quantities and cannot supply the body with energy, but they are nonetheless all essential. If any mineral or vitamin is missing from the diet then a deficiency disease results. Rickets is an unusual example of a deficiency disease as it can be due to a lack of the mineral calcium or of vitamin D. Rickets is still common in some populations despite its causes and methods of prevention being well-understood.

| **Minerals** | **Vitamins** |
|---|---|
| **Minerals** are chemical elements that are absorbed as simple compounds or ions. The body needs five of these in quite small quantities including calcium and sodium. More than ten other elements are needed in very small quantities, including the metals iron and zinc and the non-metals iodine and boron. Each mineral has specific uses in the body. Iron is needed to make hemoglobin, the red oxygen-carrying chemical in blood. Iodine is needed to make thyroxin, a hormone that controls how fast we release energy in our body. | **Vitamins** are complex carbon compounds that the body cannot produce itself. They are chemically very varied but can be divided into two groups: fat-soluble (vitamin A and D) and water-soluble (vitamin C and all the B vitamins). Vitamins have many different roles in the body. Vitamin C for example is needed during the production of a tough rope-like protein called collagen that strengthens parts of the body such as skin, tendons, ligaments and blood vessel walls. Scurvy is a disease caused by vitamin C deficiency. The symptoms are due to insufficient collagen in the body. |

Conduct some independent research to answer the following questions—the first question **a)** in each pair is easier than the second one **b)**, which is more of a challenge. Your choice!

1.  **a)** Each of the following foods is rich in one of the five nutrient types—which one? Soy beans, honey, butter, bread, cheese.

    **b)** Name a food that is rich in each of these chemicals: vitamin C, vitamin D, calcium, iodine, boron.

2.  **a)** If you measured the amounts of the five nutrient types (minerals, vitamins, proteins, lipids and carbohydrates) in your body, which would be the largest?

    **b)** Arrange the five nutrient types in order according to the amounts in your body, starting with the smallest.

3.  **a)** Water is not usually considered to be a food. Why not?

    **b)** Growth requires producing more cells and this requires producing more DNA. There is DNA in the foods that we eat.
    Is DNA therefore a sixth food type?

4.  **a)** Look at the two groups of food on the right. What are each of these two groups of foods rich in?

    **b)** Explain which is the "odd one out" in each group of foods.

---

### 📊 Should we drink smoothies or eat fruit?

Food scientists carried out an experiment on a group to compare the effects of drinking a fruit smoothie with eating fresh fruit salad—both containing the same quantity of protein, fat, carbohydrate and fiber.

Two hours after the participants had drunk the smoothie or eaten the fresh fruit, they were asked to rate how full they felt on a scale from zero (empty) to 100 (extremely full) and whether they felt more hungry or less hungry on a scale from minus 100 to plus 100. Average results are shown in the following table.

|  | **Fullness** | **Hunger rating** |
|---|---|---|
| smoothie | 31 | −21 |
| fruit salad | 48 | −34 |

1.  Summarize the differences in the table for the smoothie and the fruit salad results.

2.  A feeling of fullness is called satiety. Suggest reasons for the difference in satiety, given that the quantities of protein and other food types consumed were the same.

3.  Discuss whether it is better to drink a fruit smoothie or eat an equivalent quantity of fresh fruit.

The full results of this experiment are available online in the article *A Comparison of the Satiety Effects of a Fruit Smoothie, Its Fresh Fruit Equivalent and Other Drinks*, by Peter Rogers and Roya Shahrokni. You could carry out a similar experiment to investigate smoothies.

## How does the human body digest food?

One of our major body systems has the job of digesting the food that we eat and absorbing the products of digestion. In simple terms, the digestive system is a tube that runs from our mouth to our anus, through which food passes. This tube is called the **gut** and consists of a series of **organs** that each specialize in particular aspects of breaking down or absorbing foods. For example, the stomach stores food after a meal, kills bacteria in the food and gets protein digestion started.

The sequence of organs used in the digestive system is:

mouth → esophagus → stomach → small intestine → large intestine → anus
       (gullet)                      (duodenum    (colon and
                                 and ileum)    rectum)

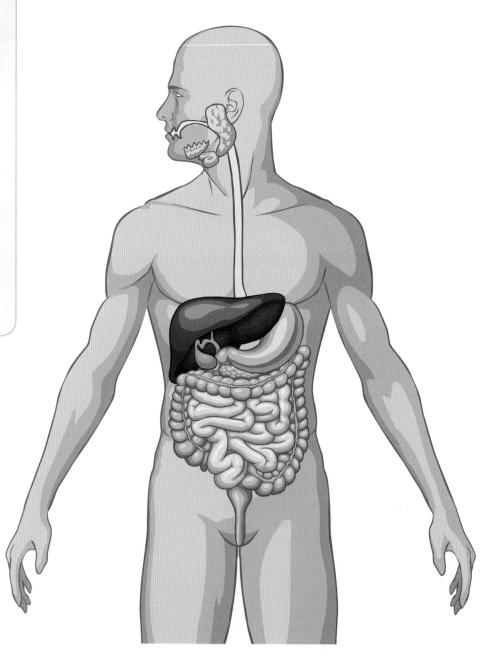

**ABC**

**Ingestion** is the taking in of food (usually through the mouth) for subsequent digestion.

**Feces** is material that reaches the end of the gut, mainly consisting of gut bacteria and undigested parts of foods such as plant fiber.

**Egestion** is the removal of feces from the gut (usually through the anus).

An **organ** is a part of an animal or plant that is composed of different tissues that work together to perform a function.

A **catalyst** is a substance that speeds up a chemical reaction.

The **gut** is the tube in the body that food passes through.

▶ Can you identify each organ and trace the route that food follows from **ingestion** to **egestion**?

# How do enzymes help with digestion?

Although teeth chop food into smaller pieces and the stomach and intestines churn this food to help break it up, digestion is mostly a chemical process. Large food molecules are broken down into smaller molecules until subunits are produced that are small enough to absorb into the bloodstream. The chemical reactions that break down food are carried out by enzymes—biological **catalysts**—which speed up the process. Digestive enzymes are made in big quantities by cells in the wall of the gut and also in special organs connected to the gut, primarily the salivary glands and the pancreas.

Over 20 different types of enzyme are used to digest our food. They are needed because each enzyme can only digest one type of chemical in food. The names of most enzymes end in –ase and the enzyme name as a whole usually tells you what it digests. Amylase digests amylose (a long chain of glucose molecules) into maltose (pairs of glucose molecules). A different enzyme is needed to digest maltose. Can you guess what this enzyme is called?

The digestion of amylose and maltose can be presented using chemical equations. The reactant (starting material) is shown on the left of the equation and the product on the right. The enzyme is shown above the arrow of the equation because it is not changed or used up during the reaction.

▲ These two cooked pasta shells were kept in a liquid for 24 hours. The one on the left was kept in saliva and the one on the right in tap water. What has happened to them? What conclusions can you draw about the properties of saliva?

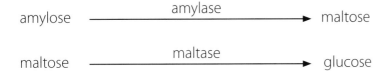

$$\text{amylose} \xrightarrow{\text{amylase}} \text{maltose}$$

$$\text{maltose} \xrightarrow{\text{maltase}} \text{glucose}$$

 **Experiment**

### Digesting starch

Starch is a carbohydrate that plants make to store glucose and therefore energy. Amylose is a common form of starch.

### Materials and apparatus needed

- Starch dissolved in water—a concentration of 1 g of starch per 100 ml of water is suitable. Heat is needed to dissolve starch.

- Amylase dissolved in water—this could be made from pure amylase powder, or from wheat seeds that have been germinated and ground up to release their enzymes.

- Iodine solution—this is used to test whether starch is present or not. If there is no starch present, the solution is brown; if starch is present the solution will be blue-black.

- Test tubes.

- Apparatus to measure quantities of liquid such as syringes, small measuring cylinders and pipettes.

- Spotting tiles for carrying out starch tests.

- Thermometer and apparatus for keeping test tubes at a constant temperature.

- Electronic timer.

**Basic procedure**

1. Put 5 ml of starch solution in a test tube.

2. Put 1 ml of amylase solution in another test tube.

3. Heat up both tubes to 40°C.

4. Pour the starch solution into the tube containing amylase solution, mix the contents and start the timer.

5. Take a drop of the starch–amylase mixture and put it into a cavity on a spotting tile. Test for starch by adding a drop of iodine solution. Does the iodine solution go brown or black?

6. Repeat the previous stage 1 minute after mixing the starch and amylase, and again after 2, 4 and 8 minutes. How long does it take for the starch to be digested?

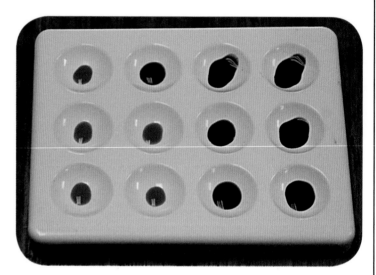

▲ Your results should look something like this

**Troubleshooting**

- If the starch hasn't been digested after 8 minutes, repeat the basic procedure with starch solution that you have diluted with water. If the starch still isn't digested, your amylase is probably inactive.

- If the starch has already gone when you first test it, repeat with amylase solution that you have diluted with water.

- If you aren't sure whether test results are brown or black, put a drop of pure starch solution in a cavity and a drop of water in another cavity. Add a drop of iodine solution to each and compare the colors.

**Going further**

When you have successfully digested some starch solution, you can devise an experiment to investigate something that might affect how fast the starch is digested by amylase. Here are some suggestions:

1. Test the effect of heat by repeating your procedure at higher and lower temperatures.

2. Test the effect of pH by repeating with different amounts of citric acid and sodium hydrogen carbonate.

## Fuelling Chris Froome's victory in the Giro d'Italia

Chris Froome won the Giro d'Italia (Tour of Italy) bicycle race in 2018. Early on in the race, Chris was suffering from an injured knee and his form was uncertain. However, in the 19th stage of the race, he was able to take the lead.

Stage 19 was a particularly gruelling one—185 kilometers with 3,500 vertical meters of ascent. Much of Chris's success was undoubtedly due to his team's plans for refuelling him far more often than is usual during cycle races. Look at the following infographic, which describes the refuelling plan.

**BREAKFAST**

200ml juice
400g rice
egg (3 whites /1 yolk)
4 pancakes with jam
green tea with honey

| | Mass (g) |
|---|---|
| Carbohydrates | 189 |
| Protein | 31 |
| Fat | 32 |
| Total energy (kcal) | 996 |

**RACE (5 h 12 min):**

14 × energy gel    2 × energy drink

| | Mass (g) | Mass per hour (g/hr) |
|---|---|---|
| Carbohydrates | 502 | 96 |
| Protein | 4 | 1 |
| Fat | 4 | 1 |
| Total energy (kcal) | 2,348 | |

1. Chris's team knew that only 90 g of carbohydrate per hour could be absorbed into the bloodstream from food in Chris's gut. How much in total could enter his bloodstream during the race?

2. What was used to supply this carbohydrate?

3. Chris's team staff were posted at key refuelling points along the race route to give Chris food. According to the plan, how many times did they aim to do this and why was this better than giving one large supply of food at the start of the race?

4. The expected energy expenditure during the race was 6,180 kJ. The amount of energy in food given at refuelling points during the race was 2,348 kilocalories. Convert this amount of energy into kilojoules (1 kilocalorie is equal to 4.2 kilojoules). Was it enough?

5. Fat contains more energy per gram than carbohydrate. Why was so much carbohydrate and so little fat given to refuel Chris during the race?

6. The content of Chris's breakfast and the food supplied to him during the race were very different. What are the reasons for this difference?

## Which is better—aerobic or anaerobic respiration?

**Respiration** happens in all plant and animal cells. Complex food molecules such as carbohydrates and lipids are broken down by a sequence of chemical reactions to release the energy stored in them. There are two ways of doing this. Human cells usually perform aerobic respiration, but sometimes they also use anaerobic respiration. This table compares these two processes in humans.

> **ABC**
> **Respiration** is the release of energy in a living organism which occurs when food molecules are broken down.

| Aerobic | Anaerobic |
|---|---|
| uses oxygen | no oxygen needed |
| produces water and carbon dioxide | produces lactic acid |
| releases the maximum amount of energy from a food | only releases some of the energy in food |
| can only release energy moderately rapidly | can release energy very rapidly |
| can continue indefinitely | can only be done for brief periods |
| can be fuelled by sugars or lipids (fats or oils) | can only be fuelled by sugars |

Both types of respiration consist of many chemical reactions but their overall effects can be summed up with a single equation each:

Aerobic respiration:    glucose + oxygen ⟶ carbon dioxide + water

Anaerobic respiration:        glucose ⟶ lactic acid

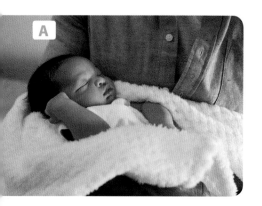

A

The oxygen used in aerobic respiration is breathed in and the carbon dioxide is breathed out through the lungs. Water produced by aerobic respiration helps to keep the body hydrated. The lactic acid produced by anaerobic respiration would be poisonous if it reached a high concentration. To prevent this from happening, we can stop respiring anaerobically, if necessary, by reducing the amount of energy that we are using.

Consider the activities in the following images (A–D) and decide which type of respiration is mainly being used to provide the energy needed in each image.

B

C

D

# What is the energy from respiration used for?

Our bodies need energy to:

- build proteins and other complex chemicals needed for growth
- keep the brain functioning and send messages using nerves
- pump blood round the body and food along the inside of the gut
- move the body by contracting muscles
- pump chemicals into and out of cells.

Whenever energy is used for these purposes, some of it is converted to heat. This helps to keep the body at 37°C, which is the average human body temperature. In cold conditions, not enough heat is generated to keep the body warm so extra respiration occurs in special tissues called brown adipose. Shivering is another way of generating extra heat.

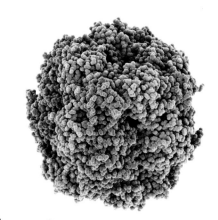

▲ The most abundant protein in leaves is rubisco (top)—an enzyme used in photosynthesis. The most abundant protein in humans is collagen (bottom). What sequence of events has to happen for rubisco, eaten as part of the diet, to be converted into collagen?

 **What is a Goldilocks diet?**

Goldilocks had porridge for breakfast. It had to be just the right temperature. A Goldilocks diet gives us just the right amount of energy. How can we make sure we get this? Firstly, we can listen to what our body is telling us. Appetite and satiety are two feelings that tell us when to eat and when to stop eating. In the  past this would have given us enough energy and also stopped us from becoming too fat. Unfortunately, we now tend to eat foods that are so rich in energy that it is easy to take in more than we need. If the body's natural system for controlling energy intake isn't working well enough, we may need to learn more about how much energy different people need and different foods contain.

Find a reliable website that gives recommendations for how much energy different people need and a database that gives the energy content of foods. Use this information to answer the following questions. Some sample websites include www.nrv.gov.au and www.foodstandards.gov.au

1.  What happens to the amount of energy needed by a child as they grow older?

2.  Compare the average amounts of energy needed by boys and girls.

3.  For a child of your age and sex, what is the difference in energy requirement between the lowest and highest physical activity level? Try to give your answer as a percentage.

4.  What happens to a woman's energy requirement during pregnancy?

5.  Using your chosen website, find the highest daily energy requirement of all and describe a person who would need it.

6.  Find three foods with a very high, and three foods with a very low, energy content.

7.  Compare the dietary energy content of your favourite snack food with that of a carrot.

8.  Foods containing starch and fiber take longer to digest and so make us feel satiated for longer, helping to reduce energy intake. Goldilocks ate porridge for breakfast. Explain whether this was a good choice, compared with other possible breakfast foods.

**Media literacy skills**

# Evaluating websites

Not all information sources are equal in value. When conducting internet-based research always ask yourself "Am I confident that this is a credible, authoritative website that can be used within a school setting?"

Here are some guidelines:

- What is the name of the creator or the author of this website? If you cannot locate the author, seek another source. There are exceptions to this—some credible sources such as the World Health Organization may not include the author on their websites.

- Is the author of this website reliable and qualified to write about the topic? If you cannot determine their credentials, seek another source. For example, a writer on nutrition should reasonably be expected to have some academic credentials.

- Is this website provided by an organization or a corporation? What does this organization or corporation do? You can determine this by clicking on a link that says "About us". Ask yourself, is it possible that their presentation of information is biased or one-sided?

- What kind of website is this? Is it a blog, an advertisement or an interview?

- Is this website appropriate for research within a school? What is the domain of the website? Typically .edu, .gov and .org organizations are more suitable sources than .com but this will still require some judgement.

 **Trekking across the South Pole**

Aleksander Gamme is a Norwegian explorer. In 2011 he completed the first ever solo, unsupported trek to the South Pole and back. Aleksander spent 90 days on skis in the icy wilderness pulling a sledge with all his equipment and food. He traveled 2,270 kilometers and endured freezing temperatures, hunger, loneliness and hard effort.

Here are some answers to questions that Aleksander answered for readers of this book. Read Aleksander's answers and then answer the questions that follow.

*How much energy were you able to take in from food per day?*

"I started with 15,000–19,000 kJ [per day] in the first week, and then going up to 27,000 kJ a day. I had a diet with a fat percentage up to 50% and used a lot of effort testing out a diet with less refined sugar and more nutritious food with good fatty acids."

*How much body mass did you lose during the expedition?*
"I started with a body mass of 100.5 kg and finished with 76 kg."

*How much mass did you pull on a sledge or carry?*
"I started with 175 kg and 15 kg in a backpack."

*How far did you travel?*
"Approximately 2,280 km."

*What were the temperatures during the expedition?*
"Pretty much between –10°C and –25°C. But it's the wind making it cold, and it's pretty much windy all the time."

"The wind falls down from the icecap, so on the way in to the pole, it's always facing the wind. And then it's a lot faster the other way, with downwind, light pulls and picking up my own caches along the way. Cache with fuel and food every second degree (of latitude)."

*Did you feel cold or warm when you were sleeping?*
"When out of the coastal climate, Antarctica is cold but dry. On sunny days it's quite comfortable in the tent, because the sun's radiation heats up the tent. I had a double sleeping bag, but used only one on most of the trip. Because it's dry air it's easier to dry up socks and clothing and wet stuff, a lot easier than in the Arctic Ocean where the humidity makes that a real fuss. I also supplied myself with two solar panels, charging up a 10,000 mAh battery pack. That made me able to charge iPods, cameras and my satellite phone."

1.  A typical adult male needs about 10,000 kJ of energy from food per day. How much energy from food did Aleksander consume per day during the main part of his expedition, expressed as a percentage of the typical adult male amount?

2.  What are the reasons for Aleksander needing more energy during his expedition?

3.  **a)** How much body mass did Aleksander lose during the expedition?

    **b)** What are the reasons for the loss of body mass?

4.  A headwind blows against the direction of the travel of an object, whereas a tailwind blows with the direction of travel. What are the reasons for a headwind making Aleksander feel colder than a tailwind or no wind at all?

5.  Why is it important for an Antarctic explorer to dry out wet clothing before putting it on again?

## What happens in photosynthesis?

- In science *synthesis* means making a chemical and *photo* means light, so **photosynthesis** is making chemicals using energy from light.

- To make carbohydrates by photosynthesis, carbon and oxygen are obtained from carbon dioxide and hydrogen from water.

- Carbohydrates such as glucose are the main foods produced by photosynthesis but other foods needed for growth can be made, such as amino acids (the building blocks of proteins).

- Leaves absorb carbon dioxide from the air and light from the sun.

- Roots absorb water from the soil and also minerals.

- Minerals are simple chemicals found in the soil that are used to supply elements other than carbon, hydrogen and oxygen. For example, nitrate and sulfate are absorbed from the soil to supply nitrogen and sulfur, which are needed to make amino acids.

**ABC** **Photosynthesis** is using energy from light to split water into hydrogen and oxygen and to produce carbon compounds by combining the hydrogen with carbon dioxide.

Synthesis of glucose in plants can be shown with a simple equation:

carbon dioxide + water ⟶ glucose + oxygen

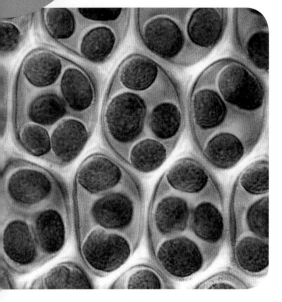

1. Plants, chloroplasts, leaves and chlorophyll are all green in color. Each of them could be 5 meters, 5 millimeters, 5 micrometers or 5 nanometers long. Find out what size each is and then arrange them in order of size, starting with the smallest.

2. Do you agree with the following claims? Explain your answers.

   a) Plants grow faster when they are given green light than when they are given blue or red.

   b) Plants acquire material for growth chiefly from air and water.

   c) Energy is produced in photosynthesis.

   d) All energy released by animals in respiration was once sunlight captured by plants.

   e) Leaves are the lungs of a plant.

 Chloroplasts in leaf cells of the moss *Atrichum androgynum*

## ATL Communication skills

### Interpreting discipline-specific terms

In the life sciences and other academic disciplines, we must be able to use and interpret discipline-specific terms and symbols. For example, terms that have a broad everyday meaning, but a more focused meaning within a discipline. The word 'food' in the life sciences is an example.

▶ Garden centers sell products that are labelled "plant food", but to a life scientist they are not real food as they do not provide the plant with any energy. They only contain minerals such as nitrate, phosphate and potassium. What discipline-specific term could be used for this product instead of plant food? Do you think that "fertilizer" or "mineral nutrient" is better?

## 👥 Opportunities for contributing to research as amateur scientists

Citizen science initiatives are opportunities for community volunteers to get involved in experiments. Often this involves members of the public gathering data and submitting their findings to an online database. Coordinators of citizen science projects usually share the data that is generated, by giving public access to it. In some cases, the aim of an experiment is to educate or change local practice.

For example, in the summer of 2018, the organization at www.permaculture.co.uk challenged the public to grow three garden crops separately, known as a monoculture, and also grow the three crops together in one plot, known as a polyculture. They provided a map of how the plots were to be constructed and a short online course on how to take measurements. Polyculture is viewed as a more sustainable form of agriculture.

Scientific American (www.scientificamerican.com) maintains a database of citizen science projects as does www.citizenscience.gov.

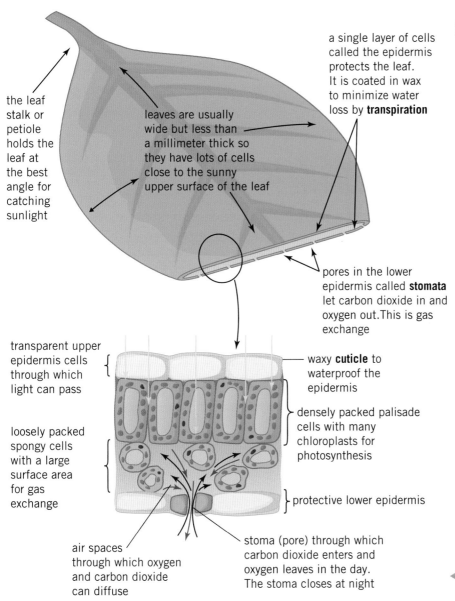

the leaf stalk or petiole holds the leaf at the best angle for catching sunlight

leaves are usually wide but less than a millimeter thick so they have lots of cells close to the sunny upper surface of the leaf

a single layer of cells called the epidermis protects the leaf. It is coated in wax to minimize water loss by **transpiration**

pores in the lower epidermis called **stomata** let carbon dioxide in and oxygen out. This is gas exchange

transparent upper epidermis cells through which light can pass

loosely packed spongy cells with a large surface area for gas exchange

air spaces through which oxygen and carbon dioxide can diffuse

waxy **cuticle** to waterproof the epidermis

densely packed palisade cells with many chloroplasts for photosynthesis

protective lower epidermis

stoma (pore) through which carbon dioxide enters and oxygen leaves in the day. The stoma closes at night

◀ What features of a leaf help with photosynthesis?

> **ABC** A **stoma** (plural: **stomata**) is a pore found in the lower epidermis of a leaf.
>
> **Transpiration** is the process in which water is lost by evaporation from the leaves through the stomata.
>
> The **cuticle** is a waterproof waxy coating that protects the leaf.

## Are leaves perfectly designed?

The answer to this is no, for two reasons:

1. Biologists don't use the word "designed" for things like leaves, because unlike buildings or machines, nobody designed them. There is fossil evidence to show that leaves have been developing by evolution over hundreds of millions of years.

2. We cannot say that any leaf is perfect because new features could develop that make the leaf even better at photosynthesis. A plant with leaves that are better at photosynthesis will have a strong advantage over other plants.

▲ Leaves of a fern fossilized more than 300 million years ago

One of the problems for plants is that a large wet surface area is needed inside the leaf for absorption of carbon dioxide and for excretion of oxygen, but valuable water tends to evaporate from this surface and be lost from the leaf. This water loss is called transpiration. When water is difficult to obtain, plants need to reduce water loss by transpiration. Use the internet to research leaf adaptations that reduce transpiration in plants living in dry areas.

## Which groups of organisms make food by photosynthesis?

Plants are not the only group of organisms that can make food by photosynthesis. Algae and some types of bacteria also do it. All bacteria and some algae are microorganisms—organisms that are so small that they can only be seen individually with a microscope.

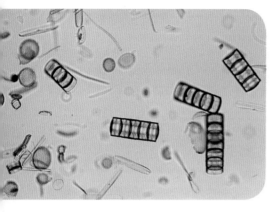

▲ Phytoplankton are very small algae, but they make vast amounts of food by photosynthesis because there are such large numbers of them in lakes and seas

▲ Seaweeds are large algae usually found in shallow seas or along rocky shores that make food by photosynthesis, even if they look red or brown rather than green

◄ Several groups of bacteria make food by photosynthesis, including the cyanobacteria (blue-green bacteria), which sometimes multiply to form vast "blooms". Brightly colored bacteria in hot springs also produce food by photosynthesis. Bacteria in this pool in Upper Geyser Basin of Yellowstone National Park are colored green and yellow

# Summative assessment

**Statement of inquiry:**

We will need to change how we transform materials and energy to achieve sustainable production and equitable distribution of food in the 21st century.

▼ Special types of bee are needed to pollinate the flowers of the Brazil nut tree, such as *Eulaema meriana*, seen here. These bees are rarely found outside natural rainforest. Without pollination, no nuts are produced

▲ Brazil nut trees (*Bertholletia excelsa*) live in moist lowland Amazon rainforests. They grow up to 50 meters tall and can survive for 500 or more years

▼ The fruit of the Brazil nut tree is a large capsule (right) that is the size of a baseball. It can contain up to 24 individual Brazil nuts, each enclosed in a woody seed case (left). One tree could produce 50 capsules of nuts per year. One nut weighs approximately 5 g and contains 137 kJ of energy

▲ Agoutis are large rodents living in the rainforest. They are able to break open the hard capsules and the woody seed cases and eat the nuts. They store Brazil nuts when they are abundant by burying them in the soil. Some of these buried nuts germinate and grow into new trees

**Growing Brazil nuts**

Use the information accompanying the photos and your own knowledge to answer these questions.

1.  **a)**  How many nuts could one Brazil nut tree produce per year? [1]

    **b)**  How much would these nuts weigh in total? [1]

    **c)**  How much energy would the nuts from one tree contain? [1]

2.  **a)**  Which part of the Brazil nut tree collects the energy needed to make food? [1]

    **b)**  What process is used to make food in a Brazil nut tree? [1]

    **c)**  What conditions in a tropical rainforest allow this process to happen very rapidly? [3]

3.  What are two reasons for agoutis needing to eat food such as Brazil nuts? [2]

 **Nutritional content of Brazil nuts**

The table shows the nutritional content of Brazil nuts per 100 g. RDA is recommended daily allowance.

| Nutrient | Content | % of RDA | Amino acid | Content |
|---|---|---|---|---|
| thiamine (B1) | 0.617 mg | 54% | tryptophan | 0.141 g |
| riboflavin (B2) | 0.035 mg | 3% | threonine | 0.362 g |
| niacin (B3) | 0.295 mg | 2% | isoleucine | 0.516 g |
| vitamin B6 | 0.101 mg | 8% | leucine | 1.155 g |
| folate (B9) | 0.022 mg | 6% | lysine | 0.492 g |
| ascorbic acid (C) | 0.7 mg | 1% | methionine | 1.008 g |
| vitamin E | 5.73 mg | 38% | cysteine | 0.367 g |
| calcium | 160 mg | 16% | phenylalanine | 0.630 g |
| iron | 2.43 mg | 19% | tyrosine | 0.420 g |
| magnesium | 376 mg | 106% | valine | 0.756 g |
| manganese | 1.2 mg | 57% | arginine | 2.148 g |
| phosphorus | 725 mg | 104% | histidine | 0.386 g |
| potassium | 659 mg | 14% | alanine | 0.577 g |
| sodium | 3 mg | 0.13% | aspartic acid | 1.346 g |
| zinc | 4.06 mg | 43% | glutamic acid | 3.147 g |
| | | | glycine | 0.718 g |
| starch | 0.25 g | - | proline | 0.657 g |
| sugar | 2.33 g | - | serine | 0.683 g |
| dietary fiber | 7.5 g | - | **Nutrient type** | **Content** |
| water | 3.48 g | - | carbohydrate | 12.27 g |
| | | | fat | 66.63 g |
| energy | 2,743 kJ | - | protein | 14.32 g |

4. Calculate the total mass per 100 g in Brazil nuts of:

    **a)** vitamins [2]    **b)** minerals. [2]

5. Display the data for the content of the main food types in Brazil nuts using the style you think is most suitable. [3]

6. The selenium content of Brazil nuts is 1.92 mg per 100 g. The RDA for adults is 0.060–0.075 mg per day. The safe limit is 0.4 mg per day and daily intake above 1 mg is toxic. What advice would you give to people about selenium in Brazil nuts? [3]

## Melting points

Vegetable oil is extracted from seeds. It varies in the content of saturated fat, monounsaturated fat and polyunsaturated fat. Vegetable oil is solid at cold temperatures and liquid at higher temperatures. The temperature at which this change occurs is called the melting or the freezing point. The table shows data for five types of vegetable oil.

| Vegetable oil | Saturated fat (%) | Monounsaturated fat (%) | Polyunsaturated fat (%) | Melting point (°C) |
|---|---|---|---|---|
| flaxseed oil | 8 | 21 | 71 | −24 |
| olive oil | 11 | 79 | 8 | −6 |
| peanut oil | 18 | 48 | 34 | 3 |
| coconut oil | 92 | 6 | 2 | 25 |
| palm oil | 52 | 38 | 10 | 35 |

Brazil nut oil contains 25% saturated fat, 40% monounsaturated fat and 34% polyunsaturated fat.

7. **a)** Using the data in the table, decide what you would expect the melting point of Brazil nut oil to be. This is your hypothesis. [2]

    **b)** Explain how you used the evidence in the table to decide on your hypothesis. [4]

    **c)** Design an experiment to test your hypothesis. [4]

## Brazil nuts and sustainable food production

8. Using scientific language, evaluate the sustainability and fairness of Brazil nut production. You could include these ideas:

    • Would it be better to clear natural rainforests and grow Brazil nut trees in plantations?

    • Which is more sustainable—agriculture, or gathering food from rainforests and other natural ecosystems?

    • Should agoutis be killed to stop them eating Brazil nuts?

    • What percentage of Brazil nuts should humans eat and what percentage should be left for other species?

    • What will happen as the human population rises and demand for Brazil nuts increases? [10]

# 4 Reproduction

**Key concept:** Relationships

**Related concepts:** Consequences, Form, Pattern

**Global context:** Personal and cultural expression

Ocean sunfish are among the largest of bony fish, growing to 1000 kilograms (1 tonne). Females produce as many as 300 million eggs. Eggs and sperm are released in special parts of the oceans called spawning grounds. The offspring increase in size by a factor of about 60 million as they grow to adulthood. By what factor does a human increase, to reach adult size? What are the advantages and disadvantages of producing so many eggs?

Kiwis are flightless nocturnal birds, native to New Zealand. Females lay a single egg that is unusually large in relation to body size—it can be as much as a quarter of female body weight and takes 30 days to be produced. How much would a human egg weigh if it was 25% of body weight? After being laid, the egg is incubated by the male until it hatches after 9–13 weeks.

What are the advantages and disadvantages of producing such a large egg?

**Statement of inquiry:**

The relationships between specific organisms are affected by their form of reproduction.

▲ Alpine salamanders (*Salamandra atra*) are 140 to 150 mm long. Males and females mate and fertilization then happens inside the female's body. Usually just a single embryo develops, feeding on the yolk from its egg until it is born. The length of time spent inside the female varies with altitude—two years for females living at 800 meters above sea level, rising to as much as three years at 1600 meters.
How does this compare with humans?

◄ Lonesome George was the last member of his species—the Pinta Island Galápagos tortoise (*Chelonoides abingdonii*). Goats introduced to Pinta reproduced rapidly, destroying the tortoise's habitat. In captivity, George was mated with females of other closely related tortoise species, but although eggs were laid, none of them ever hatched. He died on 24 June 2012 at an age of at least 80. What lessons can we learn from Lonesome George?

**Statement of inquiry:**

The relationships between specific organisms are affected by their form of reproduction.

> "
> *Sexual reproduction is the chef-d'oeuvre, the masterpiece of nature.*
> "
>
> *Erasmus Darwin, 1800*

## Introduction

Reproduction can happen without parents forming an obvious relationship if they simply release their gametes into the wind or into surrounding water. It is then up to each male gamete to find and fuse with a female gamete, making a zygote. The zygote develops into a new individual with no more help from the parents. Many plant and animal **species** reproduce in this way.

In other species, males and females form partnerships that last until death and they only reproduce with their partners. Strong parent–offspring bonds are formed that are never broken. Family groups may develop into clans where siblings, cousins and other related individuals cooperate. Between these extremes of minimal and deep relationships, there is immense variation in how reproduction happens. Even so, a common pattern is seen in most plants and animals.

- Plants and animals produce offspring by sexual reproduction.
- Sexual reproduction is the production of male and female gametes and their fusion to form zygotes.
- A zygote is the start of a new life.
- Male gametes are smaller than female gametes and travel to the female gametes.
- Gamete production involves halving the number of chromosomes per cell.
- Meiosis is a special division which halves the number of chromosomes.
- Some organisms also reproduce asexually.
- In asexual reproduction there is only one parent and all offspring have the same genes.

There are powerful forces encouraging reproduction, caused by inheritance and evolution. Organisms alive today are the result of successful reproduction, generation on generation, over billions of years. Only organisms with genes that promote reproduction will produce offspring. Offspring inherit genes from their parents and usually inherit the ability and instinct for reproduction. Individuals do not pass on their genes if they do not reproduce. If a whole species fails to reproduce, it will become extinct.

Choosing a partner is one of the most significant decisions that humans make. Another decision with very significant consequences is whether to have children or not. In the past, it was common to have 10 or more children but today nearly all people choose to have fewer. This decision is heavily influenced by the culture and traditions of the

community where we live. For example, there was a one-child policy in China for many years. Humans have a personal say in decisions about reproduction. Having a child is a creative act in a biological sense, but we may prefer to develop our creativity in other ways. In a world where the human population has increased considerably, we should look beyond ourselves when deciding on our reproductive life plan.

 **Reading a passage from Darwin's *On the Origin of Species*, 1859**

You can find the full text of *On the Origin of Species* at http://darwin-online.org.uk/

Read pages 64–66 and answer the following questions.

1. What is "geometrical increase"?

2. Darwin mentions the rapid increase in the number of cattle and horses in Australia after they were released into the wild. Can you find another example of an animal that reproduced prolifically after being introduced to Australia?

3. a) Darwin tells us that the fulmar (*Fulmarus glacialis*) is believed to be the most numerous bird in the world despite laying only one egg when it reproduces. Can you explain how there could be a very large population of a species with such a low reproduction rate?

   b) What is the difference between saying that fulmars are the most numerous bird and that they are believed to be the most numerous?

   c) Carry out some research into the number of fulmars in the world since Darwin wrote *On the Origin of Species*.

▲ Darwin revised his book repeatedly—there are six editions

## What is a species?

A species is a type of organism. Scientists use double names for species. For example, humans are *Homo sapiens* and the grape vine is *Vitis vinefera*. The second of the two names in each case is the species name. The first name is the genus. A genus is a group of similar species.

◀ These birds on the island of South Georgia are members of the same species, *Aptenodytes patagonicus* (king penguins). They are all very similar in appearance and only ever reproduce with other king penguins. Emperor penguins are quite similar to king penguins and have the name *Aptenodytes forsteri*

Members of a species share many features, including their outward appearance. The reason for this is that in most cases organisms only reproduce with other members of their own species. Offspring therefore only inherit features of that species. This gives us a definition: a species is a group of organisms that interbreed with each other and therefore have similar features.

In most cases members of different species do not reproduce with each other. This is called hybridization because the offspring are hybrids. Hybrids between species are rare in nature and are usually not able to reproduce—they are sterile.

Lions and tigers have sometimes bred with each other. The offspring are called ligers or tigons, depending on which parent is the lion and which is the tiger. Male ligers and tigons are infertile but females sometimes produce offspring. Ligers and tigons have only been produced in zoos, because lions and tigers live in different parts of the world and do not normally meet each other. This may be the reason for them not having developed natural methods to avoid hybridization.

▲ A liger is the offspring of a male lion (*Panthera leo*) and a female tiger (*Panthera tigris*)

## 📊 Naming of butterflies

An iridescent (glistening) butterfly was discovered in 1911 in the Amazon and named *Caeruleuptychia helios*. In 2012 a brown butterfly discovered in the same area was given the name *Magneuptychia keltoumae*. DNA research has now shown that they are males and females of the same species. Males and females have no difficulty in recognizing each other when looking for a mate, even if this can leave biologists confused!

| | Upper side of wings | Underside of wings |
|---|---|---|
| **Male** | | |
| **Female** | | |

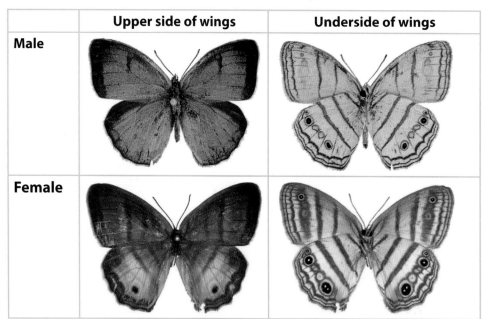

1. What are the similarities and differences between the males and females?
2. What features might the males and females use to recognize each other?
3. Why do you think the females were discovered 100 years later than the males?
4. How could biologists avoid making similar naming mistakes in the future?

1. Find out whether these are names of real species:

   *Aha ha*                          *Panama canalia*

   *Agra vation*                     *Myrmekiaphila neilyoungi*

   *Medio annis*                     *Dracorex hogwartsia*

   *Parastratiosphecomyia stratiosphecomyioides*

2. Find the scientific names of these species:

   Little bustard          Polar bear          Giant squid

   Bald eagle              Grizzly bear

3. Choose five species that you are interested in and find their scientific names.

▲ These beetles must be in the same species because they are mating. They are *Donacia* beetles but as there are there are over 70 species in this genus we would need an expert to identify which species they belong to

## How do animals choose a partner for mating?

Animals select their mates in many different ways. Their first essential step is to check that any potential partner is the right species. They can do this using distinctive features such as scent chemicals (pheromones), colored markings, or behavior patterns.

In some species, it is up to the female which male she mates with, so the males have to impress her. This can involve very elaborate courtships. In other species males compete for females by either threatening to fight other males or by actually fighting. For example, the antlers and horns of male mammals are used to intimidate or, if that fails, as weapons in fights. In some species males use cunning to mate quickly with females when the dominant male is absent or distracted.

▲ The flowers of the Australian small tongue-orchid (*Cryptostylis leptochila*) look like females of a wasp species (*Lissopimpla excelsa*) and release the same pheromones. Male wasps of this species are attracted to the orchid and vigorously attempt to mate with the flowers. If two orchid plants trick them, the male wasps transfer pollen from the first to the second

◄ The DNA of bonobo (*Pan paniscus*) babies at Twycross Zoo, UK was compared with that of the three adult males. The alpha (most dominant) male had fathered fewer babies than a less dominant male

▲ Great hornbills (*Buceros bicornis*) mainly use vocal calls in their courtship displays. Pair bonds are strong and long-lasting. After mating, the female lays one or two eggs in a nest that she has built in a hollow inside a tree. She then seals up the opening of the hollow with plaster made mainly from feces, leaving only a narrow slit through which the male can feed her. The female incubates the eggs for 40 days until they hatch and she then looks after the offspring in their first weeks of development. Only then does she emerge from her imprisonment and both male and female parents work to feed their young

▲ A peacock (*Pavo cristatus*) displays his tail feathers to peahens. If they are sufficiently impressed, mating may follow. Can you explain the reasons for peahens choosing to mate with males that have the best display of tail feathers? Charles Darwin was interested in this question

▶ Male fallow deer (*Dama dama*) fight at traditional rutting sites called leks, during the mating season in the fall. Males that are victorious in these fights then mate with any female that comes to the lek. What is the advantage of this pattern of behavior to the females?

If members of a species are very scattered, it can be an advantage to find and remain with one partner. In addition, if both parents have to work hard to rear their offspring there are advantages in having a strong and faithful partner. About 3% of mammal species choose partners for life and do not mate with any other member of their species. This pattern of behavior is more common in birds.

1. In some mammal and bird species, females only mate with one male, whereas males attempt to mate with many different females. Can you explain this difference?

2. In many bird and butterfly species, the males are brightly colored and flamboyant, whereas the females are drab and inconspicuous. Can you explain this difference?

3. In many spider species, the females are much larger than the males, whereas in most mammals the males are larger than the females. Can you explain these differences?

## What is the difference between males and females?

In most animals and some plants, adults are either male or female. They only produce male or female gametes. Adults in some species produce both male and female gametes. They are called hermaphrodites. Even in these species there are clear differences between the two types of gamete.

Consider the following examples and then decide what is the essential difference between males and females.

Atlantic purple sea-urchins (*Arbacia punctulata*) all have the same appearance but each adult only produces male or female gametes. The gametes are produced inside the body and are released into sea water. Male gametes are sperm and swim to the female gametes (eggs) to fertilize them.

▲ Adult male or female *Arbacia punctulata*

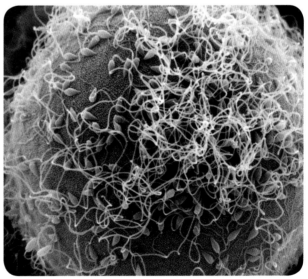

▲ In this electron micrograph of an *Arbacia punctulata* egg, many sperm are visible on its surface, but only one of them will fertilize it. In this species, the eggs are 80 μm in diameter

The fern *Ceratopteris richardii* has a tiny gamete-making stage in its lifecycle called the prothallus. Some prothalli produce both male and female gametes and some only produce male gametes. The sperm has a "head" coiled four times and about 80 "tails". The "head" is at the back and the "tails" are at the front when it swims!

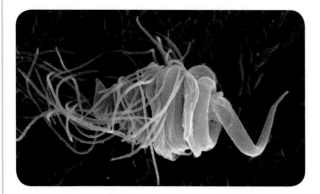

▲ Sperm with coiled "head" and many "tails". It is about 4 μm across at its widest point

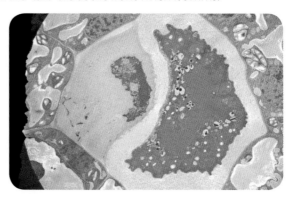

▲ The dark crescent-shaped cell with a wavy margin is an egg. It is about 30 μm across. The egg is retained in the prothallus, where the sperm fertilizes it by fusing with the concave side. Why can ferns such as this only reproduce in damp habitats?

Male and female cattle (*Bos taurus*) are similar in outward appearance but bulls are larger and their testes are prominent, whereas cows have an udder (mammary gland). There are many differences between the reproductive systems of male and female cattle. Fertilization happens inside the cow's oviduct and sperm have to swim there from the cow's vagina.

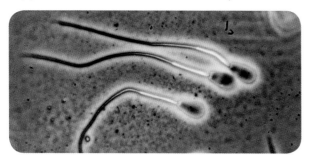

▲ The head of bull's sperm is 7 μm in diameter

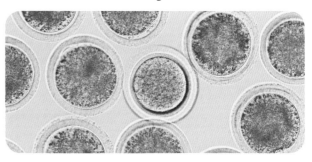

▲ Cattle eggs are 100 μm in diameter. They have a coat made of gel that helps to ensure that only one sperm fertilizes each egg. Why is this important?

Lily plants (*Lilium regale*) produce both male and female gametes inside their flowers. Male gametes are made inside pollen grains and female gametes inside an ovary in the center of the flower. The male gamete consists of little more than a nucleus. It cannot propel itself to the egg and instead is carried firstly inside the pollen grain and then in a tube that grows out from the pollen.

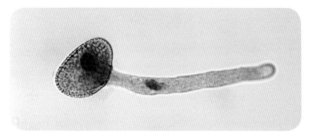

▲ A tube has grown out from the pollen grain. The male gamete is visible as a purple oval

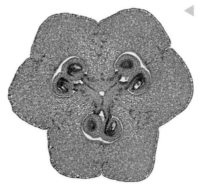

◄ In this section of a lily ovary there are six egg cells, each of which would be fertilized by a gamete from a separate pollen grain. How does the pollen get from one flower to another?

###  Growing C-ferns

The fern *Ceratopteris thalictroides* had been widely used in research. Because of its long name it is often abbreviated to C-fern. Its natural habitat is water in ponds or swamps.

Kits for growing C-ferns from spores are available from scientific suppliers. The spores grow into small flattened plants that produce male and female gametes. The sperm can be observed under a microscope. Zygotes produced by the fusion of these gametes grow into mature C-fern plants. Lots of experiments can be carried out with growing C-ferns.

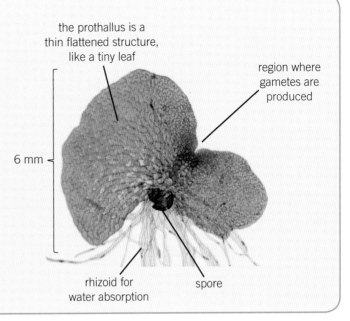

the prothallus is a thin flattened structure, like a tiny leaf

region where gametes are produced

6 mm

rhizoid for water absorption

spore

## What pattern of gamete production and release is there in humans?

Patterns can exist in time or space. They can be sequences of events or arrangements of features. All of these types of pattern can be seen in the production and release of gametes in men and women.

1.  **Where are gametes produced?**

    **Gametes** are produced in organs called **gonads**. Both men and women have a pair of gonads. Women have ovaries inside their abdomen, where egg production happens at body temperature (37°C). Men have testes (also called testicles) in the scrotum. The scrotum is a sac of loose skin outside the abdomen which provides the slightly lower temperature (35 or 36°C) needed for healthy sperm production. The positions of the gonads and other organs are shown in the diagrams of male and female reproductive systems.

    a)  When the testes start developing they are in the abdomen. In most boys they descend into the scrotum before birth. In approximately 4% of boys, one of the testes is undescended at birth and an operation may be needed to move it to the scrotum. What would be the disadvantage of leaving the testes in the abdomen?

    b)  At a very early stage in human development there are embryonic gonads that could either develop as ovaries or testes. It is extremely unlikely that one will develop as an ovary and the other as a testis. Suggest a reason for this.

> **ABC**
>
> **Gametes** are cells produced for sexual reproduction that are either male or female and have half as many chromosomes as the parent that produced them.
>
> **Gonads** are the organs in animals that produce gametes.

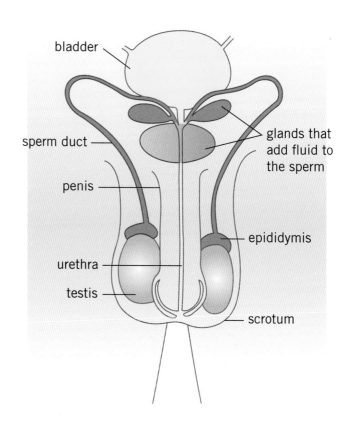

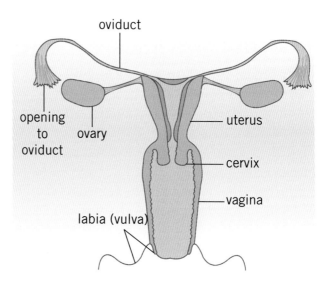

▶ 'The male (top) and female (bottom) reproductive systems'

## 2. At what times are gametes released?

A woman's body prepares again and again for pregnancy. The inside of the uterus (womb) is thickened to allow an embryo to develop there. Then an egg is released into the oviduct, where it may or may not be fertilized. If no embryo starts to develop, the thickening of the uterus lining breaks down and it is released in a process called menstruation or "a period". Preparations for pregnancy then start again.

This series of events forms a cycle—the menstrual cycle. It takes about 28 days. Release of an egg (ovulation) happens about half way between one menstrual period and the next.

The release of gametes in men does not follow such a clear pattern in time. Sperm are stored in the epididymis, next to the testis. They are released when the man ejaculates. The sperm are pushed along the sperm duct and glands near the bladder add fluids. This creates a liquid called semen, which is squeezed out through the penis in the urethra, in a series of pulses.

a) The menstrual cycle stops during a pregnancy. What is the reason for this?

b) In mothers who feed their baby solely by breastfeeding, the menstrual cycle usually does not restart until breastfeeding ends. What is the reason for this?

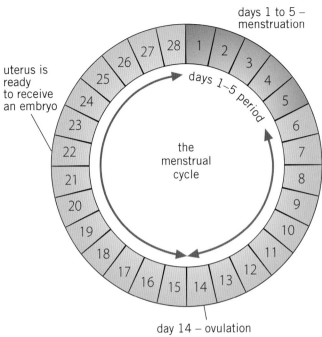

days 1 to 5 – menstruation

uterus is ready to receive an embryo

days 1–5 period

the menstrual cycle

day 14 – ovulation

▲ The events of the menstrual cycle

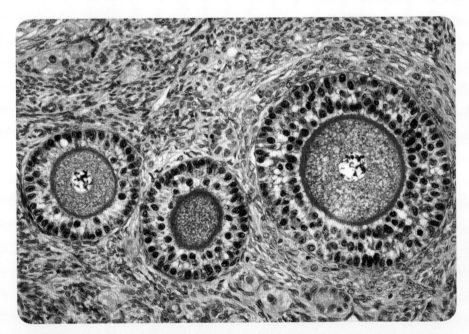

▲ The blue cells with pink coats are human eggs developing in the ovary. Fluid will build up around the egg later in development, producing a large sac called a follicle. At ovulation the follicle bursts and releases the egg from the ovary

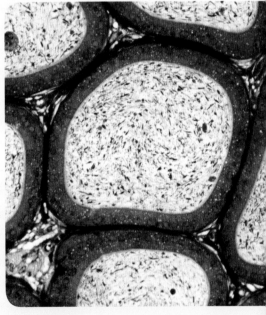

▲ The epididymis is a 6 m long coiled tube. It collects sperm from the testis, helps it to mature and then stores the sperm until ejaculation. Sperm only start to swim vigorously after ejaculation

### 3. When does gamete production begin and end?

Puberty is the time when the body goes through physical changes to move from childhood to adulthood. Girls become women and boys become men. The most significant event in puberty is the start of gamete production. Boys start to ejaculate sperm and girls start to release eggs into their oviducts. Puberty does not happen at a fixed age—it varies. Ejaculations in boys may not contain sperm for the first few months and in girls it may be a year or so after the first menstrual period that eggs start being released.

These are some examples of puberty changes:

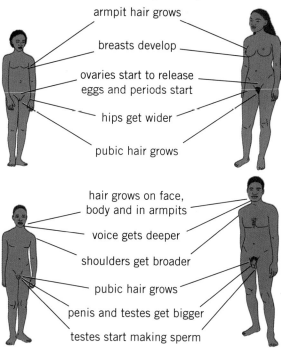

armpit hair grows

breasts develop

ovaries start to release eggs and periods start

hips get wider

pubic hair grows

hair grows on face, body and in armpits

voice gets deeper

shoulders get broader

pubic hair grows

penis and testes get bigger

testes start making sperm

> **ABC**
>
> A **zygote** is a fertilized egg produced by the fusion of the nucleus of the male and female gametes.
>
> **Mating** is the process by which sperm from a male are inserted into the body of a female.
>
> **Ovulation** is the periodic release of an egg cell from the ovaries to travel down the oviduct to the uterus, where it is available for fertilization.

Women undergo further changes in their late 40s or early 50s, known as the menopause. Levels of the sex hormone **estrogen** drop in the woman's body. A consequence of this is that eggs are not produced any more. In contrast, levels of the sex hormone **testosterone** do not drop significantly in a man's body. The consequence is that sperm production can continue until death.

a) Puberty starts at a younger age in most parts of the world than it did 100 years ago. What are the reasons for this?

b) The menopause is a developmental stage in women that is due more to genes than environment. It would not have evolved unless there were advantages for women, for families or for the community as a whole. What could these advantages be?

### 4. How many gametes are released?

Women usually release just a single egg when they ovulate. **Ovulation** happens once per menstrual cycle, so about one egg is produced per month. Sometime two or more eggs are released at the same time—this is how non-identical twins, triplets or larger numbers of babies can be born.

The number of gametes released by men is far more variable. The volume of semen ejaculated and the number of sperm per milliliter of semen both vary considerably between men. A typical ejaculation contains about 100 million sperm, so per month men can release vastly more gametes than women.

a) What are the reasons for men and women producing such different numbers of gametes?

b) The sperm count is the number of sperm per milliliter of semen. In many countries the sperm count has been falling over recent decades. What reasons can you find for this?

 **Testosterone** is a hormone that controls the development of male sex organs. It is produced in the testes.

**Estrogen** is a hormone that controls the development of female sex organs. It is produced in the ovaries.

## Providing access to menstrual hygiene products

Poverty, homelessness or cultural stigma can lead to situations where people don't have access to, or can't afford menstrual hygiene products. This can lead to students not attending school when they are menstruating.

A number of organizations exist to support education campaigns, fundraising activities and direct provision of hygiene products. Carry out some research into the activities of organizations such as Freedom4Girls, Days for Girls and Support the Girls. In your own community, if there is an organization that provides shelter for the homeless or a food bank, it is likely that they accept donations of menstrual sanitary products.

## How do male and female gametes come together in animals?

Male gametes always travel to meet female gametes, but there are many ways in which this can happen. The following table shows two strategies used in animals.

| | |
|---|---|
| Animals that live in water can easily release eggs and sperm. The sperm then swim to the eggs. To raise the chance of fertilization, all the gametes may be released at the same time in a population. | For animals that live on land it is better for males to **mate** with females and pass sperm into the female reproductive system. The sperm can then swim to the eggs. |
| Examples: bony fish, frogs, crabs and many other invertebrates, including corals and sponges. | Examples: arthropods including insects and spiders, terrestrial worms including earthworms, terrestrial slugs and snails, reptiles, birds and mammals. |

▲ Staghorn coral (*Acropora cervicornis*) releases eggs and sperm during the annual mass coral spawning on Ningaloo Reef. Why does this happen in different months in the northern and southern hemispheres?

▲ Birds have an opening to their reproductive system called the cloaca. During mating, the male mounts the female, presses his cloaca against hers and passes semen into the female. Here turkey vultures (*Cathartes aura*) are mating

1. a) How do gametes come together in marine mammals such as whales and dolphins?

   b) What are the advantages of this to marine mammals?

2. The photograph to the left shows a barrel sponge (*Xestospongia testudinaria*) that lives in shallow sea water off south east Asia and Australia. It is a male and is releasing sperm. Females look identical, but release eggs.

   a) The eggs are released from the central cup of the sponge and pour slowly down the outside. This happens at "slack water" when there are no tidal water currents, so the eggs stay close to the parent. What are the advantages and disadvantages of this?

   b) What are the advantages to this species of having separate males and females?

3. Why is the barrel sponge, which grows on Caribbean coral reefs, sometimes called the "redwood of the deep"?

## How do gametes come together in plants?

Plants don't move from place to place, so they can't meet up with each other and mate. Many plants are hermaphrodite and could therefore fertilize the eggs that they produce with their own male gametes but there are some major disadvantages to self-fertilization. To cross-fertilize, the male gametes from one plant must get to the female gametes on another plant. There are two main ways of doing this:

1. Mosses and ferns have male gametes that swim. They need a continuous layer of moisture in which to do this, from the sperm-producing plant to the plant that produces the eggs. This explains the absence of these types of plant from deserts and other dry habitats.

2. In flowering plants the journey of the male gamete to the egg happens in two stages. The male gametes are inside **pollen** grains. The pollen is transferred from where it is produced in the stamens of one flower, to a sticky pad called the stigma in another flower. Wind is used to transfer the pollen in some flowering plants, for example grasses. In other species, insects carry the pollen from stamen to stigma.

▲ This temperate rainforest in the South Island of New Zealand is an ideal habitat for plant reproduction with swimming male gametes. Mosses coat the rocks in the stream and ferns grow along the banks

▶ The cuckoo bee (*Nomada ruficornis*) covered in pollen

**Dissecting flowers**

In the image, three of the large yellow tepals have been removed from the left-hand tulip flower and all of them from the right-hand flower, to reveal the male and female parts. Pollen is produced in the anthers at the top of the six stamens. Eggs are produced inside the green ovary. Above the ovary is the sticky stigma that receives the pollen. Try dissecting some flowers yourself to see if you can find the stamens and the ovary.

The male gametes of flowering plants cannot swim, so even when they have reached the stigma, they have to be carried the last short distance to the egg. A tube grows out from the pollen grain. It grows into the ovary and to an egg cell, carrying the male gamete near its tip as it grows. The male gamete then fuses with the egg, to produce a zygote.

Conifers such as pine trees also use pollen to transfer male gametes. The pollen is produced inside male cones and is transferred by wind to female cones where the eggs are produced.

▲ Male cones are releasing clouds of pollen into the wind in this Luiang spruce tree (*Picea likiangensis*)

▲ Female cones, which contain eggs, on an Atlantic cedar tree (*Cedrus atlantica*)

1. What are the disadvantages of self-fertilization?

2. What prevents self-fertilization in humans?

3. What factors affect whether wind or insect pollination is more successful?

4. Bees and other insects cannot see the color red. What pollinates red flowers?

**ABC** **Pollen** is many tiny grains containing male gametes that are produced by conifers and flowering plants.

**Pollination** is transfer of pollen from the male parts of plants to the female parts. If the male and female parts are on the same plant it is **self-pollination**.

**Pesticides and pollination**

The most widely used pesticides globally in the 2010s were neonicotinoids. Biologists have investigated whether these pesticides harm the bees that pollinate plants. In one experiment colonies of bumblebees were treated with a low level of a neonicotinoid pesticide (10 parts per billion), a very low level (2.4 parts per billion) or none at all (control). The bee colonies were then placed with flowering apple trees. The bumblebees' behavior was monitored and their success in pollinating the apple flowers was assessed. Four types of measurement are shown in the following bar charts:

- The average number of visits to each apple flower by bees per minute.

- The number of bees that returned to the colony carrying pollen per hour.

- The length of time in seconds each bee spent on a trip away from the colony to collect pollen and nectar.

- The average number of seeds inside each apple when they were harvested.

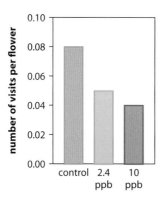 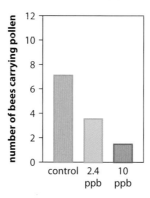 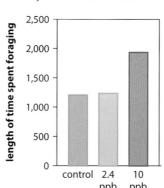 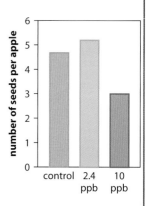

1. What effect did the pesticide have on numbers of bumblebee visits to apple flowers?

2. Bumblebees get their protein from pollen. What effect did the pesticide have on the amount of protein that the bumblebees could feed to their larvae?

3. What effect did the pesticide have on the efficiency of the bees at finding flowers and collecting pollen?

4. a) Very low levels of pesticide did not significantly affect the number of seeds per apple, but the low level of pesticide did have a significant effect. What was the effect?

   b) What are the reasons for the difference in the average number of seeds per apple?

   c) When apple seeds develop, they stimulate the growth of the fruit. What do you think the effect of the pesticide was on the size of the apples?

5. In some parts of the world, there are now too few bees for apple trees to be pollinated and humans pollinate the trees by hand. What is the disadvantage of this?

6. Bees seem to become addicted to neonicotinoid pesticides. How does this make them more harmful?

▲ A bumblebee collecting pollen and nectar from an apple flower

**Apple seeds**

In most apple varieties, the maximum number of seeds is 10, because that is the number of eggs that are made inside the ovary. Get as many apples of the same variety as you can, ranging from very small to large. Measure the size of the apples accurately, using the method you think is most suitable. Open each apple and count how many seeds there are. Display all your results using a scatter graph.

1. If you can see a trend on the scatter graph, try to find reasons for it.

2. What are the reasons for most apples containing fewer than 10 seeds?

▲ Two apples of the variety Sunset, cut in half

## What happens during and after fertilization?

Fertilization is the joining together (fusing) of male and female gametes. It is the moment when genes from two parents are combined and a new individual organism begins its life. In most plants and animals, the only parts of the male gamete that are needed are the chromosomes. The egg provides all other necessary cell structures and food stores. In mammals the egg is small, because development takes place inside the mother's body, who provides most of the food that embryo needs.

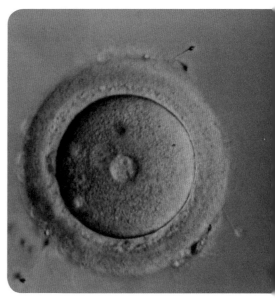

▲ This human egg is about 0.1 mm in diameter—less than the size of a full stop on a printed page! It is protected by a gel coating. Two nuclei are visible so the egg has already been fertilized—it has become a zygote

▲ In birds and reptiles, the egg is large and contains enough food (yolk) for the development of the embryo until it hatches out. This tortoise (*Testudo hermanni*) is hatching out after 100 days of development inside the egg shell

Human eggs are surrounded by a gel coating that blocks the route of the sperm to the egg. Enzymes released from the front of the sperm's head digest a hole through this gel coat, allowing the sperm to penetrate. The cell membranes of the egg and sperm then join together and the sperm's nucleus passes into the cytoplasm of the egg. The nucleus moves to the center of the egg where it joins with the egg nucleus. The egg has become a zygote.

**Meiosis** is division of a cell to produce four cells, each with half the original number of chromosomes.

An **embryo** is a plant or animal during the early stages of development from a zygote.

**Progesterone** is a hormone that maintains the lining of the uterus.

There are twice as many chromosomes in a zygote as there are in a sperm or egg. A human zygote contains 46 chromosomes, whereas the sperm and the egg each contain 23. As soon as one sperm has fused with the egg, the gel coat around it hardens, preventing any more sperm from entering. This is important, because if two sperm did fuse with the egg there would be 69 chromosomes in the zygote, and this would have fatal consequences.

A zygote soon divides to form a two-cell **embryo**. Further cell divisions and cell growth happen over the following days and weeks. Fertilization in humans occurs in the oviduct and early development of the embryo happens as it is moved towards the uterus. Seven days after fertilization, the embryo is a hollow ball of about 100 cells, called a blastocyst, which becomes implanted in the uterus wall a day or two later. The fetus will remain there, fed by its mother, for about nine months until it is ready to be born.

The yellow fever mosquito (*Aedes aegypti*) has only six chromosomes in three pairs. Therefore, the cells it produces by meiosis have three chromosomes, one each from pair one, pair two and pair three. How many combinations of chromosomes could the mosquito pass on to offspring in its gametes? How many combinations of a human's 46 chromosomes can be passed on to offspring?

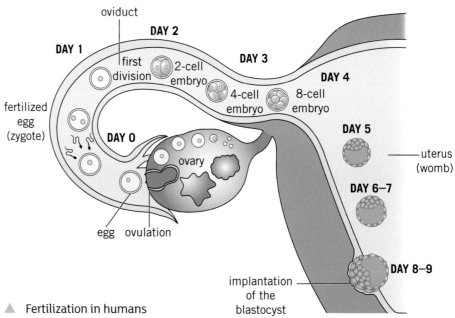

▲ Fertilization in humans

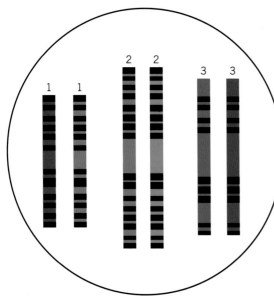

## How are gametes produced with half the usual number of chromosomes?

Fertilization doubles the number of chromosomes, because two gametes join together and they both contain chromosomes. At some stage in the life cycle of every organism that undergoes sexual reproduction, the number of chromosomes per gamete cell must be halved. This happens by **meiosis**. In humans, meiosis takes place in the ovaries and in the testes. It is an early stage in the production of gametes.

The chromosomes are in pairs. To halve the chromosome number, one of each pair is selected randomly. Because of this unpredictability, meiosis can produce lots of different outcomes—many different combinations of a parent's chromosomes could come together in a gamete. The combination that is formed is important because it decides which of a parent's genes the offspring inherit.

In meiosis, mistakes sometimes happen where either both chromosomes of a pair end up in one gamete, or neither of them. In nearly all cases this leads to the death of the gamete or of an embryo formed from the gamete. In just a few cases a baby can be born with 45 or 47 chromosomes per cell. For example, a Down syndrome baby has an extra chromosome 21.

## What are sex chromosomes?

There is one special pair of chromosomes in humans that influence whether we develop as males or females. They are the sex chromosomes. There are two types—a larger X chromosome and a very small Y chromosome. All humans have at least one X chromosome but the second sex chromosome can either be another X or a Y. Females are XX and males are XY. Therefore, females pass on one X chromosome in their eggs and males pass on either an X or a Y.

## What determines the sex and the gender of a child?

Biological differences between human males and females start with the sex chromosomes. Chains of consequences lead from X and Y chromosomes to other aspects of being male or female—what gonads and sex hormones we have, and also our primary and secondary sexual characteristics.

cell in testis
cell in ovary
XY
XX

meiosis
meiosis

**Gametes:** X  Y

50% of sperm have an X chromosome, 50% have a Y

X

all eggs have an X chromosome

X

X

XX  50% female

XY  50% male

Half the sperm swimming towards the egg are carrying an X chromosome and half a Y chromosome—it is just a matter of chance which type reaches the egg first and fertilizes it.

Gonads develop as testes if there is a Y chromosome in the embryo's cells and as ovaries if there are only X chromosomes.

From puberty testes produce sperm and ovaries produce eggs.

Testes produce testosterone. Ovaries produce estrogen and **progesterone**.

During puberty testosterone causes male secondary sexual characteristics to develop. Estrogen and progesterone cause female secondary sexual characteristics to develop.

Embryos develop male primary sexual characteristics (reproductive organs) if testosterone is present and female primary sexual characteristics if estrogen and progesterone are present.

**Before the birth of a child**

**During and after puberty**

1. a) Name any primary sexual characteristics for boys and for girls.

   b) Name any secondary sexual characteristics for boys and for girls.

2. Levels of sex hormones rise in boys' and girls' bodies during puberty.

   a) What physical changes does this cause?

   b) Suggest some behavioral changes that might be caused by the rise in sex hormones.

3. Gender is related to sex but is not the same thing. Here are definitions of sex and gender—which is which?

| The state of being male or female, especially the social and cultural differences | The two divisions of organisms, male and female, and the differences between them |
|---|---|

4. Do you accept these definitions of sex and gender? Can you find or write more helpful ones?

5. Are these personal features of an individual part of (i) sex only, (ii) gender only, (iii) sex and gender (iv) neither sex nor gender?

   a) whether they have an X or a Y chromosome or not

   b) whether they have ovaries or testes

   c) whether they like playing with dolls or kicking a football

   d) whether they make friends with boys or girls?

   e) whether they prefer to wear clothes traditionally worn by men or women.

6. Some people have a mismatch between their biological sex and gender identity (gender dysphoria). People who are experiencing these thoughts are advised to talk to their doctor. What help might doctors provide? Who else could be consulted?

## What are the differences between sexual and asexual reproduction?

Study the differences in the table and then answer the questions.

| | Sexual reproduction | Asexual reproduction |
|---|---|---|
| How many parents are involved? | There are two parents, one male and one female | There is only one parent, which could be either sex or both |
| Is there fertilization of gametes? | Male and female gametes are produced and fuse to produce a zygote | Gametes are not produced and there is no fertilization |
| Does the number of chromosomes per cell change? | Fertilization doubles the chromosome number, then later in sexual life cycles meiosis halves it | The number of chromosomes stays the same in asexual life cycles—there is no meiosis |
| Do the offspring have the same or different genes? | All offspring are genetically different from each other—every individual is unique | All offspring produced asexually by a parent are genetically identical—the offspring are clones |

1. Is each organism below reproducing sexually or asexually?

▲ Plantlets form on the leaves of the hen and chicken fern (*Asplenium bulbiferum*) and then drop to the ground

▲ If one of the five arms of the porous starfish (*Fromia milleporella*) is cut off, it can regenerate five new arms

▲ The yeast (*Komagataella phaffii*) has single cells 4 μm in diameter. The smaller cells budding off are offspring

▲ The red tomatoes (*Lycopersicon esculentum*) are fruits, each containing many seeds

▲ Violets (*Viola sororia*) sometimes produce inconspicuous underground flowers that self-pollinate.

◄ Male 14-spot ladybirds (*Propylea quatuordecimpunctata*) are smaller than females and have longer antennae

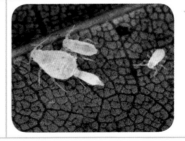

◄ Aphids sometimes live in all-female groups but they still manage to reproduce, giving birth to offspring that are already well-developed

2. Debate whether sexual or asexual reproduction is more useful to a species in these circumstances:

   a) When the environment is not changing and the species is very well adapted to it.

   b) When the environment is changing rapidly.

   c) When there are very few members of a species and they are widely scattered.

   d) When food and other resources are abundant enough to allow a rapid rise in population.

# Summative assessment

**Statement of inquiry:**

The relationships between specific organisms are affected by their form of reproduction.

## Reproduction in fulmars

Fulmars are birds that live out at sea for much of the year, in the North Atlantic and the South Pacific. The fulmars in these two areas are considered to be separate species, Northern fulmars (*Fulmarus glacialis*) and Southern fulmars (*Fulmarus glacialoides*).

1.  How can biologists decide whether the fulmars of the North Atlantic and South Pacific are the same or different species? [2]

Fulmars form pairs for life unless one dies, in which case the survivor takes a new partner. They breed on rocky cliffs, returning each year to the same nest site. Males and females mate frequently with their partner during the first part of the breeding season, after which the female develops and then lays one fertilized egg. The parents take turns (of up to 11 days) at incubating the egg. The male takes longer turns, allowing the female to feed more and replace resources used to make the yolk of the egg. The table gives data for the Northern fulmar. The hatchling is fed on the nest by both parents until it has grown to 115–119% of adult mass. The parents then stop feeding it. Four or five days later it flies from the nest and becomes independent (fledging).

| Breeding season | Late spring–early summer |
|---|---|
| **Number of eggs** | One per breeding season |
| **Time to hatching** | 47–53 days after egg laying |
| **Time of fledging** | 49–58 days from hatching |
| **Average age of sexual maturity** | 12 years in females<br>8 years in males |
| **Average lifespan** | 32 years |
| **Maximum lifespan** | Over 50 years |
| **Global population** | 7 million |

2.  Compare reproduction in fulmars and humans, giving as many similarities and differences as you can. [8]

▼ *Fulmarus glacialis* partners

▼ *Fulmarus glacialis* partners with their chick

## Measuring fertility rates

Fertility rate is the average number of young produced by a female during her life. On Orkney (Scotland) a long-running research program found that female fulmars on average raised 11 chicks to fledging (leaving the nest) during their breeding life, so that is the fertility rate of *Fulmarus glacialis*.

**3.** Explain how the fertility rate of a species could be measured. You could either describe how this would be done for fulmars, or choose any another species apart from humans. Include the observations that would have to be made and any calculations that are needed. [10]

---

## Changes in human fertility

The human population has been rising rapidly and there are concerns that it is now so high that damage to natural ecosystems is unavoidable. Further increases in human population are inevitable unless fertility rates fall. This has already happened in most developed countries.

China introduced a compulsory one-child policy in 1978–80 to reduce the fertility rate. This policy has now ended. Taiwan never introduced such a policy. The graph shows the total fertility rate (average number of children born to each woman during her whole life) in China and Taiwan from 1945 to 2015.

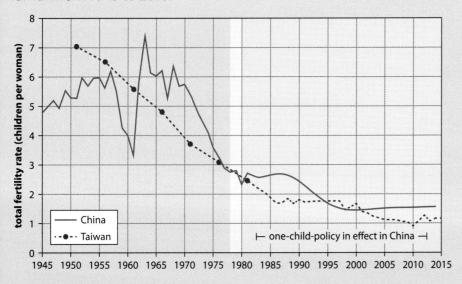

**Source of data**: Fertility in Taiwan from Taiwan's Ministry of Interior; Fertility in China before 1982 from Coale & Li (1987), later data from the World Bank.

**4.** What are the similarities and differences between China and Taiwan in total fertility rate? [4]

**5.** In 1960 a policy called the Great Leap Forward caused a famine. Explain the effect that this had on the total fertility rate. [2]

**6.** Prosperity rose in China increasingly rapidly from 1980 onwards. Some people claim that total fertility rate drops as prosperity rises, so women in China would have had fewer children even without a compulsory one-child policy. Use the data in the graph to discuss this claim. [4]

**Analyzing scattergraphs**

Scientists can influence what conclusions people draw from data by the format that they use to display it. Each point on the following graph shows the change in fertility rate and the cost of housing in one county in the US between 2010 and 2016.

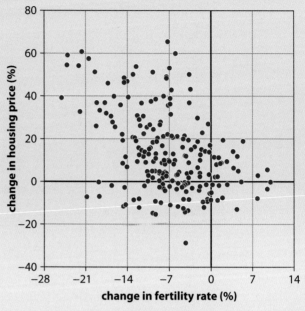

**Source of data:** Zillow Economic Research

7. What change happened to fertility in most counties between 2010 and 2016?

A. It increased

B. It decreased

C. It did not change

D. It went from negative to positive

8. What line of best fit on the graph would show the trend in the data?

A. A line joining all the points

B. A horizontal line

C. A straight line that is highest on the left and lowest on the right

D. A line that curves through the areas on the graph where there are most points

9. What conclusion do you draw from this graph?

A. An increase in fertility rate causes a decrease in house prices

B. An increase in house prices causes a decrease in fertility

C. Higher house prices are associated with lower fertility

D. There is no relationship between house prices and fertility

Evolutionary biologist Carl Bergstrom and information scientist Jevin West have suggested a new way of presenting data—a diamond plot. The following graph shows the same data as the previous graph but in a diamond plot

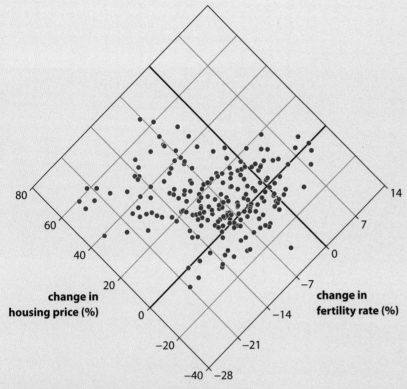

**Source of data**: Zillow Economic Research

**10.** What line of best fit on the diamond plot would show the trend in the data?

  **A.** A line joining all the points

  **B.** A horizontal line

  **C.** A straight line that is highest on the left and lowest on the right

  **D.** A line that curves through the areas on the graph where there are most points

**11.** What conclusion is most likely to be drawn from the diamond plot?

  **A.** An increase in fertility rate causes a decrease in house prices

  **B.** An increase in house prices causes a decrease in fertility

  **C.** Higher house prices are associated with lower fertility

  **D.** There is no relationship between house prices and fertility

**12. a)** Does the data in the diamond plot support the claim that women choose to have fewer children when their living standards rise? Explain your answer fully. [2]

  **b)** Discuss the factors that might influence a woman's personal choices about how many children to have. [3]

▲ The blue whale is a marine mammal. It is the largest animal ever to have lived on Earth. Blue whales are an endangered species and yet in 2018 an Icelandic whaling company killed one. Should humans protect organisms in other species or just protect ourselves?

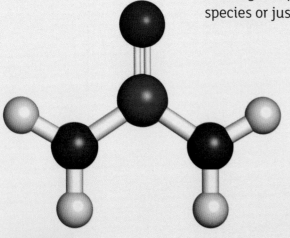

◀ In this model of a urea molecule, an oxygen atom and two nitrogen atoms are bonded to a carbon atom. Two hydrogen atoms are bonded to each nitrogen atom. Urea is a waste product that is filtered out of the blood by the kidneys and excreted. Its chemical properties are very different from those of the elements carbon, oxygen, nitrogen and hydrogen.

A group of atoms bonded together is a molecule. A molecule is the smallest separate part of a compound that has all of its chemical properties. What are the similarities between a molecule and an organism?

▶ Every organism is a separate individual. Are you an individualist, believing in personal freedom to act as you choose, or are you a conformist?

▼ This rusting wreck is unlikely ever to run again. What are the similarities between this vehicle and an organism?

**Statement of inquiry:**

Human identity includes the impulse to help family members and also those we are not closely related to.

**Key concept:** Systems

**Related concept:** Form, Function

**Global context:** Identities and relationships

**Statement of inquiry:**

Human identity includes the impulse to help family members and also those we are not closely related to.

## Introduction

The Oxford English Dictionary defines an organism as *an organized body with connected interdependent parts sharing common life*. This definition tells us that:

- All the parts of an organism are linked up—the body is a single separated whole.

- Body parts are arranged in a particular way—not randomly.

- Various body parts need each other—they interact and are interdependent.

- The body is therefore an example of a system, made up of multiple subsystems.

- Individual parts cannot survive by themselves—the whole organism lives or dies.

- Any individual animal or plant or bacterium or other form of life is an organism.

Organisms can be classified into two types: unicellular and multicellular.

| **Unicellular organisms** consist of a single cell. | **Multicellular organisms** consist of multiple cells. |
|---|---|
| The body parts acting as subsystems are structures within the cell. | Their body parts are groups of cells that make up tissues or organs. |
| Example: bacteria | Example: humans |

The organisation of single cells is considered in Chapter 2 Cells, so let's focus here on organization in multicellular organisms. Most multicellular organisms have multiple systems, each of which is composed of subsystems. Each system and subsystem has a function which other parts of the organism depend on.

Every organism produced by sexual reproduction is a separate individual with a unique identity. However, we do not live independently and relationships are important to all organisms. Humans in particular have the capacity to forge very close relationships.

▼ This family of swallow-tailed bee-eaters are huddling together to try to keep warm. How many organisms are here?

**Defining organisms**

"*Hard cases make bad law*" is a legal phrase that can equally apply to the life sciences. Test out the Oxford English Dictionary definition of "organism" by considering Cases A to F below.

▲ **Case A** When does a new generation of dandelions become organisms?

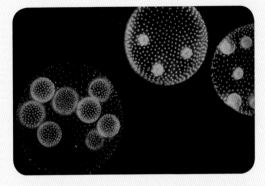

▲ **Case B** Volvox is a colonial alga. Each colony is a hollow sphere of gel, with individual alga cells stuck to the outside. Is each colony one organism or many?

▲ **Case C** Each of these mounds contains a termite colony, with a king and queen termite plus many soldiers and workers. None of these castes can live without each other. Is a termite colony one organism or many?

▲ **Case D** A lichen is a fungus with many small cells of algae growing with it. Is this one organism or many?

▲ **Case E** Identical twins are formed when an embryo splits and the two parts develop separately. Are they one organism or two?

▲ **Case F** In a lawn, the grass plants can grow and intermingle, making it very hard to count how many individuals there are. Is it possible to find out how many organisms there are in a lawn?

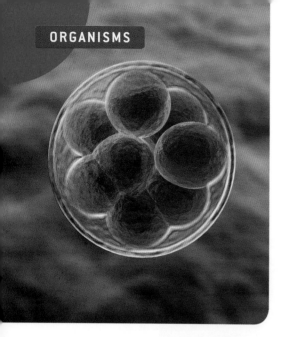

▲ In an 8-cell embryo the cells look the same, but they are already starting to communicate with each other about how each one should develop. A gel coat surrounds and protects the whole embryo

▼ Podocytes are among the strangest of cells found in the human body because of their shape. They are highly specialized and form a layer around capillaries in the part of the kidney where blood is filtered. In this photograph the podocytes are colored blue and red. Each podocyte has many narrow finger-like projections that wrap around a capillary. Fluid is filtered out of the blood through tiny gaps between these projections, in the first stage of urine production

# What is a tissue?

We start life as a single cell, formed by the fusion of a sperm and egg. This cell, called a zygote, divides to produce a two-cell embryo. After three more cell divisions and four days, a human embryo is a ball of 16 cells called a morula. At this stage the cells start to follow different paths. Depending on where a cell is in the embryo and what its neighbours are, it will develop in a particular way. By the time we are teenagers there are hundreds of different cell types in our bodies.

The function of a cell is the task that it carries out. Cells carry out a function more efficiently if their structure is suited to the task. For example, the function of a motor nerve cell (neuron) is to carry a message from the brain to a muscle. It can do this because it has a long narrow cable-like nerve fiber, along which the message can travel. There are many different functions to perform within our body and this explains why we have so many different cell types.

Cells are usually found in groups so that they can work together. A group of cells that is organised to perform one or more specific functions is a tissue. Here are some examples.

- The wall of the heart is made of *cardiac muscle tissue* and pumps blood.

- Fat reserves under the skin called *white adipose tissue* store energy and insulate the body against heat loss.

- The covering that lines the windpipe is *respiratory epithelium tissue*, which cleans the airways.

▼ The color of white adipose tissue is due to the large droplets of colorless fat that are stored inside the cells. A nucleus and small amount of cytoplasm is also present in each cell

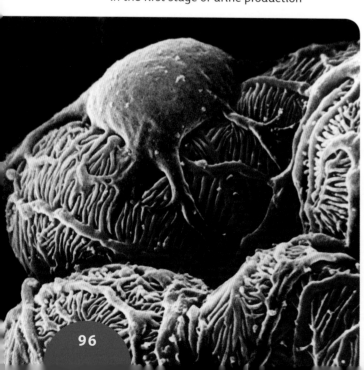

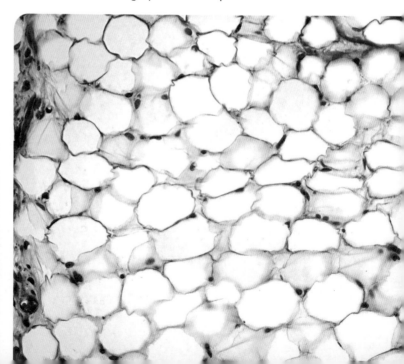

Some tissues contain large numbers of one cell type, for example the fatty tissue under the skin. Other tissues have two or more cell types that perform the tissue's function by interacting. This is seen in the alveoli—the tiny air sacs that make up the lungs. The function of alveoli is gas exchange—taking in oxygen and getting rid of carbon dioxide. This can only happen if there is a moist surface to allow the gases to dissolve. It is quicker if the gases only have to travel a short distance. The wall of an alveolus is a single layer of cells that is a mixture of two cell types. Most of the cells are very thin and permeable, allowing gases to diffuse across. The less common cells are much thicker. They produce the liquid that lines the inside of alveoli.

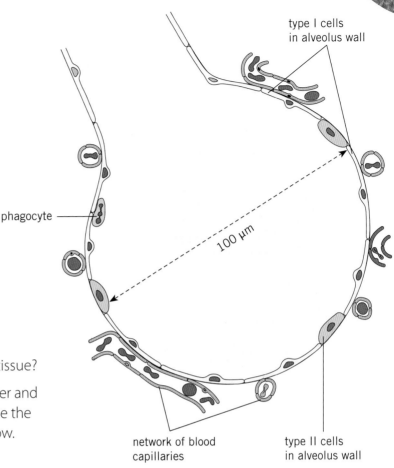

▲ This diagram shows the structure of the alveolus, where gas exchange occurs

1. What is the difference between a cell and a tissue?

2. The cells in most tissues are stuck to each other and do not change places, but in one special tissue the cells are separate and the whole tissue can flow. What is it?

3. Some tissues contain more than one cell type. Investigate the cell types in the respiratory epithelium— the tissue that forms the inner lining of the wind pipe.

    a) How many cell types are there in the respiratory epithelium?

    b) What is the function of each cell type?

    c) What is the structure of each cell type and how does it help the cell to carry out its function?

4. Brain tissues start to develop much earlier in an embryo than bone tissue. What are the reasons for this?

## What are the differences between roots and stems?

Plants are multicellular organisms. They have parts such as roots and stems, which are examples of organs. These organs have tissues arranged in such a way that functions can be carried out efficiently.

These are some similarities between roots and stems:

- Both contain xylem—a tissue that transports water and mineral ions.

- Both contain phloem—a tissue that transports products of photosynthesis such as sugars.

- Both have an epidermis—a single outer protective layer of cells.

ABC **Capillaries** are the narrowest type of blood vessel. They take oxygen and dissolved food to all cells.

**Epithelium** is tissue that lines cavities or tubes in the body such as the intestines, bladder and lungs.

The cell walls in xylem are thick and woody and are therefore very strong. They are good at resisting pulling forces. Cells in phloem are small in size, with thin non-woody walls.

1. Where do stems and roots usually grow—in the soil or in the air?

2. A chili pepper plant has stems, roots, leaves, flowers and fruits (chili peppers). Which of these parts are connected to each other when the plant is growing?

3. Consider each of the following roles in a plant. For each one, decide whether it is a function of roots or of stems.

   a) Anchorage—to prevent the plant being pulled up

   b) Absorption of water and mineral ions

   c) Holding leaves in the sunniest available position

   d) Prevention of excessive water loss

Because of the differences in function between roots and stems, their tissues are organised differently. The following diagrams show the tissues in a typical root (left) and stem (right).

4. a) What are the differences between the position of xylem tissue in stems and roots?

   b) What are the possible reasons for these differences?

5. There is a fibrous tissue that is even tougher than xylem in the corners of the stem but there is none of this tissue in the root. What is a possible reason for this difference?

▲ This photo shows the stem, leaves, flowers and fruits of the chili pepper plant

▼ The position of the xylem in the root (left) and stem (right)

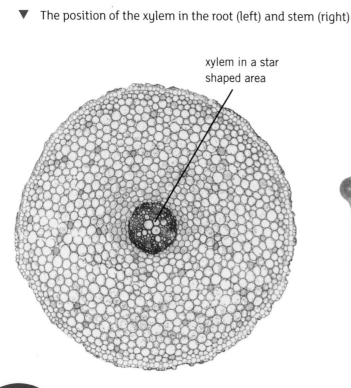

xylem in a star shaped area

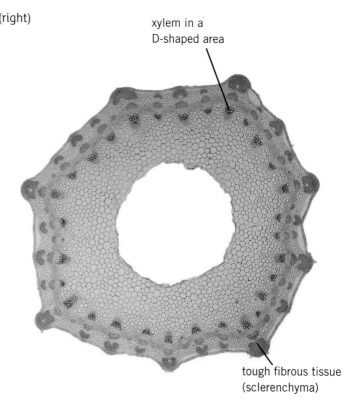

xylem in a D-shaped area

tough fibrous tissue (sclerenchyma)

# How are organs arranged in humans?

Beneath our skin there are 80 or so organs that make up the human body. We are only really aware of them when they cause problems. An organ is a group of tissues that jointly carry out a specific function.

There are some variations in the positioning of these organs but in most humans it is very similar. There are organs in the head and neck, arms and hands and in the legs and feet. The central part of the body, where all the other organs are attached, is the trunk or torso. The torso is divided into two parts by a sheet of muscle called the diaphragm. The **thorax** (or chest) is inside the ribcage and above the diaphragm. The **abdomen** is below the diaphragm and is larger in volume than the thorax.

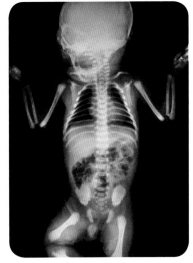

▲ In this X-ray of a small child, the bones are not yet fully formed. The dome-shaped diaphragm, which forms the junction between the thorax and abdomen, is easy to see because the lungs above it in the thorax look dark and beneath it the liver in the abdomen looks white. Gas in the intestines shows as dark blobs. Can you find the heart? Is it positioned symmetrically? Ten different bones or types of bone are visible. How many can you name?

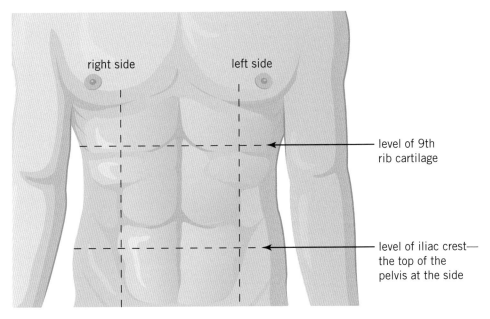

level of 9th rib cartilage

level of iliac crest—the top of the pelvis at the side

▲ To help locate organs in the abdomen, doctors divide it into nine regions with a 3 × 3 grid. The diagram here shows the position of the nine regions and the table shows the main organs in each region. Use the diagram and the table to locate these organs in your abdomen

|  | right | centre | left |
|---|---|---|---|
| **upper** | liver<br>gall bladder<br>right kidney | liver<br>pancreas<br>stomach | spleen<br>stomach<br>left kidney |
| **middle** | right kidney<br>ascending colon<br>small intestines | stomach<br>transverse colon<br>small intestines | left kidney<br>descending colon<br>small intestines |
| **lower** | ascending colon<br>small intestines<br>appendix | small intestines<br>bladder<br>sigmoid colon | descending colon<br>small intestines<br>sigmoid colon |

**ABC** The **thorax** or chest is the upper part of the trunk between the neck and the diaphragm.

The **abdomen** is the lower part of the trunk between the diaphragm and the legs.

1. Five organs are essential for us to survive: brain, heart, kidneys, liver and lungs. What distinguishes these five organs from all the others?

2. For each of the following 10 organs, describe the organ's location and function: kidneys, bladder, heart, lungs, pancreas, spleen, stomach, skin, testes, ovaries.

3. **a)** Which organs of the body can be donated?

   **b)** An organ is easier to donate than a tissue. What is the reason for this?

   **c)** A living person can donate a kidney, or part of their liver, but not their heart. What are the reasons for this?

4. Discuss the advantages of grouping together all the tissues that interact to carry out a function into an organ, rather than locating them in different parts of the body.

## What are the main systems of the human body?

The 80 or so organs of the body can be grouped into 11 body systems. An organ is therefore a subsystem within a larger system. In each system the organs interact with each other to perform an overall function. This is achieved by sending materials, forces, energy or information from one organ to another within the system. In some systems, the organs are all located in one part of the body. In other systems, the organs perform their functions better by being located in different parts of the body. The table summarises the roles of the 11 body systems.

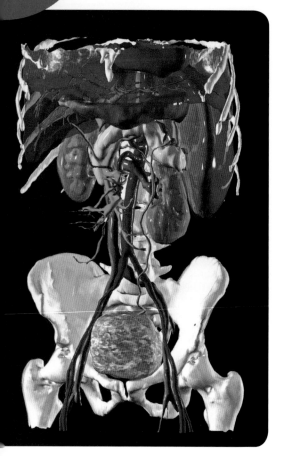

▲ Which of the following organs can you identify in this computer-generated model of a person's internal organs: the bladder (pink), the kidneys (orange), the liver (dark red), pancreas (yellow), the lungs (pink), arteries (red), veins carrying blood to the heart (dark blue) and veins carrying blood to the liver (light blue)? Can you name the different bones (white)?

| Role | Systems |
|---|---|
| growth | digestive |
| survival | integumentary, lymphatic, circulatory, gas exchange, urinary, endocrine |
| behavior | nervous, muscular, skeletal |
| reproduction | reproductive |

Choose one of these systems and find out as much as you can about it, including what organs are in it, what each organ does and what the overall function of the system is. Display what you have found in a large poster. If there are 11 students or groups of students in your class, pool together your work to produce one poster for each system.

◄ Scientists often display posters at conferences, sometimes as an alternative to giving a talk, to explain their research findings

## Working effectively with others

Scientific research is often conducted in collaborative groups with researchers of different backgrounds making unique contributions. Some important skills for collaboration include:

- Delegating and sharing responsibility for decision-making
- Helping others to succeed
- Encouraging others to contribute
- Building consensus
- Making fair and equitable decisions
- Listening actively to other perspectives and ideas
- Negotiating effectively

Reflect on a recent experience of group work that you have undertaken. To what extent were each of the criteria in the above list addressed?

## What types of sense receptor are there in the nervous system?

Sense **receptors** are the cells that we use to monitor the external environment. They are part of the nervous system of all animals. Each type of sense receptor responds to a specific input, which can either be a chemical substance or a form of energy. The input is transmitted to the brain as a signal that travels along nerve cells. The brain processes signals from sense receptors, resulting in changes in behaviour or memories.

Each sense receptor is part of a tissue in a sense organ. The range of sense receptors that an animal has reflects its environment and its activities. The table shows the types of input that sense receptors in humans can respond to and the sense organs that contain them.

ABC The **circulatory system** is the heart, blood, blood vessels, lymphatic vessels and lymph, which work together to transport materials throughout the body.

The **endocrine system** consists of glands that secrete hormones which are transported in the blood.

The **integumentary** system is the body's outer covering including skin, hair and nails.

**Lymph** is a pale-colored fluid used for transport and preventing infections.

The **lymphatic system** is the vessels and nodes (glands) that allow lymph to drain through the body.

A **receptor** is a cell that can detect information about the surroundings.

| Type of input | Sense organ | Details of input |
|---|---|---|
| electromagnetic | eye | Light of any wavelength from red (700 nanometers) to violet (400 nm) is detected by receptor cells in the retina to give us vision |
| mechanical | ear | Vibrations with a frequency of 20 Hertz (Hz) to 20,000 Hz are detected as sounds by hair cells in the cochlea inside the inner ear |
| | ear | Movements of the head are detected by hairs cells in the semi-circular canals inside the inner ear helping us maintain balance |
| | skin | Touch, pressure, stretch and vibrations are detected by different receptors in the skin |
| chemical | tongue | Five groups of chemicals are detected as the tastes of sweet, sour, salty, bitter and umami by receptor cells in the taste buds |
| | nose | Hundreds of different chemicals that can evaporate and pass through the air are detected as smells inside the nose |
| heat | skin | One type of receptor detects temperatures above body temperature (37°C) and another type detects temperatures lower than 37°C |

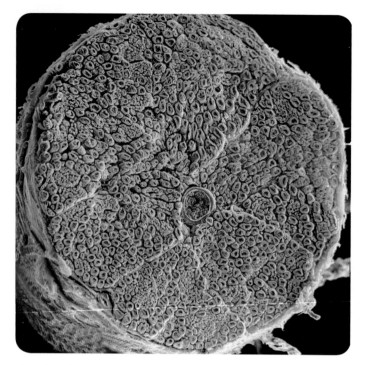

▲ This photograph was taken using an electron microscope. A nerve was frozen and then snapped. At the broken end you can see the narrow cable-like fibers that carry signals in the nervous system. They are part of nerve cells (neurons). This nerve is a bundle of hundreds of these fibers, each of which carries signals from one specific part of the body to another. In the middle of the nerve is a small blood vessel containing red blood cells.

## Which parts of the brain process sensory inputs?

Our sense receptors harvest many different kinds of information from the world around us. They then send signals to the brain. Some of these signals are filtered out before they reach the brain, to avoid overload. Even so, the brain still receives huge amounts of information. It then processes this information and uses it together with memories to guide our actions.

The signals that carry our perceptions of the environment to the brain are the same, whichever sense receptor they come from. They are electrical impulses that travel along the narrow cable-like fibers of nerve cells. The brain knows what the signals mean because each sense receptor is linked via particular nerve cells to specific nerve cells in one region of the brain, and this region does not receive signals from anywhere else. The diagrams on page 103 show the locations of regions of the brain that receive sensory inputs.

▶ In this MRI scan of the head, the skull can be seen clearly on the outside. Beneath it (in the upper part of the head) the meninges are visible—three membranes that cover the brain and spinal cord. Infection of the meninges causes meningitis, which can be a life-threatening disease. Occupying most of the head is the brain, with symmetrical left and right sides. The lower part is the cerebellum with parallel grooves. Its main functions are muscle coordination and balance. Above this is the cerebrum, consisting of the two cerebral hemispheres. It has a complex pattern of ridges and furrows because it is highly folded, to increase the area of cerebrum that can fit inside the skull. The other part of the brain, called the brainstem is further forwards in the head, so is not visible in this scan.

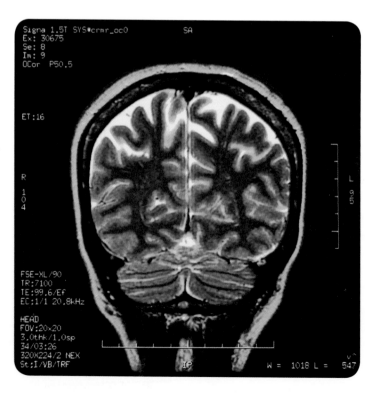

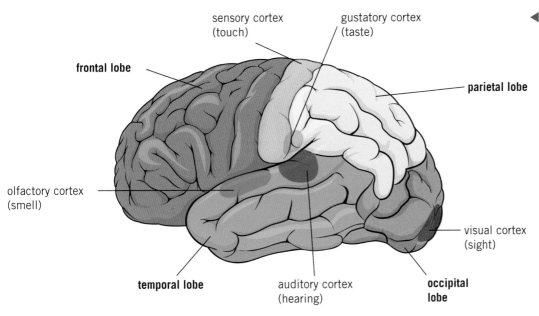

sensory cortex
(touch)

gustatory cortex
(taste)

frontal lobe

parietal lobe

olfactory cortex
(smell)

visual cortex
(sight)

temporal lobe

auditory cortex
(hearing)

occipital
lobe

◀ For each of our senses there is an area of the brain that receives the inputs. These are in the cerebral cortex—the large folded region that consists of the left and right cerebral hemispheres

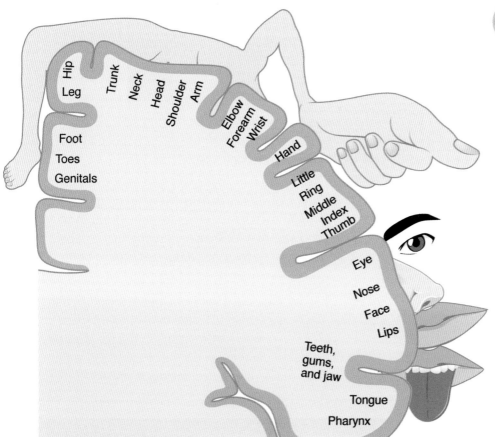

Hip
Leg
Trunk
Neck
Head
Shoulder
Arm
Elbow
Forearm
Wrist

Foot
Toes
Genitals

Hand

Little
Ring
Middle
Index
Thumb

Eye

Nose

Face

Lips

Teeth,
gums,
and jaw

Tongue

Pharynx

▲ Inputs from touch receptors can be mapped on the cerebral cortex in the sensory region at the front of the parietal lobe of the cerebrum

**ABC** The **cerebrum** is the largest and most highly developed area of the brain and it controls most physical activity and all intelligent action.

The **cerebral hemispheres** are the two halves of the cerebrum that form the main sensory and motor areas of the brain.

The **cerebral cortex** is the outer layer of the cerebrum.

The **cerebellum** is part of the brain that coordinates and controls muscle movement and balance.

A **neuron** is a cell in the nervous system that can transmit nerve impulses.

A **nerve fiber** is a long, cable-like projection of a neuron.

▲ The senses of animals vary greatly depending on lifestyle. How do a dog's senses differ from those of humans?

 **How sensitive are you?**

There are many experiments that you can perform very easily to investigate your senses. Here are some suggestions, but there are lots more.

1. Chop or crush pieces of vegetables or other plants and put them in containers so other students can smell but not see them. How many can be identified by their smell alone?

2. Gather some samples of glucose, sucrose and any other sugars. Make up solutions of each with the same concentration. Use a dropping pipette to put samples of each, one by one, on another student's tongue. Do they taste the same?

3. On your laptop, design a test where a student first sees one block of a color between blue and green. Ask them what color it is. A block of blue color then appears adjacent to the first color. Ask again what color the first block is. The blue block changes to a green block. Ask a third time what color the first block is. What conclusion can you draw about color perception?

4. Bats use sound frequencies between 11 kHz and 212 kHz for echolocation. Can you hear sounds over this range of frequencies? Carry out some research using a signal generator with a loudspeaker to find out.

5. Braille is a writing system for visually impaired people using patterns of raised dots to represent each letter of the alphabet. Using some thick paper of card and a point to push up raised dots in the paper, test how far apart dots must be for us to recognize patterns using our fingertips.

6. Find some blocks that are made out of different metals, including iron or steel. If possible, the blocks should all be the same size and shape. Magnetize the block of iron or steel—instructions for this are available on the internet. Ask other students to handle the blocks to sense any differences between them. Can they detect the magnetism?

 **Organ donation**

Locate a local government authority or non-governmental organization that promotes organ donation. Invite a representative to speak at your school to discuss the strategies they undertake to promote donation. You can also ask them to discuss the availability of different organs, and why donation is important.

# Summative assessment

**Statement of inquiry:**

Human identity includes the impulse to help family members and also those we are not closely related to.

To prepare for this assessment, find out as much as you can about organ donation. There are many websites to help you with your research. For example. the UK'S National Heath Service (NHS) website has downloadable teaching resources that you may find helpful.

## Kidney transplants

1. In the United States, there were more than 750,000 organs transplanted between 1988 and 2018. The pie chart shows the six most common transplants:

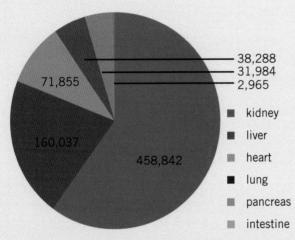

38,288
31,984
2,965

71,855
160,037
458,842

- ■ kidney
- ■ liver
- ■ heart
- ■ lung
- ■ pancreas
- ■ intestine

▲ **Source of data:** United Network for Organ Sharing (UNOS)

Suggest reasons for:

  **a)** kidney transplants being the most common [2]

  **b)** transplants of kidneys, liver, heart and lung being more common than transplants of other organs [2]

  **c)** no transplants of the brain, testes or ovaries being carried out. [2]

2. The diagram shows the position of organs in the urinary system and how a transplanted kidney is connected to other organs. Usually the diseased kidneys are left in place. The blood vessels (red) are arteries and those shown in blue are veins.

  **a)** Where in the body is the transplanted kidney placed? [1]

  **b)** Explain what connections have to be made so the transplanted kidney can carry out its function. [3]

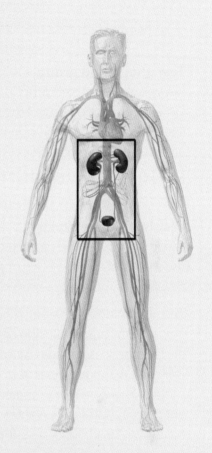

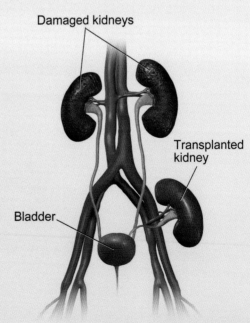

Damaged kidneys

Transplanted kidney

Bladder

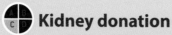 **Kidney donation**

**3.** Read the following text from a hospital website and answer the questions that follow.

---

### Tests for volunteer kidney donors

If you are thinking of donating one of your kidneys to a child or another close relative, you will first have to come into the hospital and undertake some tests. The aim of these tests is to find out whether your kidney would be a good match for the family member who needs it.

### Test one: blood group

We will test your blood group, even if you think you know it. If the family member who needs the kidney is in blood group AB, you can be a donor whatever your blood group. However, it is far more likely that the family member is blood group A, O or B, in which case you can only be a donor if you are in the same blood group, or are in blood group O.

In the future it may be possible donate kidneys to a person in a different blood group, but more research needs to be done and at present this is not possible.

### Test two: tissue typing

Assuming your blood group is compatible, we can then go on to test your tissue type, to see how good the match would be between your kidney and tissues in your child or other family member. All that is required for the test is a small blood sample.

The human body has a system of detecting viruses and any other material that is not our own tissue. This system causes rejection of transplanted kidneys that are of a different tissue type to our own. There are proteins in our tissues called HLA antigens that are a principal cause of rejection problems. We inherit HLA antigen types from our parents. Three types are inherited from our father and three from our mother. There are many different types of HLA antigen. We can use numbers to indicate different HLA antigens. If a father's HLA antigens are 1 2 3 4 5 6 and a mother's are **7 8 9 10 11 12**, their child could have 1 2 3 **10 11 12**, or 2 3 5 **8 10 12**, but not 2 4 5 6 **9 12** or 1 3 4 **8 11 13**.

The more HLA antigens that you share with the family member who needs the kidney, the better the tissue match and the more suitable you are as a donor. The more closely related you are to the family member, the more HLA antigens you are likely to share. If the family member is a stepchild or other step relation, you are unlikely to be a close enough match to be a donor.

---

**a)** What is the reason for testing blood type first, before testing tissue type? [2]

**b)** What is the advantage of a family member donating a kidney to a child, rather than a kidney being obtained from a stranger? [2]

**c)** We understand more and more about tissue types due to incredible scientific research. What are the benefits of this research for people donating or receiving a transplanted kidney? [2]

**d)** HLA antigens were discovered during research into rejection of skin grafts. Explain the reasons for them also being relevant in kidney transplantation and other human health issues. [2]

**e)** The naming of HLA antigens is much more complicated than just simple numbering. Here is an example of a name: HLA-A*02:101:01:02N. This naming system has been agreed on by a committee of the World Health Organization (WHO). Explain the advantages of international agreement over naming HLA antigens. [2]

**f)** Were the authors of the Great Ormond Street article right to use simpler names in their explanation of tissue typing? Explain your answer(s). [2]

## Ethnicity and organ donation

**4.** In the UK, there is an Organ Donation Register, where citizens can express the wish to donate organs following brain or circulatory death. The table shows kidney transplant data for the UK in 2010–2011. Data for three ethnic groups are shown. Some minority ethnic groups have been omitted.

| Ethnic group | % of population | % of organ donor register | % of kidney donors | % of kidney recipients | % of kidney waiting list |
|---|---|---|---|---|---|
| Group 1 | 89.8 | 94.2 | 96 | 80 | 71 |
| Group 2 | 4.5 | 2.3 | 1 | 12 | 17 |
| Group 3 | 2.2 | 0.8 | 1 | 6 | 10 |

**a)** Write a report comparing the data for the three ethnic groups. [4]

**b)** Suggest two factors that could cause the high percentages of Groups 2 and 3 on the waiting list for a kidney transplant. [2]

**c)** Produce a poster aimed at encouraging more people in Groups 2 and 3 to join the Organ Donor Register. [4]

## Opinions on organ donation

**5.** There is a global shortage of organs for transplantation. Some countries have an opt-in system where organs cannot be taken from a person who has died unless they or their closest relatives have given permission. Other countries have an opt-out system where doctors assume that permission is given unless the person has registered to be a non-donor. There are many different views about which system is best. Design a questionnaire that could be used to help to decide which system is best. Explain how you could ensure that the balance of views in a population is reflected in results from the questionnaire. [10]

# 6 Migration

◄ These fossils are from Mount Wild in Antarctica. They are leaves of *Glossopteris*, a seed-fern tree, which evolved 300 million years ago and became extinct 50 million years later. It only grew in warm climates, so how can there be fossils of it in Antarctica? Fossils of *Glossopteris* are also found in Australia, New Zealand, India, Africa and South America. How did this tree spread across these widely separated continents?

► This view of Hurricane Florence was taken on 14 September 2018 from the International Space Station. It was not the most powerful of tropical cyclones to hit the US and maximum sustained windspeeds were only 215 km per hour, but because it moved forward at about 4 km per hour, its effects were severe. What is the source of the energy that drives hurricanes and other movements of air in our restless atmosphere?

**Statement of inquiry:**

Evidence can be used to detect changes in the spatial patterns of migrating birds.

▲ Skaftafellsjökull is a huge mass of ice that is moving down a valley in Iceland at a rate of about a meter per day. Despite this movement, the front of the glacier is 3 km further up the valley than it was in 1890—an average rate of retreat of more than 20 meters per year. In the foreground of the photo is rock debris left by the retreating glacier and beyond is a depression which meltwater has filled to form a pro-glacial lake, with mini-icebergs covered in black volcanic ash. What causes this glacier to move down the valley? What is causing Skaftafellsjökull to retreat? Is the retreat of a glacier an example of movement?

▼ The Earth is moving at about 30 km per second in its orbit around the Sun. This orbit varies in how oval it is in a cycle that lasts about 100,000 years. This is called eccentricity. The Earth rotates once per day, on an axis between the North and South poles. The angle between this axis and the plane of Earth's orbit varies in a cycle that lasts about 40,000 years. This is called tilt. The direction of the tilt also varies in a cycle lasting about 26,000 years. This is called precession. These cycles help to explain the alternation between cold glaciations and warmer interglacial periods over the last million or so years. However, they do not explain the current warming on Earth. What explains current warming?

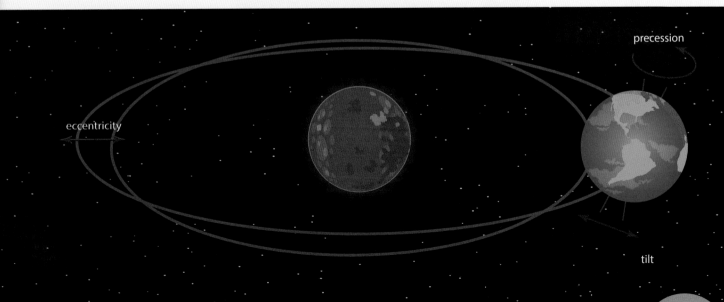

precession

eccentricity

tilt

**Key concept:** Change

**Related concepts:** Energy, Evidence, Movement

**Global context:** Orientation in space and time

**Statement of inquiry:**

Evidence can be used to detect changes in the spatial patterns of migrating birds.

ABC **Seed dispersal** is the scattering of seeds from a parent plant over a wide area.

**Germination** is the initial stages of growth of a seed to form a seedling.

# Introduction

In the US and Canada, retired people who head south to avoid cold winter weather and then move back north again in spring are commonly referred to as snowbirds. Seasonal migrations such as these are nothing new. 80% of bird species in temperate regions migrate. Some insects make amazing journeys each year, such as the monarch butterfly. There are also mammals that migrate—in Africa millions of wildebeest, zebra and gazelle move along traditional routes in a regular annual pattern.

There has been intense research into migration, initially to find evidence for its occurrence, but then to find out how it happens. How do animals move efficiently? How do they navigate? What routes do they follow? This research is particularly important because of climate change. Changes are occurring in the timing of migration and in the places where summer or winter is spent. Yellow-browed warblers, for example, breed in Asia from the Ural Mountains eastwards. Those in the western parts of this range traditionally migrated 5,500 km to spend the winter in India or South-East Asia. Increasing numbers are now migrating instead 3,000 kilometres to western Europe, where the winters have become milder. Research into migration gives us evidence of climate change and also shows us how adaptation to climate change can be achieved.

Migration is not always reversed in spring and fall. Some snowbirds decide to settle permanently in Florida or in California, for example. Animal species sometimes expand their range by spreading into new areas. Even plants have methods of dispersing their seeds so they can expand their range. These migrations into new areas are particularly important when the environment is changing and former habitats are no longer suitable.

◀ Part of a vast herd of wildebeest on annual migration (together with seven zebras)

# What provides the energy for seed dispersal?

A seed is an embryo plant, packaged up so that it can be transported. It has a protective seed coat and food reserves. When a seed **germinates**, the embryo grows a root down into the ground, anchoring it and making further movement unlikely. The seedling also grows a stem and leaves to harvest light. If the seeds produced by a plant all germinate close to it, there will be competition for light, water and mineral nutrients. **Seed dispersal** mechanisms help to prevent this and also allow a plant species to spread into new areas.

In flowering plants, seeds are contained inside fruits. A fruit is any structure that develops from the ovary of a flower. The job of a fruit is to disperse the seeds inside it. There are many different types of fruits because there are many different strategies for seed dispersal. Consider the following fruits and research the strategy that each uses when growing wild. In each of the fruits, what provides the energy for the seeds to move?

 A dandelion "clock" is a spherical array of fruits that are dispersed in dry, windy conditions. In 2018 it was discovered that as a dandelion fruit falls, a low-pressure vortex forms in the air above the fruit, generating lift. In contrast, winged fruits such as maple generate lift in the same way as the wings of a gliding bird or an airplane

- Tomatoes
- Squirting cucumbers
- Cocklebur
- Prickly Russian thistles
- Pecans
- Plums
- Maples
- Dandelions
- Coconuts

Can you find another example for each of these seed dispersal strategies?

▼ *Allium schubertii* produces a spherical head with many small fruits on radiating stalks. When the seeds inside the fruits are mature, the whole head breaks off and can roll along the ground, blown by the wind. How does the spherical shape help? The stalks to which the fruits are attached are rather brittle and are of different lengths. How does this help disperse the seeds? Which other plants use this strategy?

---

📋 **Measuring seed dispersal**

Collect wind-dispersed fruits of different types, for example winged fruits (such as maples) and puffy fruits with many hairs (such as dandelions). Your teacher may have a store of fruits that you can use.

- Design an experiment to find out how far each type of fruit is carried by the wind. In science experiments, it is best to get quantitative results, which in this case is the distance traveled by the fruits. You may need to do some initial trials to find out what height of release and what wind speed is best. Make sure all variables are the same apart from the type of fruit. An electric fan can be used to simulate wind.

- You could extend your experiment by finding the mass of each fruit and seeing whether there is any relationship between mass and distance traveled.

- You could investigate the effect of changing the wind speed on the distance traveled.

## Do lemmings jump off cliffs?

Myth-busting is an important part of science. It can be done by finding evidence to prove that a claim is false. Scientists usually call a claim a hypothesis. Sometimes in attempting to prove a hypothesis wrong, the evidence can point towards an alternative hypothesis.

A claim has frequently been made that lemmings jump off cliffs in mass. Lemmings are small mammals that live in the tundra ecosystems of the Northern Hemisphere. There are more than 20 species of lemming. For example, the Norway lemming (*Lemmus lemmus*) lives in northern Scandinavia.

Lemmings feed on plants. Weather conditions affect plant growth. In years when plants grow well, there is plenty of food for lemmings and they reproduce prolifically. A litter of six to eight offspring can be born every four weeks and those offspring can themselves reproduce when about four weeks old. Numbers of lemmings can rise very quickly during the summer. This population explosion happens approximately every four years.

Lemmings do not share out the available food equally. Instead, dominant adults defend territories and force younger and weaker lemmings to migrate. This can cause a mass migration from higher to lower ground, and can be hazardous for the lemmings. Perhaps this behavior, along with claims made in popular media, caused the myth that lemmings have this self-destructive behavior?

1. How many lemmings would there be after six months, if a pair produced eight offspring every month and those offspring were able to mate a month after being born?

2. If something is sustainable, it can carry on forever. A population that increases faster and faster is growing exponentially. Can exponential growth of a population ever be sustainable?

3. Is it better for dominant lemmings to get exclusive access to food in their territories, or would it be better for all lemmings in a population to share out the food equally?

4. Are there any other species that do mass migrations when their population rises above a critical level?

## What is the evidence for bird migration?

In parts of the world where weather conditions in summer and winter are very different, some bird species are only seen in summer and others only in winter.

1. How much difference is there in weather conditions between summer and winter in the area where you live? Can you give average temperature and rainfall statistics to support your answer?

▲ Norway lemming

**ABC** **Hibernation** is a deep sleep that helps animals to save energy and survive winter without eating.

▲ Olaus Magnus was Swedish but he migrated to Rome for religious reasons. This woodcut is from his book *A Description of Northern Peoples*, published in 1555. It shows fishermen in winter catching hibernating swallows from a lake

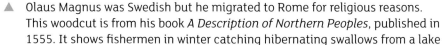

Spring    Fall

**2.** If summers and winters are different in your area, which bird species are only present in summer and which only in winter?

Differences in bird populations between summer and winter have been known for thousands of years, but the reasons were not clear. Large birds such as cranes were seen migrating in opposite directions in spring and fall but for smaller birds other hypotheses were used to explain summer–winter differences. Two common hypotheses were **hibernation** and changes in body form between summer and winter.

The long-running controversy between "migrationists" and "hibernationists" carried on through the 18th century but evidence for migration in barn swallows (*Hirundo rustica*) and other birds built up.

- There were reports from travelers on ships of swallows flying along migration routes across the Mediterranean and off the coast of west Africa.

- Dissection of swallows showed that they could not survive underwater so could not hibernate in lakes.

- Swallows kept in a cage through the fall remained active and did not prepare for winter by going into hibernation.

- The only reports of hibernation were unreliable and despite much searching, no swallows or other birds that disappeared in winter were found hibernating.

▲ In the 4th century BC, Aristotle wrote that garden warblers (*Sylvia borin*) change into blackcaps (*Sylvia atricapilla*) in the fall and back to garden warblers in the spring

> 66
> What becomes of swallows in winter time, whether they fly into other countries or lie torpid in hollow trees and the like places, neither are natural historians agreed, nor can we certainly determine. To us it seems more probable that they fly away into hot countries...
> 99
>
> *John Ray, 1678*

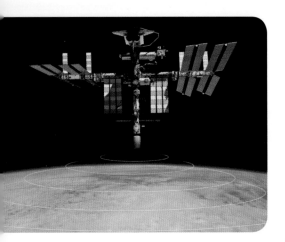

▲ As part of a project called ICARUS (International Cooperation for Animal Research Using Space) an antenna for tracking animals has been placed on the International Space Station

Stronger evidence of migration came in the 20th century. Bird banding allowed individual birds to be identified and their different wintering and summering habitats to be confirmed. A metal or plastic band with a unique number is placed on the bird's leg. For example, in May 1911 a swallow chick was banded in England with the number B830. In December 1912 this bird was found nearly 10,000 kilometers away in South Africa.

Small radio transmitters were attached to birds, allowing their position to be tracked. The route taken by each bird can be determined, not just the starting and finishing points of the journey. Initially the tracking was done in road vehicles or with small aircraft, but now satellites are used.

3. What are the benefits of researching bird migration?

4. Find a non-bird example of an animal that undergoes seasonal migrations each year. Research when the migrations happen, what routes are taken and the total distance traveled.

## How does a bird fly?

Birds must generate two forces to fly from one place to another:

- **lift** to stay airborne and not be pulled to the ground by gravity

- **thrust** to move forwards in the intended direction.

In powered, flapping flight, lift is generated by moving the wings up and down. The forces that cause these movements are generated by muscles. Only pulling forces can be generated, so different muscles are needed for the upward and downward movement of the wings. Muscles that generate opposite movements are called antagonistic muscles. The diagram shows **antagonistic muscles** that move the wings up and down.

**ABC** **Contraction** is the use of energy to generate pulling forces in muscle by making the muscle tissue shorter in length or more tense.

**Antagonistic pairs** of muscles are needed to cause opposite movements of the body, because muscle tissue can only exert a pulling force in one direction.

▶ The downstroke generates most of the lift, because the wing pushes against the air underneath it. During the upstroke the wing is folded slightly inwards and the feathers partly separate, preventing generation of downward forces

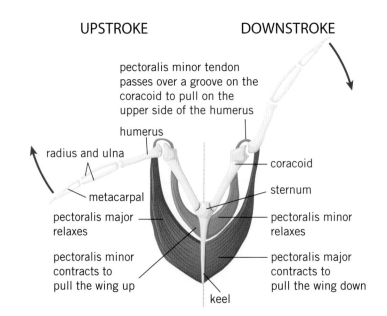

UPSTROKE          DOWNSTROKE

pectoralis minor tendon passes over a groove on the coracoid to pull on the upper side of the humerus

humerus

radius and ulna

metacarpal

pectoralis major relaxes

pectoralis minor contracts to pull the wing up

coracoid

sternum

pectoralis minor relaxes

pectoralis major contracts to pull the wing down

keel

1. Pectoralis major is a more powerful muscle in birds than pectoralis minor. What are the reasons for this?

2. Birds can generate some lift even without flapping their wings. This happens during gliding flight. The method is the same as with an aircraft wing. How do a gliding bird's wings or an aircraft's wings generate lift?

3. Some birds gain height by soaring on thermal air currents. Typically, they rise along a helical path and can reach great heights. Videos of this are available online using search terms such as "storks thermalling". Soaring is also used by non-powered paragliders or hang gliders. What provides the energy for birds or paragliders to soar?

 **Experiment**

### Dissection of a bird wing

This experiment can be done with the wing of a chicken, turkey or other bird. It can also be done with a chicken leg, though the joints and the muscles will be different.

1. Rinse the wing under running water and thoroughly dry it with a paper towel, as the surface may be contaminated with *Salmonella* bacteria.

2. Cut the skin along the entire length of the wing, pointing the scissors up to avoid cutting tissues under the skin.

3. Remove the skin from the wing by placing your finger under the skin and lightly tearing at the **connective tissue** below it.

4. Use a blunt probe to separate the individual wing muscles from each other without tearing them. The muscles will be a pale pink color. If there is any fat tissue it will be yellow or cream colored.

5. Pull on each of the muscles and note the movement that results. Determine pairs of muscles that are antagonistic.

6. Follow a muscle to where it connects to bone by means of a **tendon**. Note the appearance of the tendon.

7. Carefully remove all the muscles by cutting the tendons. This should reveal the elbow joint.

8. Identify the humerus on one side of the elbow joint and the radius and ulna on the other side.

9. The bones above and below the elbow are connected by **ligaments**. Cut through these ligaments and separate the humerus from the radius and ulna. Note the shape of the bones and how they fit together at the joint.

10. The ends of the bones at the elbow are covered in **cartilage**. Note the smoothness of the cartilage surface. Note also the oily feel of the cartilage. This is due to the presence of a natural lubricant called synovial fluid. The smoothness of the cartilage and the synovial fluid reduce friction when the bones move at the joint.

▲ Pectoralis major and pectoralis minor are called "breast meat" when birds are cooked as a food. The breast meat in this photo is from a pigeon. The dark color shows that there is myoglobin in the muscle. Myoglobin stores oxygen. It allows pigeons to make longer flights than chickens or turkeys, where the breast meat is pale in color and oxygen is not stored

**ABC** **Connective tissue** is strong, tough tissue that holds organs or other tissues together.

A **tendon** is a tough band of tissue that connects a muscle to a bone.

A **ligament** is a tough, elastic tissue that connects bones together at movable joints.

**Cartilage** is smooth, tough tissue that covers the surface of bones where they meet at a joint, reducing friction.

## How do birds get energy for migration?

Energy is needed to fuel migration. Consider the strategies used by bar-tailed godwits and white storks. What are the differences? What are the reasons for these birds adopting such different strategies?

▼ Tracks of white storks equipped with GPS loggers

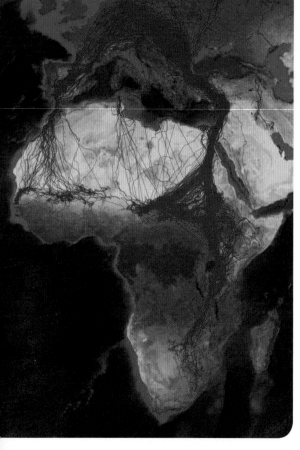

1. Bar-tailed godwits are wading birds that feed by probing wet mud to find worms and other animals. Their flights from Alaska to New Zealand in September and October have been investigated. Godwits can fly 11,000 km at between 15 and 25 metres per second and without any stopovers for rest or refueling. The journey takes about nine days.

   After a period of intense feeding before departure 55% of their body mass is fat. They use up 0.42% of their body mass per hour of flight. Before departure their gizzards, liver, kidneys and digestive organs are reduced to a very small size. Flight muscles and heart are enlarged. On arrival in New Zealand, the bar-tailed godwits cannot feed until they have rebuilt their digestive system, which takes about a week.

2. White storks feed on insects and many other types of animal. They migrate from Europe to Africa in August and September. The routes they follow are up to 10,000 km long and are almost entirely over land. They usually travel in the middle part of the day and rest at night. The storks search for thermals, which are rising currents of air caused by heat from the Sun. They use them to gain altitude, minimizing the amount of flapping flight needed.

   They do not eat extra food or accumulate stores of energy before the migration, but feed whenever possible during the journey in the morning and evening. When the storks travel across areas lacking food such as deserts they lose body weight but regain it afterwards at stopover sites, where they may spend several weeks.

## Which birds hold migration records?

| Longest migration route | Fastest speed of migration |
| --- | --- |
| Arctic terns migrate 15,000 km between the Arctic and Antarctic seas, so they spend much of the year in continuous daylight of polar summers. | Great snipe have been recorded flying 4,600 km from Sweden to central Africa non-stop in two days, which gives an average speed of 97 km per hour. |
|  |  |

## Longest non-stop sea crossing

Bar-tailed godwits migrate 10,400 km from eastern Siberia to New Zealand in 7–8 days. They double their body weight with fat reserves before this journey.

## Smallest migrant

Blackpoll warblers with a mass of only 12 g migrate from eastern Canada to Colombia and Venezuela, including a three-day non-stop flight over 2,500 km of ocean.

## Highest mountain crossing

Demoiselle cranes ascend to 7,900 metres above sea level when crossing the Himalayas from China and Mongolia to India in flocks of up to 400 cranes.

## Largest migrant

Great bustards weighing up to 16 kg migrate as much as 2,000 kilometres from northern Mongolia to Shaanxi province in China, but take long layovers during the journey.

1. Can you find any birds that beat these migration records?

2. Think of another migration statistic and find out which bird holds the record.

3. Most birds migrate north and south, rather than east and west. What are the reasons for this?

4. Some birds fly continuously when they are migrating and others only fly by night or day. More fly only by night than only by day. What are the advantages of flying:

   a) continuously        c) only in daylight

   b) for only part of the day    d) only at night.

5. The largest types of bird do not migrate. What are possible reasons for this?

6. Parkrun is an organization that organizes free, weekly, 5 km timed runs all over the world. Typically, the runners do several laps of a circular course. What are the similarities and differences between parkruns and bird migration?

▲ Have you ever been on a parkrun? Did you keep track of where you traveled and the distance?

## Is there evidence of movement by plants and animals in response to climate change?

The distribution range of a species is the geographical area where it lives. It can be shown using a distribution map.

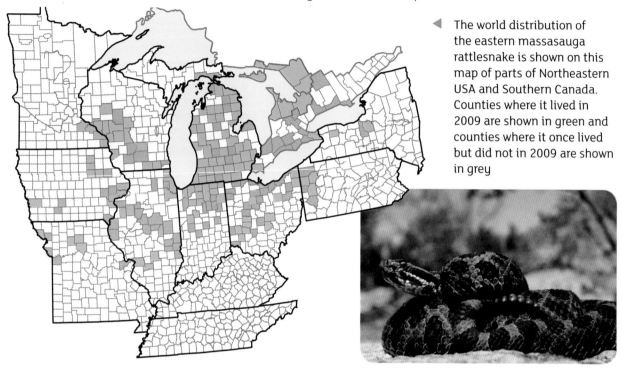

◀ The world distribution of the eastern massasauga rattlesnake is shown on this map of parts of Northeastern USA and Southern Canada. Counties where it lived in 2009 are shown in green and counties where it once lived but did not in 2009 are shown in grey

**Source of data**: J. W. Ray (2009) and United States Fish and Wildlife Service (2009).

1. Using the data in the map, give a brief summary of the distribution range of this snake.

It is natural for plants and animals to change their range by spreading into new areas or by disappearing from areas formerly occupied. This can be in response to a change in environmental conditions or changes in interactions with other organisms. For example, more intense competition or predation could eliminate a species from an area.

Changes in species distribution seem to be particularly rapid at the moment and there is evidence that climate change is the major driving force. Animals and plants are adapted to particular temperatures and if the climate changes, migration to a new area may be vital.

2. If the climate becomes warmer, in which direction would you expect plants or animals to move:

a) in the northern hemisphere

b) in the southern hemisphere

c) on mountains.

The graph at the top of page 119 shows the change between 1968 and 2015 in the average location of three marine species off the east coast of the USA. An interactive version of this or similar graphs may be available on the EPA website.

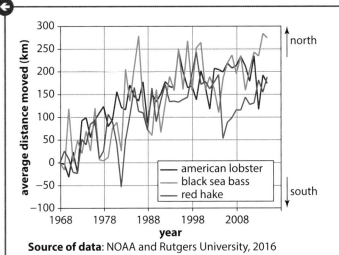

average distance moved (km) / year

— american lobster
— black sea bass
— red hake

**Source of data**: NOAA and Rutgers University, 2016

▲ The Arctic river beauty (*Chamaenerion latifolium*) grows in Iceland. What would happen if the climate became too warm for it?

**3. a)** What is the overall trend in the distribution of these species?

**b)** What might cause the fluctuations from year to year?

**c)** Can you find examples of plant species moving north in response to climate change?

The bar chart on the right shows the change in the northern margin of the spider distribution range in Britain. In each case the data are from a 25-year study period towards the end of the 20th century. Positive numbers are movements of the margin northwards. Negative numbers are movements southwards.

**4.** Which of these claims is supported by the data in the bar chart?

**A.** Spiders extended their range northwards.

**B.** There was no clear trend in changes to the northern margin of distributions.

**C.** There were larger northward range extensions than southward retreats.

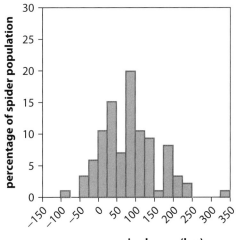

percentage of spider population / range margin change (km)

**Source of data**: I-C. Chen, J. K. Hill, R. Ohlemüller, D. B. Roy and C. D. Thomas, *Science*, 2011, **333**, 1024–1026

**5.** In the Alps, researchers have monitored the range in altitude of 183 different species of mountain plants. On average, the lower edge of the range has moved upwards by 30 m and the upper edge by 34 m.

**a)** What is causing the ranges of mountain plants to move higher up mountains?

**b)** Among the 183 species there is a lot of variation in the changes in range.

**c)** What are some possible reasons for the differences between the species?

**d)** What is the reason for conservationists being concerned about the species that live highest in the Alps and other mountains?

**Preserving the habitat of migrating species**

▲ Larva and pupa of monarch butterfly

The monarch butterfly is an important species of insect that undertakes migrations from North America to Central America annually, thus having an impact on the ecology of the entire migration corridor. The number of monarchs has decreased significantly over the last 20 years.

This demise has prompted a number of volunteer actions. The US Fish and Wildlife Service, for example, maintains a website entitled "Save the monarch butterfly" which details a number of actions people can take. Examples include:

- citizen science projects involving submitting observation data to researchers

- planting milkweed, the preferred food source of the monarch larva

- undertaking campaigns to limit the use of pesticides in local gardens

- campaigning to preserve or enhance habitat along the migration corridor or adding features to backyard gardens that enhance butterfly habitat.

Research a migratory species in your community and undertake actions to support its survival.

## How did humans spread through the world by migration?

Humans have migrated to almost all parts of the world. Evidence for when and how this happened comes from a variety of sources:

- fossilized bones and teeth, which can be dated using radioactive isotopes including carbon

- stone tools, carvings and cave paintings which are part of human culture

- base sequences of genes in DNA extracted from fossils and from modern humans.

This evidence tells us that humans (*Homo sapiens*) evolved in Africa between 315,000 and 250,000 years ago. It also tells us that there were several waves of migration of humans out of Africa. The first was to the Middle East between 120,000 and 90,000 years ago. Later migrations took humans through Asia and on to Australia.

Some of the migration routes used would be impossible today. The area now covered by the Sahara Desert had woodland and grassland with lakes and rivers during some periods in the past. Until about 10,000 years ago, sea levels were low enough for there to be a land bridge between Siberia and Alaska, so humans were able to spread from Asia to North and South America.

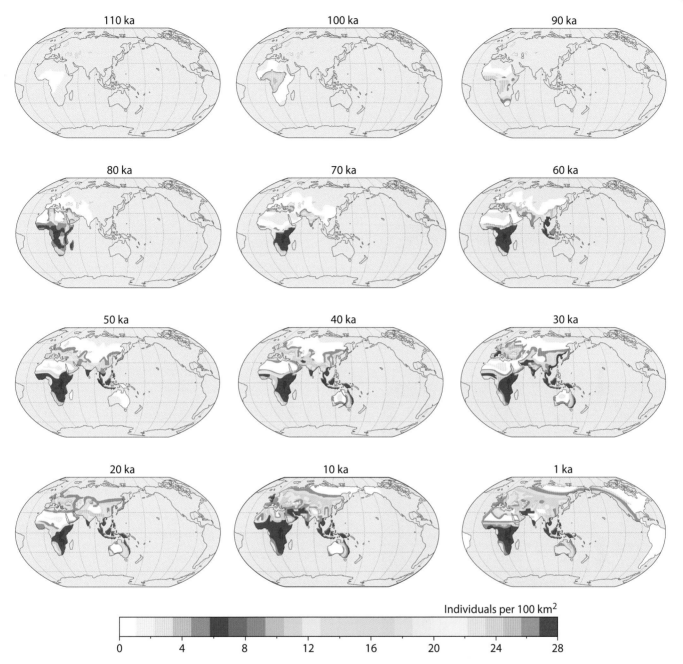

110 ka  100 ka  90 ka

80 ka  70 ka  60 ka

50 ka  40 ka  30 ka

20 ka  10 ka  1 ka

Individuals per 100 km²

0   4   8   12   16   20   24   28

**Source of data**: A. Timmerman and T. Friedrich, *Nature*, 2016, **538**, 92–95

▲ The maps show the densities of human populations around the world at different times since 110,000 years before the present (110 ka). The timings of human migration can be deduced from the maps. Grey indicates no humans

1. Work out when, according to these maps, humans reached

   a) India   b) Australia   c) North America   d) South America

2. Research when humans reached these islands and where they migrated from:

   a) Hawaii   b) Madagascar   c) New Zealand   d) Iceland

3. Find examples of parts of the world where humans have visited but never permanently settled.

4. Find out which other planet in the universe would be most habitable, for any humans deciding to migrate from Earth.

A

## What are the reasons for human migration?

Consider photos A–F, which show different examples of migration. In each case, try to find a similar example in your part of the world. When you have studied all the examples, try answering these questions:

1. Discuss the differences between these types of human traveler:

   - nomad
   - evacuee
   - colonist
   - refugee
   - tourist
   - migrant

2. Are there any other types of human traveler?

3. Debate whether all humans should have the freedom to move to all parts of the world.

4. Discuss the environmental costs of human travel.

B

A. These Bakhtiari herdsmen and women spend their winter in the lowland plains of Khuzestan Province of Iran and then walk over mountain passes into the green valleys of the Zagros Mountains for the summer. The summer quarters are called yaylāq and winter quarters are qishlāq. These annual migrations have been done for thousands of years. The photo was taken in April 2009. Fewer members of the Bakhtiari tribe now travel between these summer and winter quarters. Young men in particular are reluctant to do so after experiencing a different lifestyle during military service.

B. This photo, taken on 7 September 2017, shows Rohingya people crossing a mangrove swamp on a journey from Northern Rakhine in western Myanmar to neighboring Bangladesh. They were fleeing from violent conflict and persecution in the villages where they had been living. On 29 September 2017 the United Nations reported that the number of Rohingya in Bangladesh had risen beyond half a million. UNHCR nutrition experts estimated that nearly 20% of those arriving in camps in Bangladesh were suffering from acute malnutrition with breastfeeding mothers severely traumatized, sick and malnourished.

**C.** St Kilda is an isolated archipelago in the Atlantic Ocean, 180 km to the west of mainland Scotland. A population existed on the main island of Hirta for hundreds of years, surviving by growing crops and catching seabirds. The photograph shows some of the inhabitants in the 1800s. From the mid-19th century the population of St Kilda started to decline. In the 1920s crop failures, influenza and possibly lead poisoning caused severe difficulties. In 1930, the remaining 36 people on St Kilda decided collectively that they wanted to leave. On 29 August they were transported by boat to the mainland of Scotland.

**D.** Maori arrived in New Zealand as early as the 13th century. From the early 19th century onwards, Europeans started to arrive and settle there. In 1840, a treaty was signed between Britain and the Maori, who had been concerned about the increasingly lawless behavior of some settlers. More settlers arrived, establishing communities with British names and ways of life. The Maori population dwindled, in part due to European diseases, but is now higher than ever, though only 18% of the total New Zealand population. The young men in the photo were brought to New Zealand in 1929 by the Salvation Army. Under New Zealand government schemes, another 76,673 people from Britain migrated to New Zealand between 1947 and 1971.

**E.** These women are planting rice in a paddy field in rural Xizhou, in Yunnan Province, China. The International Labour Organization estimates that between 1979 and 2009 about 340 million people in China migrated from rural to urban areas. This may be the largest migration in human history. In 2017, over 800 million people lived in cities in China, but over 230 million of these were migrant workers from families that were still registered in rural areas. There is evidence that migration to cities leads to an increase in average income but a significant reduction in wellbeing.

**F.** The cruise ship Azura has 19 decks, weighs 105,000 tonnes and carries 3,100 passengers with 1,250 crew members. The passengers in the photo sailed from Southampton, UK to the Azores and on to the Caribbean. They are seen disembarking on 11 November 2013 for a sightseeing tour of Antigua. After visiting several other islands, the passengers flew back to the UK from Barbados. Azura offers "an incredible choice of bars, restaurants, sports and spa facilities, entertainment including an 800-seat theatre, plus lots of other exciting and unique features".

# Summative assessment

**Statement of inquiry:**

Evidence can be used to detect changes in the spatial patterns of migrating birds.

The map shows the areas where American redstarts (*Setophaga ruticilla*) breed in summer (yellow) and where they live in winter (blue).

▲ This distinguished male American redstart was banded at Powdermill Nature Reserve, Pennsylvania on 28 May 2010 when two years old, so he was almost 8 years old when re-caught and photographed on 25 April 2015

## Migration methods in American redstarts

1. What is the advantage to American redstarts of migrating southwards in the fall?
   - **A.** It would be boring to live in the same area throughout the year.
   - **B.** Offspring need to find new territories to avoid competing with their parents.
   - **C.** In winter there are too few insects to eat in areas where American redstarts breed.
   - **D.** They have a better chance of finding a partner to mate with in the south.

2. What requires most energy during migration of American redstarts?
   - **A.** Contracting flight muscles
   - **B.** Keeping the body warm
   - **C.** Using up body fat reserves
   - **D.** Navigation using the stars.

3. Redstarts migrate at night. What is an advantage of this?
   - **A.** There is less danger of collisions.
   - **B.** The sun is dazzling in daylight.
   - **C.** The moon is used in navigation.
   - **D.** There is less risk of predation.

4. How many migrations will an 8-year-old American redstart have done?
   - **A.** 2      **B.** 4      **C.** 8      **D.** 16

5. How do American redstarts get the energy that they need for migration?
   - **A.** By basking in the sun
   - **B.** By waiting for favorable winds
   - **C.** By flapping their wings
   - **D.** By eating insects

## Migration routes in American redstarts

6. American redstarts are classified as "Extremely Rare Vagrants" in Britain and Ireland, where they have only ever been recorded eight times. All of these sightings were between September and November and nearly all were young birds, located near western coasts. What do the sightings tell us about American redstarts and about weather conditions in the Atlantic? [5]

7. Explain the evidence from the map for migration of American redstarts in spring and fall. [2]

8. Most of the American redstarts that spend winter on Cuba, or islands to the east, breed in the Mid-West and North-East of the USA and Canada. What route do you think these birds will follow when they migrate in spring? (Unless you already have evidence for the route, your suggestion is a hypothesis.) Explain the reasons for your hypothesis. [4]

9. Plan out a scientific investigation to test your hypothesis. Include the methods to be used and the type of data that would be collected. [4]

## Tracking reproduction in redstarts

The graph shows results of over 55 years of research at Powdermill Nature Reserve in Pennsylvania. American redstarts and other birds are caught throughout the year using mist nets. Over 750,000 birds have been caught in this way. Bands allowing individual birds to be identified are put on the birds' legs, unless they are already banded. The age and sex of each bird is recorded. In spring females are checked to see whether they are developing an egg. At the end of each year, the data are analyzed to find 10th centiles for recording dates. A 10th centile is the date when the first 10% of all records for the year have been made. 10th centiles were obtained each year for these stages in migration and breeding:

- Spring arrival—a measure of when the birds arrive after their migration.

- Breeding initiation—a measure of the start of reproduction as females are gravid (developing an egg).

- Juvenile appearance—a measure of completed reproduction as young birds have flown from the nest.

The graph shows these dates for each year, plotted against the average temperature 1–21 April of that year. The dates are shown as Julian days, which is the number of days since 1 January.

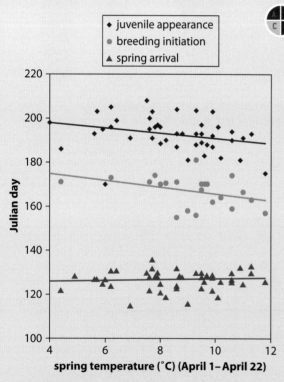

**Source of data**: M. E. McDermott and L. W. DeGroote, *PLoS ONE*, 2017, **12(4)**

**10. a)** What was the warmest average spring temperature? [1]

    **b)** What was the coldest average spring temperature? [1]

**11.** What effect (if any) does average spring temperature have on:

    **a)** spring arrival [2]

    **b)** breeding initiation? [2]

**12.** Use the data in the graph to deduce:

    **a)** how many days there are on average between breeding initiation and juvenile appearance [1]

    **b)** whether this period is shorter if the spring is warmer. [1]

**13.** Using the data in the graph and your understanding of the energy requirements of migration and egg production in birds, deduce what problem American redstarts may have if springs became much warmer in the future. [2]

## Journals and scientific language

Read the following extract, taken from the PLoS ONE scientific journal.

> "Migratory animals comprise a significant portion of biodiversity worldwide with annual investment for their conservation exceeding several billion dollars. Designing effective conservation plans presents enormous challenges. Migratory species are influenced by multiple events across land and sea regions that are often separated by thousands of kilometres and span international borders. To date, conservation strategies for migratory species fail to take into account how migratory animals are spatially connected between different periods of the annual cycle bringing into question the utility and efficiency of current conservation efforts."

**14.** Using language that non-scientists can understand, explain the problems encountered in ensuring the survival of birds such as the American redstart. Base your explanation on the text from PLoS ONE. [5]

**15.** PLoS ONE is an online, multidisciplinary, open access, peer-reviewed science journal, that publishes primary research including negative results. Explain the advantages of having these features in a science journal. [5]

No man is an island, entire of itself; every man is a piece of the continent, a part of the main; if a clod be washed away by the sea, Europe is the less, as well as if a promontory were, as well as if a manor of thy friend's or of thine own were; any man's death diminishes me, because I am involved in mankind. And therefore never send to know for whom the bell tolls; it tolls for thee.

John Donne (1623) Part of *Meditation Number 17*, from *Devotions upon Emergent Occasions*

What meaning do you take from this poem?

▲ British sculptor Antony Gormley placed 100 identical cast-iron models of his own body, facing out to sea along almost 2 miles of beach. What message do you think is intended by the artist?

▶ The artist Alexander Calder was the originator of a form of kinetic art called a mobile. This piece was made in 1937. Although the shapes can rise or fall they return to balance. Can you make a mobile that moves in air currents but regains its balance? What causes any displacement of a shape in the mobile to be reversed?

Jan Brueghel the Elder painted *The Entry of Animals into Noah's Ark* in 1613. How many different species of animal can you see? Communities cannot be conserved by simply keeping a male and female of each animal species alive. What else needs to be done?

**Statement of inquiry:**

To achieve fairness, development must balance the needs of current communities with the needs of future communities.

This street art was painted in the Santo Domingo district of Medellín. Why did the artist show such anger in the animals? Santa Domingo was once one of Colombia's most notorious *comunas* (slums) with high rates of drug-related crime. In 1982 a "Medellin without Slums" program was launched, to promote fairness for the urban poor. Public spaces were transformed into places where communities could come together

ABC    A **community** is the total collection of living organisms (including plants and animals) living within a defined area or habitat.

**Dynamic equilibrium** is a type of equilibrium where a balance is reached because movement in one direction is canceled out by the same rate of movement in the other direction.

# Introduction

A group of organisms living together in an area is called a **community**. The organisms in a community have many effects on each other. These effects are called interactions. If two organisms interact with each other, there is a relationship between them, so research into communities is a study of relationships.

Communities are complex, with many different species present. There must be producers such as plants or algae that make food. There must be decomposers that recycle materials. Communities also contain consumers that feed on other organisms. Within these groups there are many ways of living that help organisms avoid competing with each other too much. Communities therefore include a great diversity of organisms.

Natural communities usually stay in balance. The numbers of each type of organism do not stay constant, but interactions within the community limit the variations in number. Typically, an increase in the numbers of a species is followed by a decrease and vice versa. This is called **dynamic equilibrium**.

Experiments with artificial communities tell us that a community is unlikely to stay in balance when the number of species is small. The more species there are, the more interactions there can be, making balance within the community more robust. Biodiversity is therefore the key to the sustainability of communities.

Over hundreds of thousands of years, humans have spread geographically and have become part of many of the world's natural communities. We have learned to catch and consume many other species. With the development of farming we have created artificial communities and bred plants and animals to suit our needs. The rising human population places great pressure on natural communities and on farmland. Overexploitation could cause irreversible losses in biodiversity and make it much harder for communities of the future to remain in balance.

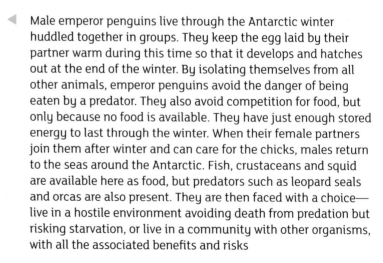

◁ Male emperor penguins live through the Antarctic winter huddled together in groups. They keep the egg laid by their partner warm during this time so that it develops and hatches out at the end of the winter. By isolating themselves from all other animals, emperor penguins avoid the danger of being eaten by a predator. They also avoid competition for food, but only because no food is available. They have just enough stored energy to last through the winter. When their female partners join them after winter and can care for the chicks, males return to the seas around the Antarctic. Fish, crustaceans and squid are available here as food, but predators such as leopard seals and orcas are also present. They are then faced with a choice— live in a hostile environment avoiding death from predation but risking starvation, or live in a community with other organisms, with all the associated benefits and risks

# What does a food chain tell us?

All organisms need food, but there are many different ways of getting it. Food chains show how organisms in a community get their food.

Some organisms make their own food, using an energy source and simple materials such as water and carbon dioxide. These organisms are called producers, for example, aspen trees.

If the energy source is light, food is made by photosynthesis. There are three groups of organisms that use photosynthesis to make food: plants, algae and photosynthetic bacteria.

Consumers feed on other organisms. Special adaptations are needed to do this effectively, so most consumers only eat certain types of food. Elk, for example are adapted to feed on plants. They prefer to graze on grasses and herbs but they have a digestive system that can break down tough fibrous material, including twigs and bark from trees such as aspen. Wolves feed on other animals, outrunning them and then killing them using their teeth. By hunting in packs wolves can catch elk, despite them being larger in size.

Consumers are placed in numbered groups according to what they eat:

- Primary consumers feed on producers. They are also sometimes called herbivores.

- Secondary consumers feed on primary consumers (herbivores).

- Tertiary consumers feed on secondary consumers.

Aspen, elk and wolves together form a food chain:

aspen ⟶ elk ⟶ wolves

▲ The last wolves in Yellowstone National Park were killed in 1926, but in the 1990s they were reintroduced

▲ Mature aspen trees and saplings in Yellowstone National Park

◀ Elk are large deer that are native to eastern Asia and North America including Yellowstone National Park

This food chain shows us that elk eat aspen and wolves eat elk. We know that food contains materials and energy. Therefore, the arrows tell us how materials and energy can be transferred in a community.

The first species in a food chain does not get food by eating other organisms, so it must be a producer. The second organism eats a producer, so is a primary consumer. The third organism must be a secondary consumer. Therefore, the food chain shows us that elk are primary consumers and wolves are secondary consumers.

A food chain cannot tell us everything about feeding relationships in a community. For example, elk not only eat aspen—they eat other trees and actually prefer non-woody plants. Elk are the primary prey of wolves but not their only prey. A diagram that combines food chains to show the different possible food sources for each species in a community is called a food web.

▼ Food web for Yellowstone National Park. Can you identify producers, primary consumers and secondary consumers?

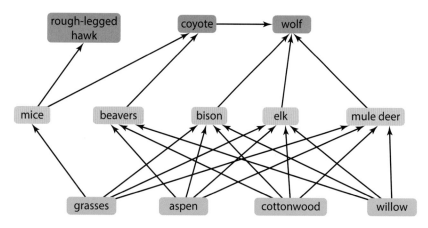

This food web for Yellowstone National Park does not show all the feeding relationships. A full food web for a community would be extremely complicated and have hundreds of species and arrows. This food web was constructed to study the interactions that took place when wolves were reintroduced to Yellowstone National Park.

## Reintroducing wolves to Yellowstone

Wolves were eliminated from Yellowstone National Park when the last ones were killed in 1926. For 70 years there were no wolves in the park apart from occasional strays. During the years without wolves there were some significant changes in Yellowstone with numbers of elk rising significantly and numbers of beavers and various types of tree reducing. However, in the 1990s wolves were reintroduced. The graphs show the numbers of wolves, elk, beaver and bison in the northern ranges of Yellowstone in the years after the reintroduction. They also show data about three tree species from survey areas in the northern ranges.

▲ Bison grazing near a hot spring in Yellowstone National Park

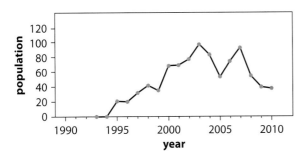

▲ Graph A Numbers of wolves

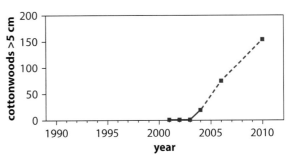

▲ Graph E Numbers of cottonwood trees with a trunk wider than 5 cm

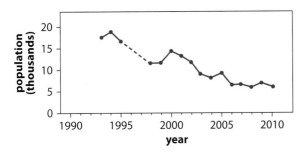

▲ Graph B Numbers of elk

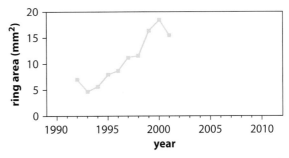

▲ Graph F Average growth in cross-sectional area of willow stem per year

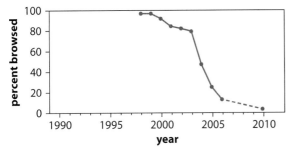

▲ Graph C Percentage of top shoots of aspen trees eaten

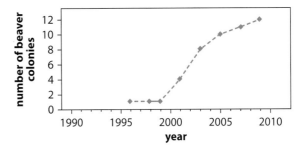

▲ Graph G Number of beaver colonies

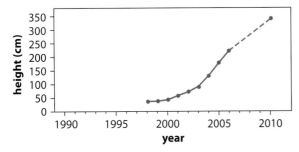

▲ Graph D Average height of aspen trees

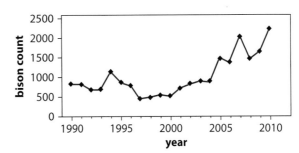

▲ Graph H Summer counts of bison

1. In what year were wolves reintroduced to Yellowstone?

2. a) What happened to the numbers of elk after wolves returned?

   b) What are the reasons for this change?

3. a) What happened to the size and numbers of the trees after wolves returned?

   b) What are the reasons for the change?

4. Beavers feed on trees and also need tree trunks to make their dams.

   a) What happened to the numbers of beavers after wolves returned?

   b) What are the reasons for the change?

5. Bison feed on mostly grasses and other non-woody plants, but also on leaves and twigs of trees.

   a) What happened to the numbers of bison after wolves returned?

   b) What are the reasons for the change?

6. a) Would you say that the reintroduction of wolves caused biodiversity in Yellowstone to increase or decrease?

   b) Would you say reintroduction of wolves made the community more balanced or less balanced?

 **Participate in contributing to ecosystem balance**

In many places, the balance of natural communities is disrupted by the introduction of species that are not normally found in an area. These species can end up dominating natural communities. When this happens, they are referred to as invasive species.

Conservation groups often seek volunteers to remove invasive species from public areas. They also often provide directions to citizens about how to act so as to limit the spread of an invader. For example, in the Great Lakes Region of North America, the emerald ash borer is an invasive species that destroys ash trees. People are advised not to transport cut wood from the affected area to other areas. Another example is in the UK, where the Scottish National Trust sponsors Rhododendron eradication programmes.

## Which organisms compete in a community?

**Competition** happens in communities when organisms need the same scarce resources. We see this in crowded forests where trees compete for light. Trees also compete for water and mineral nutrients from the soil. Foresters try to prevent competition by thinning out some trees thus allowing remaining trees to grow more strongly.

Animals compete for food and space. Animals can use behavior patterns to compete with each other. They may use aggressive behavior, but other types of strategy can also be used.

Competition can be a harmful interaction because it reduces how much of a useful resource an organism can get. Growth of organisms is likely to be reduced by competition and also reproduction. It is better to avoid competition. If two species are competing for the same resource, competition can be reduced if one or both species change to use different resources.

Competition is most intense with members of your own species, because the needs for resources are exactly the same. Some species show a behavior pattern called territoriality. Pairs or small groups defend an area and prevent other members of the species from coming into it. The territory is usually more than large enough to provide sufficient food for the animals defending it. If food is abundant then territories may become smaller.

Wolf packs are highly territorial. Their territories can extend over 30 or more square kilometers. Territorial behavior explains why the numbers of wolf packs in Yellowstone National Park soon reached a peak after reintroduction. Because of territoriality, wolves are unlikely to ever eliminate their prey species—the numbers of wolves are kept below the level where this might happen.

▲ There is intense competition for light between the trees, shrubs and lianas in this tropical rainforest community in Thailand

◄ Gannets nest on top of this rock pillar at Muriwai in New Zealand. Each pair of gannets requires a certain minimum area therefore limiting the number that can nest there

 **Experiment**

### Competition in plants

Cardboard egg boxes are ideal for growing plants from seed. You may have already done this when you were younger. Because the cups in the egg box are the same size, egg boxes are also ideal for competition experiments.

Design and carry out an experiment to test a hypothesis. Here are some possible hypotheses, but you may prefer to propose and test one of your own.

- The more cress seeds that are sown per cup the smaller the weight of each plant.

- The more radish seeds that are sown per cup the taller the plants grow.

- A mixture of mustard and cress gives more total weight of plants than the same number of plants of just mustard or just cress.

**Bird species in Wytham Woods**

Wytham Woods near Oxford have been used for research into forest communities for many years. Each year a census is done on the number of breeding pairs of two bird species, *Parus major* and *Cyanistes caeruleus*. The results for *Parus major* are shown in the left graph and for *Cyanistes caeruleus* in the right graph. Both *Parus major* and *Cyanistes caeruleus* show territorial behavior and use song to defend their territories.

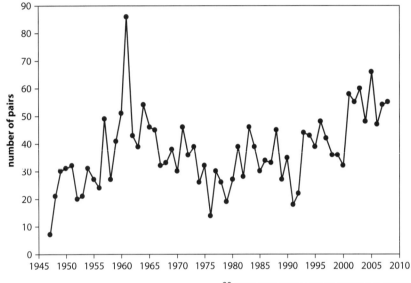

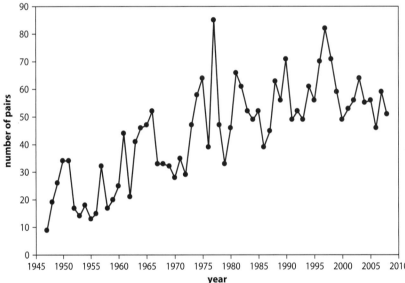

1. The start of 1947 was extremely cold in Wytham Woods. What was the effect of this weather on the bird populations?

2. If the *Parus major* population rises in one year, it tends to fall again in the following years and similarly if it falls it tends to rise again. Can you suggest reasons for this?

3. The population of *Cyanistes caeruleus* goes through cycles of rising and falling but also it shows an overall long-term trend. What is this trend? Can you suggest a reason for the trend?

4. The *Parus major* population is in a dynamic equilibrium. What does dynamic mean? What does equilibrium mean?

5. *Cyanistes caeruleus* and *Parus major* both nest in holes in trees or in bird boxes that have been designed to be like tree holes. How could you find out whether the *Cyanistes caeruleus* and *Parus major* populations are competing for nest sites or for food?

# Which relationships in a community benefit both organisms?

So far in this chapter we have looked at organisms that harm other organisms by eating them and also at organisms that harm each other by competing. The table shows these types of relationship, with blue upward arrows representing benefits and red downward arrows representing harm. There is a third type of relationship in communities where both organisms benefit from the interactions. These are called **mutualistic** relationships.

| Organism A | Organism B | Interaction |
|---|---|---|
| ↑ | ↓ | One organism gains a benefit from the relationship but the other organism is harmed. Example: **predator–prey relationships** |
| ↓ | ↓ | Both organisms are harmed by the relationship. Example: **competition** |
| ↑ | ↑ | Both organisms gain from the relationship. Examples: **mutualistic relationships** |

There are many examples of mutualistic relationships. Two examples from Yellowstone are given here.

- Willow trees need wet ground to thrive. Beavers cut the trunks of willow trees near the base to get material for making their dams. The willows can easily regrow so are not seriously harmed by being cut. Damming of rivers creates wet areas some distance upstream of the dam and therefore more sites on which willow trees can grow.

- Bison and elk both have a digestive system similar to cattle, with a large stomach called the rumen. Billions of bacteria live there. The bacteria release enzymes to digest the plant matter eaten by the animal. In particular, cellulose in plant cell walls is digested. The bison and elk couldn't otherwise digest cellulose so they benefit from having the bacteria in their rumen. The bacteria also benefit by having somewhere to live as well as a supply of food.

Some other examples of mutualism that you could research are shown in the photos on this page.

▲ Removal of parasites by cleaner fish or (as here) by oxpeckers

▲ Algae and fungi living together in lichens

▲ Pollination of flowers by birds or insects

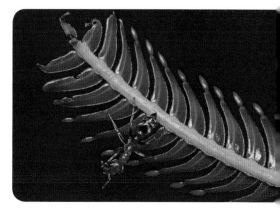
▲ Ants living on acacia trees

**ABC** **Competition** is the relationship between two organisms that strive to use the same resources.

**Predators** are animals that hunt, kill and eat other animals called their prey.

**Prey** is an animal that is a source of food for a predator.

**Mutualism** is a relationship between two organisms from which both benefit.

# What interactions are there in social groups?

Social animals live in groups rather than alone. Wolves for example live in packs. Groups can vary in size from just a few to thousands of individuals. In honey bee colonies, there are thousands of workers, smaller numbers of drones and just one queen. Leafcutter ant colonies can contain millions of individuals.

An individual honey bee or leafcutter ant cannot survive alone—they always live in a colony. Some animals only form groups at certain times, when there are benefits in cooperation.

▲ These geese are flying in a V-shaped group, taking turns to fly at the front. What benefit(s) do they gain from this?

▲ Chimpanzees remove harmful parasites from each other during grooming. Can you find any other benefits that grooming behavior brings to chimpanzees?

▲ Yellow-rumped caciques breed in a bag-shaped nest that hangs from the end of a tree branch. They breed in groups, with up to 100 nests in a single tree. Usually there is also a wasp nest in the same tree. Predators that try to take eggs or young from the nests are mobbed by the adults nesting in the tree. Do you know any other species that increase their success rate by breeding in groups?

▲ These leafcutter ants take pieces of leaf back to their nest and add them to a large heap. Warm conditions develop there, allowing a special type of fungus that lives nowhere else to digest the leaves. The ants feed pieces of the fungus to their growing larvae. What type of relationship is there between the leafcutter ant and the fungus? Carry out some research to find out why one leafcutter ant could not live by itself

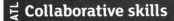
## Use social media networks appropriately to build and develop relationships

There are places on Earth such as Okinawa in Japan and Sardinia in Italy where people live much longer on average. These places are known as Blue Zones. What people in Blue Zones share, among a number of factors, are strong community connections.

For young students who have grown up as "digital natives", social connections can be helped through the positive use of social media, for example by maintaining contact with distant friends and relatives, or by connecting to people with similar concerns or interests. However, social isolation is not healthy and can be an outcome of excessive use of social media.

Discuss with other students in your class ways in which social media can *enhance* community connections and ways in which social media can *impede* social connections.

Create an infographic summarizing the outcomes of your class discussion and post it near the place where you sit to do your homework.

## What are the similarities and differences between predators, parasites and pathogens?

Predators, parasites and pathogens all harm animals by feeding on their tissues.

- Predators catch and kill their prey and then eat all or most of it. The prey is unlikely to survive when caught.

- Parasites and pathogens both live inside their **host** or on its outer surface. They get their food from the host and therefore weaken it. They may eventually kill the host, but only after some time has passed.

Parasites and pathogens are similar in some ways, but there are also differences.

- A pathogen is a microorganism that causes a disease. Because pathogens are too small to see with the naked eye, the causes of infectious diseases were uncertain until microscopes came into use. It was only in the 19th century that the "germ theory" of disease was widely accepted and other bizarre ideas were shown to be false. For example, the cause of the disease brucellosis was not understood until Scottish microbiologist David Bruce showed that it is due to infection with the bacterium *Brucella abortus*. Brucellosis affects various mammals including bison and elk in Yellowstone National Park.

ABC A **host** is the organism on which a parasite lives.

**Antibodies** are proteins that attach to one specific foreign substance in the body to help fight an infection.

**Immunity** is the ability to resist and overcome one specific infection.

A parasite is a larger organism than a pathogen. Most are large enough to be seen without a microscope so many were discovered long ago. Chimpanzees pick ticks, fleas and lice off each other during grooming, so we might argue that they discovered these external parasites before we did. Because parasites reproduce more slowly than pathogens, the harm caused by them usually develops more gradually and is milder, so the host can tolerate it for a long time. Generally, parasites on the skin only cause minor harm, but internal parasites can eventually be life-threatening if uncontrolled.

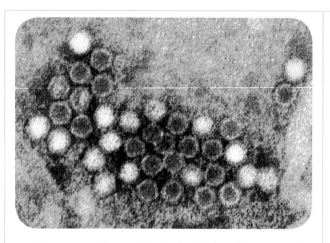

▲ Viruses are the smallest microbial pathogens and can only be seen using very high magnification with an electron microscope. These bocaviruses were discovered as recently as 2005. They are icosahedral in shape and only 20 nanometers in diameter. Bocaviruses cause respiratory tract infections, mainly in children.
Why are adults less likely to be affected?

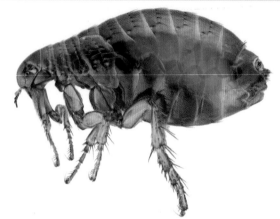

▲ Fleas are bloodsuckers that live on the skin. They have flattened bodies so they can move between hairs or feathers. Despite being insects, they do not have wings and instead use their powerful hind legs to jump as much as 50 times their body length.
How does their jumping ability help them?
Is a flea a predator or a parasite?

▲ This ruby-tailed wasp enters a mason bee's nest and lays an egg next to one of the mason bee's eggs. Both eggs hatch into larvae, but the wasp larva eats the bee larva.
Is the ruby-tailed wasp a predator or a parasite?

▲ The pathogens that cause Ebola are ebolaviruses. Ebola is a virulent disease affecting humans, killing up to 90% of those infected, but the viruses that cause it can live in fruit bats and other host animals without making them ill.
What is the reason for the advice on this sign?

A major challenge for a host is to control pathogens or internal parasites when they have entered the body. This is done by recognizing parts of the pathogen or parasite as foreign and by making **antibodies** against them. Once the host's body can make these antibodies it is **immune** and can kill the invaders. Some parasites are particularly good at evading detection by avoiding having chemicals that the host can recognize as foreign.

A major challenge for both pathogens and parasites is transfer from one host to another. To ensure long-term survival this must happen before the host finds a way of killing them or they kill their host. Pathogens can spread from host to host in the air, fluids, food, or by bodily contact. Many internal parasites have complicated life cycles that help them to spread, with each stage in the life cycle living on a different kind of host.

---

 **Population case studies**

1.  a)  Bison can extend over large areas in Yellowstone National Park and have relatively few internal parasites. However, bison herds kept in crowded conditions on farms often have severe problems with parasites such as intestinal roundworms. How do you explain this difference?

    b)  Some bison in Yellowstone National Park are infected with the bacteria that cause brucellosis, but they do not develop the disease. Cattle on farms do develop the disease when they are infected. If they are pregnant with a calf they usually lose it by miscarrying. How do you explain this difference?

    c)  In recent years large numbers of bison that venture out of Yellowstone National Park in search of food in winter have been culled, with the stated aim of reducing brucellosis infection in cattle. This policy is very controversial. Do you support it? Give your reasons.

2.  Records of furs sold by fur trappers to the Hudson Bay Company give estimates of the numbers of snowshoe rabbit and their predator, the Canada lynx, over a long time period. The results are shown on the right. Can you explain the cycles in the numbers of prey and predator?

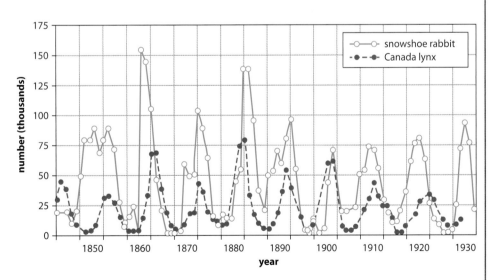

3.  An experiment was carried out to investigate fluctuations in the numbers of the adzuki bean weevil and a type of wasp that is its parasite. The results are shown on the right. Can you explain the results of the experiment?

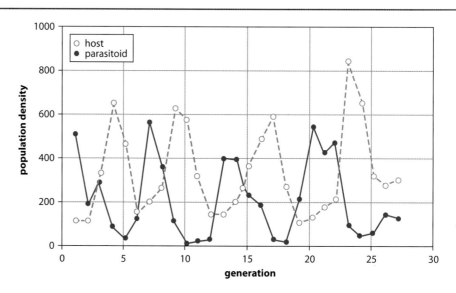

4.  Four moose were introduced to the island of Newfoundland in 1904, to attract big game hunters. The graph shows estimates of the resulting population. There has been concern about the effects of moose on the natural communities of Newfoundland. Moose on the island of

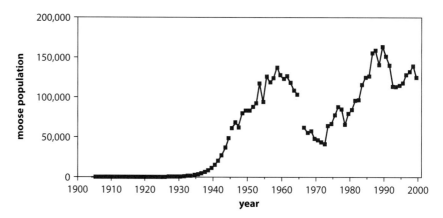

**Source of data**: B. E. McLaren, B. A. Roberts, N. Djan-Chékar and K. P. Lewis, *Alces*, 2004, **40**, 45–59

Newfoundland have been described as "a wrecking ball". Research the effects of the moose population to find out whether this description is justified.

## Should we expect all organisms to do something useful for a community?

What is the point of a parasite? This is a question that is often asked, because parasites seem so harmful. We might also wonder whether communities would be better off without pathogens causing disease. The catching and killing of prey by predators can seem very brutal. The phrase "nature red in tooth and claw" from one of Tennyson's poems sums up this feeling. Consider the four arguments on the following page:

1. Predators, pathogens and parasites help to prevent any single species from becoming too dominant in a community. This is because their effects become more intense on a species as its population increases. Pathogens and parasites can spread from host to host more easily so affect a higher percentage of their hosts. Predators build up in numbers if there is more of their prey. If large increases of any one species are prevented in a community, there will be more biodiversity and better balance.

2. Predators catch and kill the least fit individuals among their prey, causing abilities such as speed of running, sharpness of hearing and effectiveness of camouflage to improve by evolution. In a similar way, pathogens and parasites cause antibody production and other defences to improve in their hosts.

3. Humans have had damaging effects on many natural communities so it is hypocritical to expect other organisms to contribute in a useful way.

4. Biodiversity encompasses all the species in terrestrial and oceanic communities, including predators, pathogens and parasites, so we should value these groups of organisms as a part of biodiversity.

Using these four arguments and any others that you think are important, debate this question: Should we expect all organisms to do something useful, either for humans or for the ecological community where the organisms live?

# Summative assessment

To prepare for this assessment, carry out some research. What methods are used to fish for scallops by dredging? Are scallops eaten in your part of the world and if so, where do they come from? Find a map on the internet of the Southern Scallop Fishery in New Zealand and familiarize yourself with the geography of this area.

Read 'What we do in the shallows' written by Naomi Arnold: https://www.nzgeo.com/stories/what-we-do-in-the-shallows/

▲ Cooked scallops ready to be served

## Ecology of scallops

1. The part of the scallop that we eat is a powerful muscle linking the two valves of the shell. When this muscle contracts it closes the shell, squeezing out water at high velocity and causing the scallop to make a sudden movement. What does this sudden movement achieve?

   A. The scallop catches its prey

   B. The scallop escapes from a predator

   C. The scallop swims into the dredging net

   D. The scallop burrows into the sea bed

Questions 2–5 relate to scallops in the Southern Scallop Fishery and in each question the possible answers are:

   A. Producer

   B. Primary consumer

   C. Secondary consumer

   D. Tertiary consumer

2. Scallops (*Pecten novaezelandiae*) feed on microscopic algae floating in sea water (phytoplankton). What is the trophic level of scallops?

3. Scallops have various predators, such as sea stars (*Astropecten polyacanthus*), octopus (*Pinnoctopus cordiformis*) and blue cod (*Parapercis colias*). What is the trophic level of scallop predators?

4. Scallops compete for food with oysters (*Tiostrea chilensis*) and green-lipped mussels (*Perna canaliliculus*). What is the trophic level of these competitors?

5. What is the trophic level of the phytoplankton on which scallops feed?

6. Some sponges live attached to the outside of scallop shells, making it harder for other animals to attach. These other animals are larger than the sponges and can impede the movement of the scallop. The sponge cannot move from place to place by itself but is carried by the scallop to safer areas or areas with more food availability. What sort of relationship is there between the sponge and the scallop?

   A. Competition       C. Mutualism

   B. Interaction       D. Parasitism

7. Draw a food web that includes scallops and as many other organisms as possible. [4]

## Harvesting a natural resource

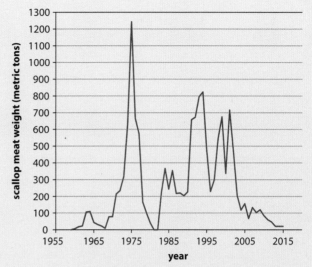

8. The graph shows the quantity of scallops (*Pecten novaezelandiae*) collected from the Southern Scallop Fishery each year from 1959 onwards. The fishery was closed in 1981–2. Suggest reasons for the:

   a) small harvest of scallops in the 1960s [2]

   b) huge increase during the first half of the 1970s [2]

   c) decrease in the second half of the 1970s [2]

   d) recovery in the 1980s and the high levels of harvesting in the 1990s [2]

   e) decrease in harvest after 2001. [2]

**Source of data**: New Zealand Ministry for Primary Industries (2016).

## Investigating the decline in scallops

9. Many causes have been suggested for the decline in scallops since 2001:

   - silt entering rivers due to agriculture and forestry, then being carried to sea and covering the sea bed
   - changes in weather patterns and climate due to the greenhouse effect
   - intensive scallop fishing by ocean-floor dredging
   - disease, toxins and pollutants.

   a) Choose the hypothesis that you think is most likely to have caused the decline in scallops since 2001. Use scientific ideas to explain your reasons for thinking that this is the most likely cause of the decline. [3]

   b) Design a scientific investigation to test whether your chosen hypothesis is affecting scallops in the Southern Scallop Fishery, including how you would control the variables and how you would collect data. [7]

## Ecological restoration

10. a) Discuss how science can help with attempts to restore the Southern Scallop Fishery and protect it for the future. [4]

    b) Fishery workers in Tasman Bay, Golden Bay and other parts of the Southern Scallop Fishery are keen to restart dredging for scallops. Write an article for them to read. Explain the importance of balancing the needs of current communities with those of future communities. [6]

Dredged and undredged areas of Lyme Bay on the south coast of England. Can you tell which is which?

# 8 Ecosystems

◀ European starlings fly in huge flocks in the minutes before they land and roost overnight. Together the starlings are less likely to be caught by predators than if they fly alone. The flock is a self-organized system—nothing plans or supervises the movements. How does this work? Do you know any other examples of self-organized systems?

▶ This trickling filter bed is used to treat sewage at a small community in Wales. The sewage trickles from a rotating boom onto a bed of small stones. As it drains down through the bed, bacteria in a layer on the surface of the stones break down solids in the sewage. The bacteria form the base of food chains in the filter bed. The liquid reaching the bottom is usually clean enough to be discharged into a river. The trickling filter bed is an example of an open system. What materials enter and leave the system? Why are both stones and bacteria needed in the filter bed?

**Statement of inquiry:**

The Earth will become uninhabitable for humans and many other organisms if we continue to damage the environment.

▲ NASA launched the Parker Solar Probe in August 2018. The probe has heat shields, solar panels to supply energy, propellant thrusters for changing trajectory, antennae for radio communication with Earth plus many different sensors for collecting scientific data. The aim is to swoop closer to the Sun's surface than any other spacecraft has ever done and collect important data, without being damaged by the brutal conditions. Failures in any of the components of the probe could prevent the success of the mission. Is the probe one system with a number of subsystems, or are there separate systems within the probe?

▶ This famous image of the Earth was taken from Apollo 8 when it was orbiting the moon. Pilot Jim Lovell is quoted as saying, "The vast loneliness ... is awe-inspiring and it makes you realize just what you have ... on Earth."

What would you say to someone from another planet if they asked what we have on Earth?

▲ Three ecosystems can be seen in this view: Can you identify them?

# Introduction

Organisms live together in communities and interact with their environment. Because of these interactions, living organisms and the environment operate as an ecological system. We call this an ecosystem. Living organisms are the **biotic** components and all parts of the non-living environment are the **abiotic** components. A forest is an ecosystem. A lake is an ecosystem. Anywhere that organisms live sustainably has an ecosystem, so the Earth's surface is almost covered with them, from rocky mountain peaks to deep ocean trenches. This thin but precious layer of ecosystems is called the ecosphere.

Ecosystems are complex and unplanned. They seem chaotic and disorderly, with each organism selfishly taking what it wants from the environment and discarding its waste products. Nevertheless, ecosystems survive for long periods of time—they are an excellent example of sustainability. This is because interactions between components of the ecosystem prevent essential resources from running out or toxic wastes from accumulating. The key to it is recycling. Resources move from organism to organism and between organisms and the environment, in complex repeatable cycles.

However, there is no guarantee that the natural order we see in any ecosystem will continue. Sometimes changes cause an ecosystem to collapse. The changes could be triggered by a shift in climate, or the arrival of a new species, or by damage due to human activities. Ecosystems on Earth are sustainable and resilient only because those that aren't do not survive.

Systems are divided into two types:

- open systems: materials are able to enter and leave

- closed systems: materials do not enter or exit.

Ecosystems are open, which has advantages and disadvantages. Leaves falling into a lake from trees in a forest bring food and therefore energy that organisms in the lake can use. On the other hand, rain may bring acid into the lake from air pollution in industrial areas. Rises in atmospheric carbon dioxide from human activities can also cause acidification of the water. Even in Arctic and Antarctic ecosystems toxic lead is detectable from human activities in the past. No ecosystem is therefore truly independent. They are part of an overall global system that is threatened in many ways by current human activities.

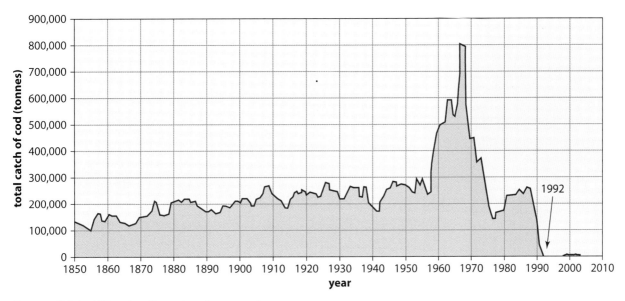

**Source of data:** Millennium Ecosystem Assessment

## What are the characteristics of aquatic ecosystems?

Life first existed in the oceans and for over a billion years all ecosystems were aquatic, as no organisms could live on land. Water is abundant on Earth and covers more than 70% of the Earth's surface. Most of this is sea or ocean where sodium chloride and other salts from rock have dissolved, making the water saline.

Water evaporates from the surface of seas and oceans and then condenses, falling as rain. Rainfall on land drains downward in streams and rivers and also forms ponds and lakes. The water contains low concentrations of salts, so is called freshwater. Thus, we can divide aquatic ecosystems into two groups, **freshwater** and **marine**. Aquatic ecosystems are mostly hidden from us because we cannot easily see beneath the water surface, but they are rich and varied.

The depth of the water affects what type of ecosystem there is. In shallow water plants or algae can attach to the underlying mud or rock, anchoring themselves to prevent movement. Animals live among them. In freshwater lakes where there is calm water, floating plants can cover the surface, creating cooler shady conditions below. Rocky shores can be harsh environments where organisms have to survive destructive wave action. In warm shallow seawater corals can grow and reefs can develop.

▲ The Grand Banks are shallow seas off the coast of Newfoundland, where ocean currents combine to create ideal conditions for plankton to grow and provide abundant food for other marine life. For hundreds of years cod was fished in these waters, but unsustainable overfishing from the 1950s onwards led to an ecosystem collapse. The population of cod was reduced by more than 99% and it has never recovered

▼ Coral reef ecosystems can only develop close to the water surface where sunlight penetrates and algae inside hard corals can make food by photosynthesis

Plants and large algae do not usually exist in deeper open water. Photosynthesis is only carried out by microscopic algae and bacteria that live close to the surface where sunlight can penetrate. These organisms and the small animals that feed on them are the plankton that drifts in seas and oceans. Large animals can swim faster than the currents, so move through the water to feed, or avoid being fed on.

In deep water it is mostly very cold and it is dark because sunlight does not penetrate. There is little oxygen in the water because it also does not penetrate from the air and is not being made by photosynthesis. The ecosystems here are very different from those near the surface, with organisms that are adapted to the conditions. Because of the difficulty of exploring deep in the oceans these ecosystems are still relatively unknown.

◀ In the depths of the ocean near hydrothermal vents there are ecosystems where no photosynthesis occurs and the only light is generated by living organisms. Here deep ocean fish swim among giant tube worms

 **Setting up an ecosystem in an aquarium**

▲ Collecting pondlife

You do not need a special tank to set up an aquarium—a large glass jar will do. You will need to have a balance of organisms—an aquarium with one type of fish, plastic plants and food added artificially each day is not an ecosystem. Visit a local pond where you have permission to collect material. You will need buckets and nets. Collect some mud from the bottom of the pond and enough water to fill your aquarium. Take some water plants and use a net to collect pond animals. Resist the temptation to take large numbers of animals—your ecosystem will only stay in balance if you have relatively small numbers and no very large animals.

Put your aquarium in a place that has light but is not too hot. The water will probably be cloudy for a time when you have put everything in, because of the mud, but it will settle. Any pondweeds with roots should be planted in the mud. When the water is clear you can see what organisms there are. If you have done a good job, the aquarium should remain in balance for as long as you keep it. When you have learned as much as you can, return the water and all the organisms to the pond where you got them—remember, this ecosystem needs to stay in balance.

Extension activity: You could put probes in the water and use a data-logger to monitor the temperature and pH of the water in your aquarium ecosystem.

# What are the components of terrestrial ecosystems?

Terrestrial ecosystems are those that are on land rather than in water. The environment in terrestrial ecosystems is a complex mixture of solids, liquid and gases.

Air is a mixture of gases. It supplies organisms in terrestrial ecosystems with vital resources—oxygen, carbon dioxide and, in some bacteria, nitrogen. All organisms release waste gases into the air, including methane from some bacteria. Winds move the air between ecosystems. For this reason, all ecosystems are interconnected via the atmosphere and if humans change the atmosphere it affects *all* ecosystems.

Water is liquid in most terrestrial ecosystems, so is also is free to move. Water from rainfall drains into the soil though spaces between the solid particles. It can then drain out of the soil into streams and rivers. In some dry ecosystems with little rainfall, water is drawn up through the soil from underground reserves and evaporates from the soil surface. Water changes state when it evaporates from soil or from plant leaves, and water vapor in the air condenses to form dew in cool conditions.

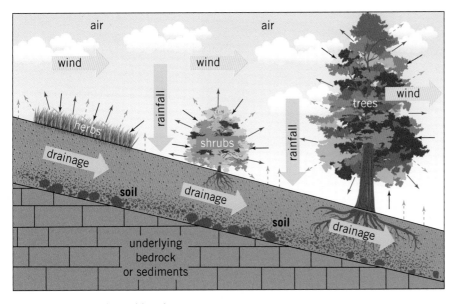

key  → oxygen released by plants
    → CO₂ absorbed by plants
   - - → water evaporating from plants (transpiration) or from soil

◀ Forests, shrubland and grassland are open systems because materials are free to move in and out of the ecosystem. Animals, sunlight and heat transfer are not shown on this simplified diagram

Soil is an important part of most terrestrial ecosystems. The solids within it are dead matter from organisms and fragments eroded from rock. These solids attract and hold both water and mineral nutrients. Unless waterlogged, soil has air spaces that contain the same gases as the air above the soil. However, soil usually contains less oxygen and more carbon dioxide, due to respiration by the organisms living in the soil.

Soil does not usually move much and in natural ecosystems it tends to become deeper and deeper. Soil erosion can sometimes occur as a result of wind or water movements. This can occur naturally (during storms, for example), but is often a consequence of human activity (after deforestation, for example).

Plants gain a stable anchorage by being rooted in soil and therefore the whole plant does not move. Plants obtain water and mineral nutrients from the soil. Many animals live in soil, such as earthworms, springtails and mites.

There are also vast numbers of bacteria and fungi, many of which act as decomposers, breaking down dead matter from organisms and releasing mineral nutrients back into the soil.

 **Finding animals that live in soil**

▲ Earthworms feed on dead matter from organisms in the soil, such as dead roots or leaves

Visit a forest or another local ecosystem. Obtain a sample of soil, including any organic matter on the soil surface, such as dead leaves. You could use a trowel or small spade to dig out the sample. Put it in a tray or bowl and sort through to find any living organisms present. Try to identify each organism that you find in the soil and then return it to its habitat.

Bacteria will be present in huge numbers but they are microscopic and therefore invisible. Can you find any thread-like fungal hyphae?

## What is the link between ecosystems and climate?

There are many different types of terrestrial ecosystem. The map on the following page shows natural ecosystem types in North America. It was produced by the Commission for Environmental Cooperation. Study the distribution of ecosystem types. There is a huge range, including many different types of forest.

Is rainfall or temperature more important in deciding what type of ecosystem there is in an area? You can try to decide this by comparing the ecosystems map with maps for annual precipitation (rainfall and snowfall) and for annual mean (average) temperature. You can find maps of temperature and precipation for North America at the CEC website (www.cec.org/map/climate).

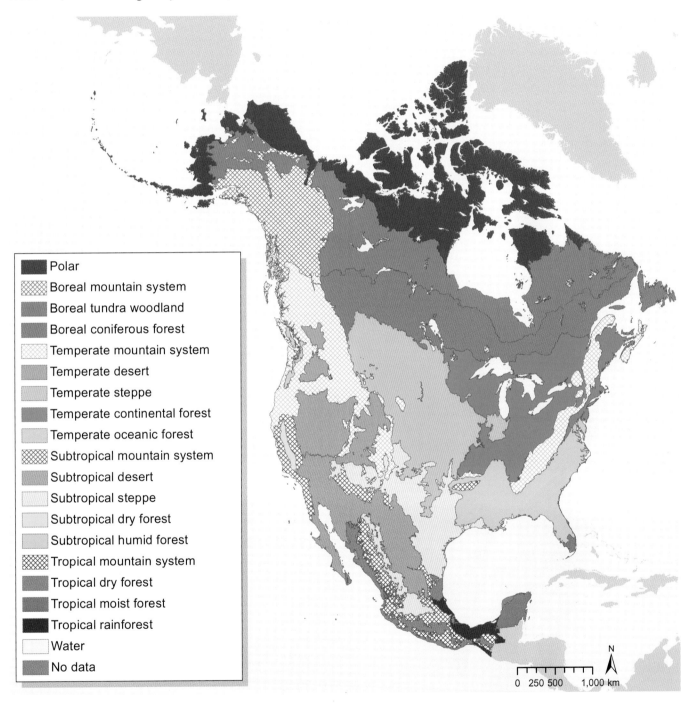

Legend:
- Polar
- Boreal mountain system
- Boreal tundra woodland
- Boreal coniferous forest
- Temperate mountain system
- Temperate desert
- Temperate steppe
- Temperate continental forest
- Temperate oceanic forest
- Subtropical mountain system
- Subtropical desert
- Subtropical steppe
- Subtropical dry forest
- Subtropical humid forest
- Tropical mountain system
- Tropical dry forest
- Tropical moist forest
- Tropical rainforest
- Water
- No data

0  250 500    1,000 km

N

# What types of organism are there in ecosystems?

There are three main types of organism in ecosystems—producers, decomposers and consumers.

## Producers

These are the organisms that can build up complex carbon compounds from much simpler substances, such as water and carbon dioxide. They take these substances from the environment. They also need a source of energy, which is usually light. The main waste product that they release is oxygen. All other organisms rely, directly or indirectly, on the complex carbon compounds made by producers and many organisms also rely on the oxygen.

*Types of producer:*
> *plants and also algae and certain bacteria.*

## Decomposers

These break down dead organic matter. This could be whole dead animals or plants, dead parts of organisms such as fallen leaves, a dead branch on a tree, or animal feces. Decomposers release simple substances such as carbon dioxide back into the environment. Without decomposers, dead organic matter would accumulate in an ecosystem and the simple substances required by producers would run out.

*Types of decomposer:*
> *microbes which are either bacteria or fungi.*

Producers and decomposers rely on each other. Decomposers need the complex carbon compounds that producers make and producers need the simple compounds that decomposers release. We could imagine an ecosystem with only these two groups of organisms. In real ecosystems there is always another group.

▲ Producers, consumers and decomposers are all involved in the production of food for humans. What examples can you see in these photos?

## Consumers

These eat material from other organisms and digest it in their gut or another structure inside their body. Many consumers eat living organisms, for example when an elephant feeds on the leaves of a tree, a tick feeds on human blood, or a baleen whale swallows krill. Some consumers eat dead organisms, such as a vulture feeding on carrion or an insect larva boring holes as it feeds on the dead wood of a tree. These examples also show that some consumers eat a whole organism and others just consume part of an organism.

*Types of consumer: animals and also certain protozoa.*

## How does a decomposer feed and grow?

Decomposers need a supply of dead material from other living organisms—this is their food. It could be dead plants and animals, feces or even crude oil spilt from a tanker.

Decomposers release digestive enzymes into their food. For example, decomposers that feed on dead wood release enzymes to digest the two main chemicals in it: cellulose and lignin. Each type of decomposer is adapted to break down a particular type of dead material and releases the enzymes that are needed to do this.

Decomposers are either fungi or bacteria. Bacteria are unicellular, often with spherical or rod-shaped cells. Many of them can move through fluids, which means they can swim to their food supply. Most fungi have a body made of thread-like hyphae, which grow over a food supply or into it.

Enzymes released by decomposers move through the food, digesting it as they go. Water is needed both for the movement and for digestion. Therefore dry materials do not decompose. Decomposers absorb as many of the useful products of digestion as they can, but inevitably other organisms absorb some of them. Many fungal decomposers release antibiotics to kill bacteria that might absorb digested foods.

Once absorbed by decomposers, the products of digestion can be used. Amino acids are made into proteins. They can also be converted to sugars by removing a nitrogen-containing part of the amino acid. This part is changed into ammonia ($NH_3$) and released into the environment.

▲  Is the fungus on these tomatoes a decomposer?

The release of ammonia is an example of an important activity of decomposers—complex compounds made by other organisms are broken down and simple substances are released as waste products. As a result, elements that producers have taken in from the environment are returned to it. Decomposers therefore play a very important role in ecosystems. The table shows the form in which the different elements are released.

| Element | How released |
|---|---|
| carbon | carbon dioxide ($CO_2$) |
| hydrogen | water ($H_2O$) |
| oxygen | $CO_2$ and $H_2O$ |
| nitrogen | ammonia ($NH_3$) |
| phosphorus | phosphate ions ($PO_4^{3-}$) |
| sulfur | sulfate ions ($SO_4^{2-}$) |

1.  The elements in the table are all non-metals. Which metallic elements are released during decomposition?

2.  Some elements are released as part of molecules and some as ions. What is the difference between an ion and a molecule?

3.  If supplies of an element run out in an ecosystem, can living organisms make more by converting another element?

## Researching wetlands

▲ The raft spider can walk over the surface of the water in bogs, hunting for insects to catch

Research these questions to find out more about wetlands.

1. What prevents dead organic matter from decomposing in some wetlands, and peat to accumulate?

2. How do producers in wetlands such the Venus fly trap obtain nitrogen, despite the lack of nutrient recycling?

3. What causes peat to decompose very quickly when it is added to soils in gardens?

4. What are the consequences of draining wetlands, for organisms such as this raft spider, and for atmospheric carbon dioxide concentrations?

# Experiment

### Decomposing tea bags

Tea bags can be used to investigate rates of decomposition as a part of the global carbon cycle. An international organization called the Tea Bag Index (TBI) has been coordinating this research and has collected results from around the world. You can find out more about it from the teatime4science website. TBI has developed a standard method, which scientists call a protocol. If everyone follows this protocol then results can be compared, because the only variables in the experiment are the ones being investigated.

▲ Burying a tea bag in the Ethabuka reserve in an Australian desert

### Questions

1. What types of tea bag are used? (You will have to look at the teatime4science website to answer this.)

2. Why are these types of tea bag chosen for the investigation?

3. Why would tea bags with a bag that can decompose be unsuitable?

The tea bags are weighed while they are still dry and unused. They are then buried 80 mm deep in soil and left for 90 days. They are then dug up. As much soil as possible is removed from the outside of the tea bags and they are dried. The tea is then removed from the bags and weighed.

4. How could you dry out the tea bag?

5. Why is it necessary to dry out the tea bag?

6. Why is the tea removed from the bag before being weighed?

▲ Drying tea bags

7. Why would it be better to bury more than one bag at each location investigated?

8. How can you tell how fast the tea decomposed from the results?

9. If you buried tea bags in a desert and in a tropical rainforest, where would you expect faster decomposition? Explain your reasons.

10. Make another prediction about how fast dead matter from organisms decomposes. How could you test your prediction using tea bags?

## Why must carbon be recycled?

Carbon is a central part of all of the main biochemicals, but it is not a very common element on Earth. Fewer than two in a thousand atoms are carbon. If plants are in sunny and warm conditions, the rate at which they can make food by photosynthesis is often limited by the concentration of carbon dioxide in the air—close to 400 parts per million or 0.04%. Carbon must therefore be endlessly recycled to avoid it running out.

Carbon exists in many forms in ecosystems.

- The main inorganic reserve of the element is carbon dioxide, either as a gas in the air or dissolved in water.

- Living organisms contain a huge range of carbon compounds including carbohydrates, proteins and lipids.

- Dead matter such as fallen leaves and animal feces contains many different carbon compounds.

The two main processes in the carbon cycle are photosynthesis and respiration.

- Carbon dioxide is converted to carbon compounds in photosynthesis.

- Carbon compounds are converted to carbon dioxide in respiration.

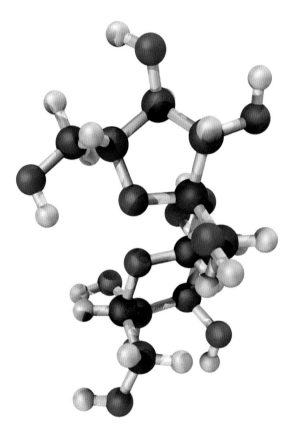

▲ Sucrose, also known as table sugar, is a carbon compound. Its chemical structure is pictured here

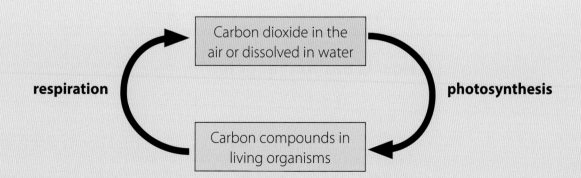

Carbon dioxide in the air or dissolved in water

respiration

photosynthesis

Carbon compounds in living organisms

### Mauna Loa and CO$_2$ concentrations

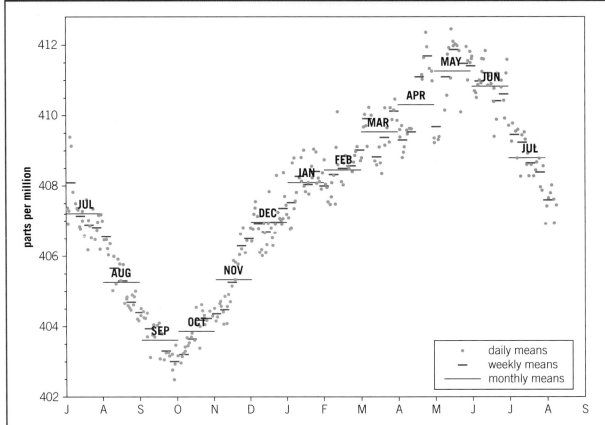

▲ The carbon dioxide concentration of the atmosphere fluctuates during the year. The graph shows the concentrations during a recent year at Mauna Loa on Hawaii

1. During which months did the carbon dioxide concentration of the air **a)** rise **b)** fall?

2. The rises and falls in carbon dioxide concentration are mainly due to photosynthesis and respiration. During which months was there

   **a)** more photosynthesis than respiration

   **b)** more respiration than photosynthesis?

3. What factors could cause the amount of photosynthesis to rise or fall during the year?

4. The data in the graph was collected by carbon dioxide monitors at Mauna Loa Observatory, which is 3,397 meters above sea level on the slopes of a volcano.

   **a)** What are the advantages of monitoring carbon dioxide at high altitude on an island in the Pacific Ocean?

   **b)** What are the disadvantages of monitoring carbon dioxide on a volcano?

## How is carbon recycled?

Respiration occurs in all organisms, but photosynthesis only occurs in producers. Instead of taking in carbon dioxide from air or water, consumers and decomposers obtain complex carbon compounds from other organisms. Movement of carbon compounds from one organism to another is therefore part of the carbon cycle. It happens when a consumer eats another organism or a decomposer breaks down dead matter.

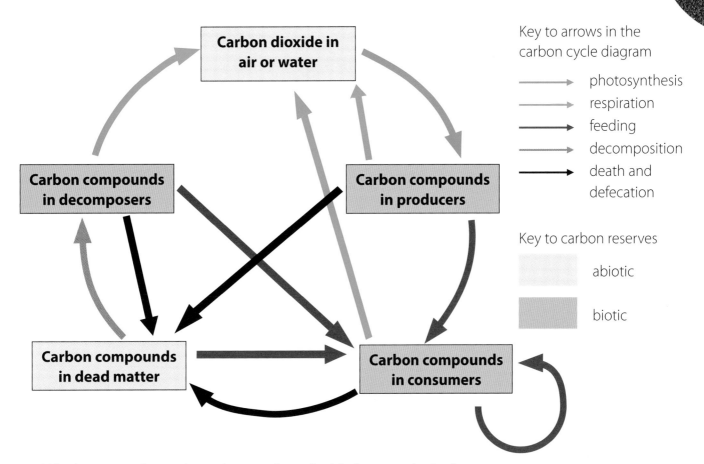

Key to arrows in the carbon cycle diagram

→ photosynthesis
→ respiration
→ feeding
→ decomposition
→ death and defecation

Key to carbon reserves

abiotic

biotic

1. Which groups of organism release carbon dioxide from respiration?

2. Deduce which arrow shows carnivores feeding.

3. Try to find an example for each of the arrows on the carbon cycle.

4. Discuss what sequence of arrows a carbon atom would pass through if it:

   a) was taken in by the leaf of a hickory tree and used to make glucose, which was moved to the root of the tree and used in respiration.

   b) became part of the wood in the trunk of an oak tree and a long-horned beetle larva ate the wood and was then eaten by a woodpecker which used the carbon compounds from it in respiration.

   c) was in cattle feces used to grow mushrooms, which were eaten by a person, who respired and released carbon dioxide, which was used in photosynthesis by grass, which was eaten by a cow.

5. Imagine some other sequences of moves that a carbon atom could make, by which the atom ends up back where it started. You could try to think of a sequence that takes as long a time or as short a time as possible to be completed.

**ABC** **Biotic** components are the living organisms in an ecosystem.

**Abiotic** components are the non-living parts of an ecosystem.

## What is causing carbon dioxide concentrations in the atmosphere to rise?

During the Carboniferous era, huge tree ferns and other plants absorbed carbon dioxide from the atmosphere and used it in photosynthesis. Some of the forests that grew were killed by rising sea levels and buried under deposits of mud. The plants did not decompose fully and were converted to coal. Carbon atoms have remained trapped in this coal for 300 million years. In a similar way, carbon from plankton in the marine ecosystems was trapped in rock as oil and natural gas, for example in the Permian basin of Texas, formed over 260 million years ago.

Coal, oil and gas are known as carbon sinks, because they can hold carbon taken from the atmosphere for an indefinite length of time. Carbon in coal is inert and organisms cannot use it. Carbon in oil and gas reserves cannot be used by organisms either, because of a lack of oxygen in the rocks where they occur.

Huge quantities of carbon have accumulated in these sinks, but we are now releasing it. When coal, oil and gas are burned, carbon atoms that have been trapped in rock for hundreds of millions of years are returned to the atmosphere as carbon dioxide. The amount of fossil fuel burning started to rise during the industrial revolution. Before this, in the late 18th century, the atmospheric carbon dioxide concentration was only 280 parts per million (ppm). Data from Mauna Loa shows that it is now over 400 ppm.

1. Describe the changes in atmospheric carbon dioxide concentration since 1958.

2. Discuss what is likely to happen to carbon dioxide concentrations during the rest of the 21st century.

3. Explain what has caused the rise in carbon dioxide concentrations.

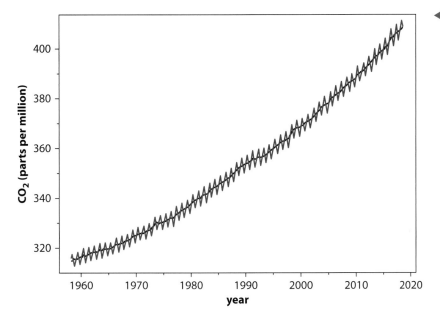

◀ Atmospheric carbon dioxide concentrations have been monitored at an observatory high on Mauna Loa, a volcano in Hawaii, since 1958. The red curve includes seasonal fluctuations and the black curve is the change year-on-year with the fluctuations removed

## ATL Reflective skills

# Consider ethical, cultural and environmental implications

IB students are encouraged to reflect on the implications of what they have learned. The implications of rising carbon dioxide concentrations are potentially enormous.

The environmental implications are obvious but are there also ethical and cultural implications?

On reflection, how do you think we should be responding to what is increasingly being called the climate emergency?

Scientists are concerned that there could be very rapid and uncontrollable rises in atmospheric carbon dioxide concentration during the 21st century, even if we reduce the amount of fossil fuels burnt. This is because some of the carbon dioxide released into the atmosphere by burning fossil fuels in the past was absorbed by oceans, forests and soils but it might be returned to the atmosphere in the future. A vicious cycle of cause and effect could develop that would threaten all of the world's ecosystems. This is shown in the flow chart.

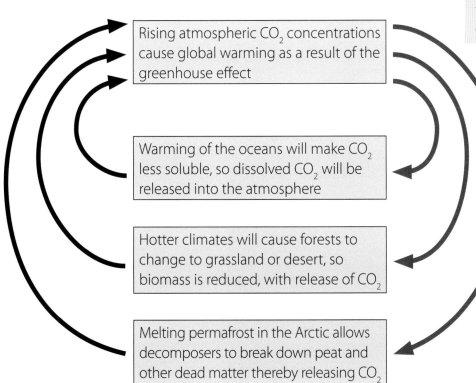

Rising atmospheric $CO_2$ concentrations cause global warming as a result of the greenhouse effect

Warming of the oceans will make $CO_2$ less soluble, so dissolved $CO_2$ will be released into the atmosphere

Hotter climates will cause forests to change to grassland or desert, so biomass is reduced, with release of $CO_2$

Melting permafrost in the Arctic allows decomposers to break down peat and other dead matter thereby releasing $CO_2$

It is not clear what global temperatures might cause this vicious cycle to begin and it is possible that it already has. Scientists refer to it as a tipping point, beyond which the Earth's ecosystems release rather than absorb carbon dioxide. "These tipping elements can potentially act like a row of dominoes," said Professor Johan Rockstrom, Executive Director of the Stockholm Resilience Centre. "Once one is pushed over, it pushes Earth towards another. It may be very difficult or impossible to stop the whole row of dominoes from tumbling over. This cascade of events may tip the entire Earth system into a new mode of operation."

With record high temperatures in many parts of the world in the summer of 2018 and widespread forest fires, concerns about the Earth reaching tipping points led to news headlines such as "Earth at risk of entering 'hothouse' state from which there is no return, scientists warn".

4. In a hothouse state, the average temperatures on Earth could be up to 6°C higher than they were at the start of the industrial revolution. What problems would this cause to ecosystems and to humans?

5. A rise of 6°C would cause sea levels to rise by about 60 meters.

   a) What are the reasons for sea level rises when the Earth's temperature rises?

   b) What problems would a 60-meter rise in sea level cause to ecosystems including coral reefs and mangrove swamps, and what problems would it cause to humans?

6. To try to prevent a hothouse Earth developing, what should be done by:

   a) individual people

   b) governments of individual countries

   c) international organizations?

▼ Rising global temperatures are causing Arctic ice to melt, depriving polar bears of their hunting grounds

# Summative assessment

**Statement of inquiry:**

The Earth will become uninhabitable for humans and many other organisms if we continue to damage the environment.

## Earthwatch

The following extract is part of an online document produced by Earthwatch Europe, for participants in an ongoing research project at Wytham Woods near Oxford (Northwest Europe). Read the text and then answer the questions that follow.

As an Earthwatch participant, you will spend time each day assisting scientists with data collection. Some of this work will be repetitive, but it is fundamental to our scientific understanding of nature. Ecosystems are incredibly complex. The only way to begin to unravel this complexity is by designing good experiments, and carefully collecting as much data as possible. Without the work of thousands of dedicated scientists, we would know nothing about climate change, the effects of pollution, the extinction of species, or how to find cures for diseases and improve crops. This is your chance to be part of the scientific effort, to find solutions to pressing environmental and cultural problems, and to enjoy the beauty and diversity of nature as you work.

Forests hold more carbon in trees and soils than any other terrestrial habitat. Climate change and elevated carbon dioxide in the atmosphere will increase the growth of trees that live in colder climates, thereby capturing more carbon. However, climate change will also increase the activity of the bacteria and fungi that break down carbon compounds stored in forest soils, releasing carbon dioxide back into the atmosphere. If decomposition outpaces tree growth, then these forests will paradoxically increase the carbon dioxide concentration of the atmosphere.

Logging can increase forest susceptibility to the droughts that are expected to become more frequent in many regions under climate change. Droughts make forests flammable, and large areas of tropical forests have burned during droughts in recent years. More subtle perturbations of the ecological interactions among trees, herbivores, predators, parasites and diseases are also likely to alter the structure and functioning of the world's forests.

There is a need for research and better understanding of the likely impacts of climate change on forest ecosystems, biodiversity, biomass production, and ultimately the implications to the local communities and the economy. The main goal of our research programme is to develop a better understanding of the role that disturbed forests, i.e. those modified by humans, play in the carbon cycle, and how this could be influenced by future climate change.

1. Explain the importance of the work of scientists for humans and all other organisms on Earth. [5]

2. The participants in this research project in 2018 were people who worked for a major oil company. Discuss the reasons for an oil company wanting its workers to be part of the research. [5]

3. Explain how planting a forest in an area that has been deforested could help reduce the carbon dioxide concentration of the atmosphere. [3]

4. Explain how the spread of tree diseases could increase the carbon dioxide concentration of the atmosphere. [2]

### Analyzing oak tree growth

A small sample of data from the Earthwatch research project at Wytham Woods is shown in the table below. It shows the initial diameter of the trunks of ten oak trees and increases in trunk circumference in 2010, 2011 and 2012. In 2010 there was cold weather in spring and then high temperatures and drought conditions in the summer.

| Tree number | | 2424 | 2399 | 2111 | 2446 | 2323 | 2174 | 2443 | 322 | 2422 | 2363 |
|---|---|---|---|---|---|---|---|---|---|---|---|
| Initial diameter (cm) | | 107 | 69 | 64 | 49 | 47 | 39 | 34 | 31 | 29 | 20 |
| Cumulative increase in trunk circumference (mm) | April 2010 | 0 | 0 | 0 | 0 | 0 | 0 | 0 | 0 | 0 | 0 |
| | July 2010 | 7.87 | 1.34 | 0.9 | 7.91 | 1.06 | 1.87 | 5.25 | 2.84 | 0.95 | 0 |
| | October 2010 | 8.47 | 3.18 | 1.24 | 10.17 | 2.4 | 2.88 | 6.28 | 2.14 | 1.31 | 1.11 |
| | April 2011 | 3.47 | 2.3 | 1.14 | 10.22 | 1.71 | 3.56 | 6.44 | 0.88 | 0 | 0.41 |
| | July 2011 | 10.82 | 6.07 | 0.91 | 18.5 | 4.81 | 6.42 | 11.14 | 1.6 | 1.3 | 1.09 |
| | October 2011 | 13.4 | 7.69 | 2.2 | 20.65 | 4.34 | 6.35 | 12.9 | 2.34 | 1.13 | 1.38 |
| | April 2012 | 15.74 | 8.67 | 3.59 | 22.61 | 6.1 | 8.54 | 13.7 | 1.5 | 1.54 | 2.45 |
| | July 2012 | 27.81 | 13.83 | 3.6 | 38.08 | 10.88 | 15.3 | 28.17 | 3.11 | 3.74 | 3.45 |
| | October 2012 | 32.41 | 15.97 | 3.31 | 43.85 | 12.31 | 18.52 | 33.29 | 3.7 | 3.86 | 4.71 |

5. Develop a hypothesis about the growth of trees in Wytham Woods and use the data to evaluate the validity of the hypothesis. [10]

- Process the data by using whatever mathematical procedures you decide are suitable.
- Choose a suitable table, chart or graph to display the transformed data.
- Interpret the data and explain it using scientific reasoning.
- Evaluate your hypothesis, using evidence from the data.

The carbon dioxide concentration of the Earth's atmosphere has already risen from about 280 parts per million (ppm) to more than 400. It is forecast to rise to 550 ppm by 2050. To investigate the effects of this on forests, a series of experiments are being done around the world. These are FACE experiments (Free-Air Carbon dioxide Enrichment). The first was started in a eucalyptus forest in Australia (EucFACE) and the second in an oak forest in England (BIFoR FACE).

▶ A circle of steel towers forms the edge of a FACE experimental area. Carbon dioxide is released from holes in the black vertical pipes that are supported by these towers. Carbon dioxide concentration is monitored by sensors on the central tower

## FACE experiments

A circle of towers is used to release carbon dioxide into the air. Whichever way the wind is blowing the $CO_2$ is released so that it blows into the circular experimental area rather than immediately away from it. Monitors check that the concentration is close to 550 ppm—the rate of $CO_2$ release is adjusted if it is not.

6. Far more $CO_2$ has to be released in FACE experiments on windy days than on calm days. Explain the reasons for this. [2]

7. Less $CO_2$ would have to be released if the circular experimental areas were enclosed with glass, but then it would not be a free-air experiment. Explain the disadvantages of doing the experiment in enclosed forest. [3]

8. Explain the reasons for thinking that the oak trees will grow faster and store more carbon if atmospheric $CO_2$ concentration rises to 550 ppm. [3]

9. Suggest a way of measuring whether the oak trees are growing faster and storing more carbon with a higher atmospheric carbon dioxide concentration. [2]

   The growth of trees does not only depend on $CO_2$—it is also affected by the amounts of mineral nutrients in the soil. Some scientists think that forest won't grow faster and store more carbon with higher $CO_2$ concentrations because trees will run short of mineral nutrients such as nitrate and phosphate.

10. Design a FACE experiment to investigate whether shortage of mineral nutrients will prevent forests from storing more carbon in the future when atmospheric $CO_2$ concentrations are much higher than they are now. [5]

▼ This map shows the layout of one of the experimental areas. The towers cannot be in an exact circle as they have to be positioned between the trunks and major branches of the trees

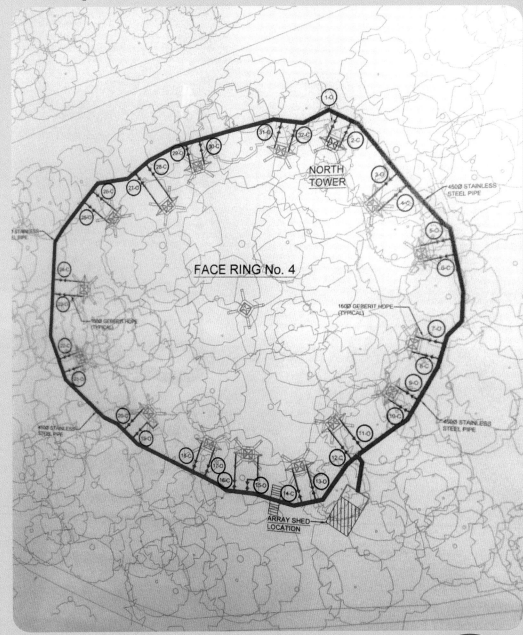

# 9 Evolution

◀ The French artist Odilon Redon created some disturbing images of metamorphosis in *Origines*, a series of lithographs. In his 1903 painting *Flower Clouds*, shown here, two figures look into the distance at the sea and the sky. What forms are appearing there?

▶ These pages are from *The Tale of Genji*, written by Murasaki Shikibu in the 11th century. It is considered to be a masterpiece and perhaps the first example of a novel. It is hard for modern readers to understand the text unless translated, because the Japanese language has changed so much over the last thousand years. Can we expect the quality of novels to have improved over the centuries or are works from all ages just as great?

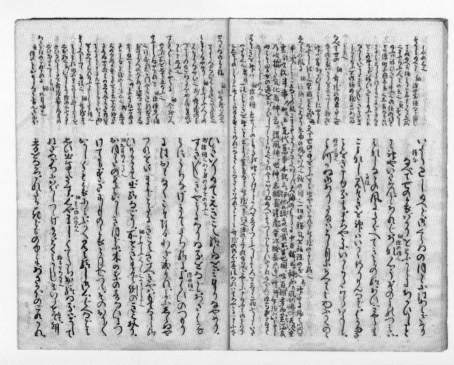

**Statement of inquiry:**

Evidence of past changes helps us understand life today and how it might be transformed in future.

▲ Many movies have been based on novels. *To Kill a Mockingbird* is highly regarded both in the original novel by Harper Lee and the movie adaptation in 1962, directed by Robert Mulligan and starring Gregory Peck. Can you think of any movie adaptations that you think are better than the novel? Which great novels became box-office flops as movies? What other adaptations of one art-form to another are possible?

▼ Fashion can change rapidly. One possible reason is teenagers not wanting to look like their parents. Are there other reasons for such changes in clothes, shoes or hairstyles? Can you identify the decade when this photo was taken? What styles of jeans are fashionable now? What style of jeans do you think will be fashionable in, for example 30 years?

**Key concept:** Change

**Related concepts:** Environment, Evidence, Transformation

**Global context:** Orientation in space and time

**Key concept:** Change

**Related concepts:** Environment, Evidence, Transformation

**Global context:** Orientation in space and time

**Statement of inquiry:**

Evidence of past changes helps us understand life today and how it might be transformed in future.

▲ This statue at Shrewsbury School of Charles Darwin shows him as a young man. He was a pupil at the school between the ages of 9 and 16.

## Introduction

Charles Darwin's book *On the Origin of Species by Means of Natural Selection* was published in 1859. It changed forever our understanding of the natural world. Darwin explained the mechanism that causes organisms to change over time—the process that we call **evolution**. His explanation shows how all forms of life could have evolved from a universal common ancestor. A consequence of this is that humans share kinship with all other living organisms. This was a deeply shocking idea to many people living in the 19th century, who had been taught that God created humans and that humans have a special place in creation.

Darwin probably realised in 1838 that natural selection was the cause of evolution, but he waited over 20 years before publishing this discovery. He has been accused of fearing too much how religious leaders might react. The real reason for such a long a delay is that Darwin was accumulating evidence. In the *Origin of Species,* he presents a wealth of evidence for evolution by natural selection. This is what all scientists, and indeed all non-scientists, should do when trying to change our understanding. Darwin even anticipated counter-arguments, by explaining how transformations could occur to produce complex structures, such as the eye.

Since 1859 there have been many more discoveries that have changed our understanding of the natural world. We now know that the universal common ancestor lived far longer ago than Darwin imagined—perhaps 4 billion years ago. We know how environments on Earth can change and how this can cause extinction of some species and opportunities for others. We also know that humans are not only affected by environments on Earth, but that we can profoundly change them. For these reasons, it has never been more important to study the life sciences, and base our actions on an understanding of the impact that we are having on planet Earth.

## How were breeds of dog developed by humans?

The DNA of wild grey wolves (*Canis lupus*) and dogs such as beagles or bulldogs (*Canis familiaris*) is so similar that we can be confident that all breeds of dog were developed from grey wolves. A process called selective breeding or artificial selection was used to achieve this. This diagram shows the basic process.

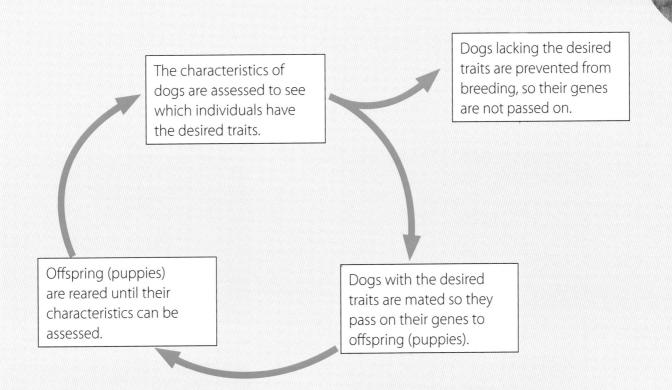

The changes in the **traits** of dogs may be very small with each new generation of dogs, but if the process of artificial selection is repeated over many generations, there can be massive changes—traits can be transformed. This is how dogs have become so different from grey wolves and how so many breeds of dog with strikingly different appearance and behaviors have been developed.

It is important to remember three things about artificial selection:

- Artificial selection can only change traits if they are due to the dogs' genes and not to the environment.

- If something is changed during a dog's lifetime, the offspring of that dog will not inherit the changed trait—for example if a dog's tail is docked (cut shorter) its offspring will not be born with docked tails.

- Artificial selection can only work if there is variation in the genes. If there is no genetic variation in a breed, then it is impossible to select individuals with more desirable traits to breed the next generation.

1. Dogs are often kept as pets, but most breeds were originally developed to do something useful for their owners. Find out what work these breeds originally did:

   a) Alaskan Husky
   b) Bouvier des Flandres
   c) Catahoula Cur
   d) Doberman Pinscher.

**ABC** **Evolution** is gradual change in traits of living organisms that are determined by genes.

**Traits** are characteristics or features of living organisms, that are determined either by genes or by the environment.

2. What traits does a Dachshund have that make it ideally adapted to help hunt animals such as badgers and rabbits?

3. What could a dog breeder do if they wanted to develop a particular trait, but none of the dogs in their favourite breed had the genes for that trait?

▲ Dalmatian (25 kg)

▲ Papillon (2 kg)

▲ Great Dane (55 kg)

▲ Nova Scotia Duck Tolling Retriever (33 kg)

▲ Dog breeds show amazing variety in size, length of fur, color of fur and behavior. A grey wolf is shown on page 131

## How are genes transformed by mutation?

A gene is a sequence of bases in a DNA molecule. There are four different bases in DNA, usually referred to by their initials A, C, G and T. They can be arranged in any sequence. Typical genes are at least a thousand bases long.

**Mutations** are changes to genes. The smallest but most important type of mutation is when one base changes to another base, for example C to G. This is called a base substitution. The change usually happens when DNA is being copied and a small mistake happens. It can also happen when high-energy radiation or certain substances (**mutagens**) cause chemical changes in DNA.

These are the most important features of gene mutations:

- Mutations are *random*—any base in a gene can change, and it can change to any of the other three bases.

- Mutations are *heritable*—although changes to base sequences in skin or other body cells are not passed on to offspring, mutations in the ovary and testis cells that develop into gametes can be inherited.

- Mutations are *rare*—in the DNA that we inherit from each of our parents there are about 3 billion bases but there will only be a few base substitutions. Nearly all of our 25,000 or so genes are passed on to our offspring unchanged.

- Mutations can *change protein structure*—most of our genes are used to guide the production of a specific protein. A mutation in such a gene may result in a change to the protein, which can affect the structures and functions of an organism and thus its traits.

- Mutations can be *beneficial, harmful or neutral*—most mutations are neutral because they do not occur in a critical part of a gene. Some are harmful. A tiny minority of mutations are beneficial.

▲ These "identical" twins developed from one fertilized egg, but during their development mutations will have occurred in some genes, so the twins are genetically extremely similar but not truly identical. A study of the DNA from body cells of two 100-year old identical twins found just eight base differences out of 3 billion

One of the most famous mutations in human history happened near the start of a gene called HBB. This gene codes for one of the subunits of hemoglobin, the protein in red blood cells that carries oxygen. Here are the first 21 bases in the gene:

G T G C A C C T G A C T C C T G A G G A G

1                        10                        20

The mutation changed the 17th base from A to T. This changes the structure of hemoglobin only very slightly, but the change has major consequences. It causes sickle-cell disease, which is a serious and lifelong condition. However, it also provides increased resistance to malaria. As a result, in parts of the world where malaria is common, it can be an advantage to have a copy of the HBB gene with this mutation. The mutation has therefore been passed on to offspring and millions of people have inherited it.

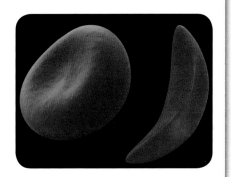

▲ The red blood cell on the left is normal, but the one on the right has become sickle-shaped, due to a mutation in the hemoglobin gene HBB

The different versions of a gene produced by a mutation are called alleles of the gene. The normal HBB allele is called $Hb^A$ and the allele with the sickle-cell mutation is called $Hb^S$. A few of the 25,000 or so human genes only exist as one allele, but with most genes there are two or more different alleles. In some cases, there are many different alleles. This explains why no two humans have exactly the same genes, apart from identical twins.

## How much variation is there in wild populations?

We are very good at seeing the differences between humans, but are usually slower to see variation in other species.

- Visit a park, garden or wild area and take a look at the organisms that are living there. Find a species that is common, so you can quickly examine many individuals. Avoid organisms deliberately grown by humans such as crop plants or farm livestock. Do not cause any harm to organisms or the environment.

- Find a trait that seems to be variable in the species that you have chosen. It should be something that is at least partly heritable, not just due to the environment.

- Choose a reliable way of measuring or recording the trait in each individual. Collect this data from as many individuals as you can.

- Display the data using the most appropriate medium. A bar chart might be suitable, but not for some traits such as bird song.

- Present the results to your class, explaining how much variation you found in the trait you investigated.

▲ Snowdrops (*Galanthus plicatus*) flower in the spring. Gardeners have discovered many different varieties growing in wild populations. A few of these are shown here

## Water lilies and cacti

The white water-lily (*Nymphaea odorata*) grows in freshwater ponds and lakes, with its leaves floating on the surface and its roots in the mud below. The stems are short and fat. They grow horizontally over the surface of the mud.

1. What is the advantage of the following features in a leaf floating on the water surface:

    a) large air spaces

    b) a coating of wax on the upper surface, but not the lower surface

    c) pores (stomata) in the upper surface, but not the lower surface?

2. What is the advantage of these other features found in water lilies:

   a) thin, flexible leaf stalks that can grow to any length

   b) air canals in the leaf stalks, which are connected to air spaces in the leaves

   c) roots that grow downwards into the mud?

Cacti grow in dry or drought-prone environments in North and South America. In Africa there are plants that have very similar features but they are called euphorbias, not cacti. The most famous type of cactus is the saguaro (*Carnegiea gigantea*).

▲ These water lilies, photographed from underwater, were growing in a lake near Cape Cod, Massachusetts. The vertical structures are leaf stalks (petioles)

3. What is the advantage of the following features in the stem of a saguaro cactus:

   a) many cells that can store water

   b) folds in the surface of the stem (fluting)

   c) vertical growth with few if any side branches?

4. What is the advantage of these other features in a saguaro cactus:

   a) spines instead of leaves

   b) pores (stomata) for absorbing carbon dioxide that open at night rather than in the day

   c) roots that spread through the soil over a large area around the stem?

▲ These saguaro cacti growing in the Sonoran desert are at least a hundred years old

5. What would happen if we planted a water lily in a desert, or a saguaro cactus in a lake?

6. Choose some other examples of plants or animals that have features that adapt them to their environment.

   • You can choose any type of organism because all organisms need to be adapted to the conditions in which they live.

   • Find out what the adaptations are and how they help the organism to survive.

   • The adaptations could be external appearance, internal structure, behavior or any other type of trait.

▲ A young herdsman in Nigeria (latitude 9°N) with his cattle at a watering place

▲ Uyghur boy with his goats in Xinjiang Uyghur Autonomous Region, China (latitude 42°N)

# What is an adaptation?

In life sciences, the concept of adaptation is very important. These are the most important features:

- Adaptations are features (or changes to features) that make an organism better fitted to its environment.

- Different adaptations are needed if an organism's environment changes.

- Only heritable traits are considered to be adaptations. For example, having dark skin is an adaptation to living in a very sunny climate, but developing a sun-tan is not.

- Adaptations are not developed deliberately by living organisms— they develop naturally and without planning. They are not developed by design.

- We can never say that something is perfectly adapted—there is always the possibility for further improvements.

- Being better adapted gives an organism more chance of survival. This is sometimes referred to as survival of the fittest.

Skin color in humans is an example of adaptation. Skin cells can produce a black pigment called melanin. The amount of melanin is influenced by several genes that we inherit from our parents. Melanin stops ultra violet light (UV) from penetrating the skin. UV has two effects on skin cells:

- It causes sunburn and, more seriously, it causes mutations in the DNA of skin cells, which may lead to skin cancer.

- It provides the energy needed for skin cells to make Vitamin D. Without sufficient Vitamin D, the body can develop rickets.

Dark skin is therefore an adaptation to living in an area with bright sunlight containing lots of UV and there is more risk of developing skin cancer than rickets.

Light skin is an adaptation to living in an area with weaker sunlight and less UV, where rickets is more of a danger than skin cancer.

Nearly all human populations that have been settled in an area for more than just a few generations have skin colors that are adapted to the intensity of UV light. There are a few populations whose skin colors do not match the amount of UV in the area where they live. This is generally where a population has migrated north or south and has not yet adapted to the change in UV intensity. This shows that it takes thousands of years for a population's skin color to adapt to its new environment—it does not happen by individuals becoming more tanned or less tanned and passing this change on to offspring.

1. Discuss which of the boys in the photos is most at risk of

   a) skin cancer

   b) rickets.

2. Humans now often migrate to a part of the world where their skin color is not well adapted. Explain the health risks for these two people and what they can do to avoid health issues:

   a) someone with light skin who moves from a northern area to the equator

   b) someone with dark skin who moves from the equator to a northern area.

## What happens in the struggle for existence?

Organisms live in crowded communities. Even in a desert, where there seem to be large gaps between the plants, roots are growing everywhere in the soil. In a forest, every suitable tree-hole is likely to contain a nesting bird during the breeding season. Predators that are few in number in a community are probably each defending a territory and all available territories are occupied.

The reason for this crowding is overproduction of offspring. Any population that is thriving will tend to produce more offspring than needed just to replace individuals that grow old and die. If every individual survives and grows to reproductive age, the numbers in a population rise faster and faster. This is called an exponential increase.

The resources available to the population don't usually increase. For plants, there are limited amounts of light, water and minerals. For animals, there are limited amounts of food and space for breeding. As a result, most organisms have to compete for resources. Survival is unlikely for the individuals that get least resources.

▲ An Icelandic boy with a black and white lamb (latitude 65°N)

◀ These are seedlings of Himalayan balsam (*Impatiens glandulifera*) that have germinated on a river bank in spring. This plant grows rapidly to about 2 meters in just a few months, then flowers and disperses its seeds. How many seedlings are visible in the photo? There are only enough resources for one or two of these seedlings to reach flowering size. What will happen to the rest? Which seedlings will be the winners?

Competition is not the only hazard of living in a community. Most organisms are in danger of being eaten by another organism. To survive, an organism needs to prevent this from happening. Prey must evade their predators and plants must deter the herbivores that might eat them.

▶ This green spiny organism is a larva of the thistle tortoise beetle (*Cassida rubiginosa*). It is camouflaged against the spiny leaves of its food plant. When its sensitive spines are touched, the larva quickly presses itself against the leaf. The larva carries a lump of feces on its back. What are the advantages of these behaviors?

The abiotic environment can also threaten survival—droughts, fires, floods and storms can all kill, especially if an organism is not well-adapted to survive such events.

▶ A forest fire in 2003 killed some trees in Pusch Ridge Wilderness, Arizona. In 2010, this was followed by heavy snowfall and winter storms, which felled many trees. The survivors of these natural disasters should have plenty of resources available to them to reproduce, and therefore pass on their genes

Charles Darwin referred to the challenges of life as the "struggle for existence". In this struggle there are two rewards for winners— they survive and they have a chance of reproducing.

Even at this stage though there are still challenges. In animals, reproduction depends on the success of mate selection. In plants, it depends on getting gametes from one plant to another.

Who will the winners be? There is an element of chance, but survival also depends on being well-adapted. The best-adapted individuals tend to survive, find a mate, reproduce and pass on their genes. The less well-adapted usually fail to do these things. This difference, based on adaptation, is called **natural selection**.

### ATL Affective skills

## Analyzing and attributing causes of failure

During research projects there are often setbacks and failures. We have to bounce back by finding the reasons for failure and overcoming them. If we succeed, we are showing resilience.

An example of this happened during research into the evolution of the peppered moth. A junior researcher was having no success at finding specimens of this moth at night in a forest where it was known to live. He was using a male moth to try to attract females. The researcher considered many possible reasons for failure, but rejected them all. It was only when a supervisor came with him that the real reason was found—the researcher was applying midge-repellent to his face and hands before entering the forest and this was repelling the moths along with the midges!

Have you ever experienced failures when you tried to do something? Were you able to practice resilience, i.e. step back, analyze the reasons for this failure and then find ways of overcoming them?
Share your experiences with others in the class.

## What features can natural selection change?

Natural selection can change any feature, as long as it is **heritable**. This includes features as small as the structure of an enzyme, up to patterns of behavior in animals. The photos on page 178 show recent cases where it is evident that natural selection causes change. The environment changed in each case and natural selection then favoured different features, causing the population to adapt to the new conditions.

In each of these examples, the changes were relatively small and they happened over just a few years. With a longer time period, natural selection can cause more significant changes, but only if these three conditions are met:

- There is **variation** in the population.

- The variation is at least partly heritable.

- Better-adapted individuals produce more offspring than others in the population.

**ABC** **Natural selection** happens when the best adapted individuals in a species survive and reproduce, passing on genes to their offspring.

Characteristics that can be passed from parents to offspring are **heritable**.

**Variation** is the range of differences between members of a species.

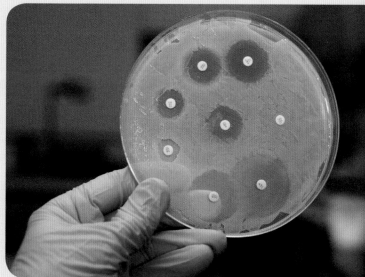

▲ The peppered moth (*Biston betularia*) is easily seen on this twig but is well camouflaged on branches covered in lichens, especially birches. During the 19th century, air in parts of Britain became very polluted, killing lichens and covering trees in dark soot. Natural selection then favoured a form of moth that had all-brown wings (melanic), rather than white wings with brown peppering. Over a few decades populations in polluted areas changed until the melanic form was dominant and the peppered form was very scarce. After pollution control measures in the 1950s, the air became cleaner and natural selection caused the peppered form to become dominant again and the melanic form to be suppressed.

How did natural selection, through the actions of predators, cause these changes?

▲ On this plate there is a thin layer of gel mixed with one strain of bacteria. Discs containing different antibiotics have been placed on the gel. A clear area around a disc indicates that an antibiotic has killed the bacteria. The bacteria must be resistant to one of the antibiotics because they have grown right up to the disc. Within a few years of the introduction of an antibiotic to control a bacterial disease, the percentage of bacteria that are resistant to it starts to increase.

How does natural selection cause this?

▶ The medium ground finch (*Geospiza fortis*) has been studied for many years on Daphne Major, one of the smallest of the Galápagos Islands. It feeds on seeds. After a severe drought in 1977, there were fewer small soft seeds on which this finch usually feeds, and more large hard seeds that are produced by drought-tolerant plants. After the drought, average beak size of the finches was found to have increased.

How does natural selection cause beak size to change?

The changes caused by natural selection are called evolution. It may seem hard to believe that structures as complex as the human eye, or the flower of a wild orchid are the product of evolution, but scientists do not base their ideas on beliefs. They look instead for evidence. There is powerful evidence for the evolution of life on Earth and for natural selection as the mechanism that causes it. In fact, it is reasonable to assume that all life on Earth is the product of natural selection, acting relentlessly, over vast periods of time.

## What can we learn about evolution from anatomy?

Anatomists study the structure of living organisms. There are some surprising similarities in the **anatomy** of organisms, for example in the pattern of bones in vertebrate limbs and in the development of vertebrate embryos.

Vertebrates with limbs are called tetrapods, which means having four limbs. The main groups are amphibia, reptiles, birds and mammals. Tetrapods use their limbs in many different ways, yet they all have the same general pattern of bones. This similarity seemed odd when Richard Owen (a 19th century biologist) first discovered it.

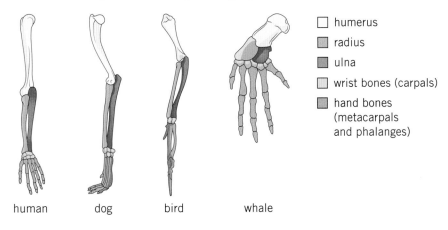

humerus
radius
ulna
wrist bones (carpals)
hand bones (metacarpals and phalanges)

human    dog    bird    whale

1.  Which tetrapods use their forelimbs in these ways: walking, running, digging, climbing, gliding, flying, swimming?

2.  Can you think of any other uses of tetrapod forelimbs?

3.  Use the images to deduce the general pattern of limb bones in tetrapods.

4.  The photograph on the right shows the first discovery of the long hind leg of the dinosaur *Diplodocus*, by Henry Fairfield Osborn in 1898. Did *Diplodocus* have the same general bone structure as modern vertebrate tetrapods?

5.  What would have been surprising to Richard Owen about tetrapod forelimbs all having the same general bone structure?

When Darwin published the *Origin of Species* in 1859, he gave us a very plausible explanation. All tetrapods are descended from one ancestral species, so they have all inherited the pattern of limb bones of that species. In some species the use of the limb changed and the bones became adapted to a new use. Particular bones changed in size or shape, or in some cases were lost, but the general pattern of bones remained unchanged.

6. Discuss whether evolution by natural selection, or design offers a more convincing explanation of similarities in the bone structure of tetrapod limbs.

## What can we learn about evolution from DNA?

It is now relatively quick and easy to discover the base sequence of a gene, or even of an organism's entire genome. Ever-increasing numbers of base sequences from many different species are available to researchers in open access international databases. Base sequence data provides very powerful evidence for evolution and helps to reveal the evolutionary history of groups of organisms. Here are some of the key findings from such research:

- Organisms that are in the same species have genes with very similar base sequences.

- Organisms that are in different species have far more differences in their genes.

- The more closely related two individuals are, the fewer differences in the base sequence of their DNA.

- Differences in the base sequence of DNA accumulate over time, so are used to estimate how long it is since two species diverged from a common ancestor.

- Computer analysis of base sequences can generate "tree of life" diagrams which show the likeliest evolutionary history of a group of organisms.

- All organisms can be traced back to a universal common ancestor, about 4 billion years ago.

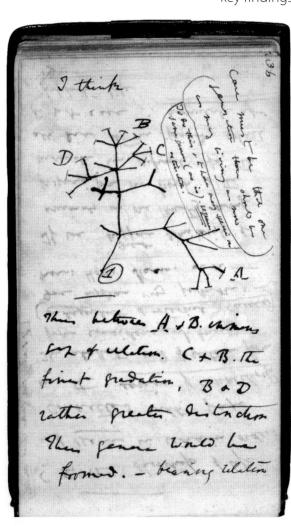

◀ This is a page from one of Charles Darwin's notebooks, dating from 1837. The tree diagram shows that he was thinking that species can split by evolution to form new species

# Evolution of canids

Evidence from DNA was used to produce this tree diagram of canids (species closely related to dogs). Divergence time in millions of years (Myr) is shown at three points on the diagram.

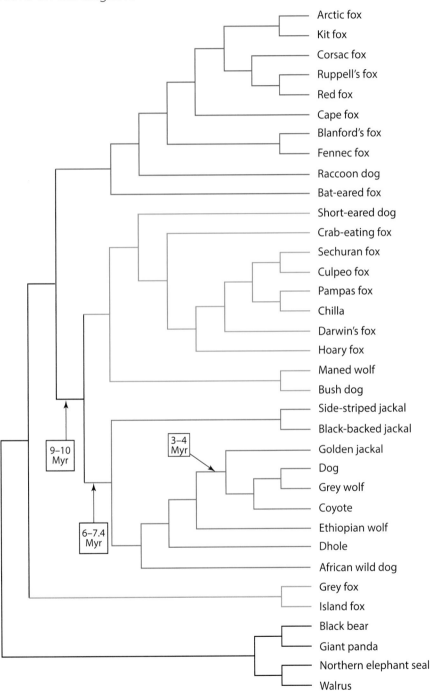

Use the diagram to answer these questions.

1. To which species is the dog most closely related?

2. Is a maned wolf more closely related to a golden jackal or a bat-eared fox?

3. How long ago did a dhole and a chilla have a common ancestor?

4. How closely related are the three species of jackal?

## What can we learn about evolution from embryos?

Fish, amphibians, reptiles, birds and mammals live in a wide range of environments and their anatomy varies greatly when fully formed. We might expect them to show different embryonic development, but instead there are strong similarities. All vertebrate embryos go through the same early stages in their development. For example, a human embryo develops a tail, like all vertebrate embryos. It also develops gill slits which continue to develop in fish. Both of these features disappear in later stages of human embryonic development.

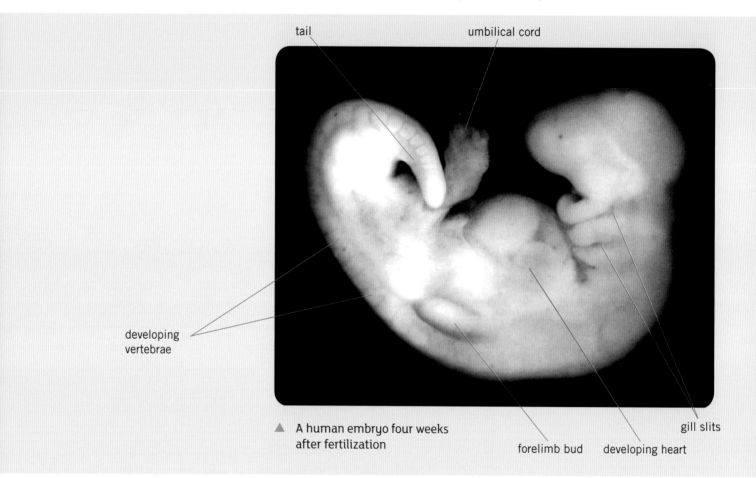

tail          umbilical cord

developing vertebrae

gill slits

forelimb bud     developing heart

▲ A human embryo four weeks after fertilization

Patterns of development in vertebrate embryos are controlled by genes—they are heritable traits. The remarkable similarities in development are explained by all vertebrates having genes inherited from a shared ancestor. The differences between vertebrates are due to evolution from that ancestor along different lines.

1. Can you explain features of human embryos, such as the tail and gill slits, in any way that does not involve evolution?

2. There are structures in a fully-formed human that do not seem to have a purpose such as the appendix and the coccyx. What are the reasons for them?

# What can we learn about evolution from fossils?

Fossils are the traces in rocks of organisms that lived on Earth in the past. They tell us about the structure of these organisms. In the best-preserved fossils, it is even possible to see what the soft internal parts were like.

Fossils occur in sedimentary rocks, which are laid down in a series of layers (strata), one on top of another. Geologists have built up a very accurate sequence of these rock strata, so they can place fossils in chronological order according to the strata in which they are found. This is called the fossil record.

Most recently, techniques have been developed to date rocks using radioactive isotopes. It is therefore possible to deduce when a fossilized organism was living on Earth. The time scale is in millions of years before the present (BP). From these dates we can work out when groups of organisms first appeared on Earth and, in the case of extinct groups such as trilobites, when they disappeared.

The evidence from fossils to support evolution can be summarized using a series of general observations:

- Organisms that lived in the past were different from organisms alive today, so there has been change.

- Sequences of fossils show progressive change over time, including gradual transformations from one life form to another.

- There is an increase in the complexity and diversity of organisms from the oldest to the youngest rocks that matches how we would expect life to have evolved.

- Some major groups of organisms have disappeared permanently from the fossil record.

1. What is the earliest evidence for these groups in the fossil record?

    a) eukaryotes—organisms whose cells have a nucleus

    b) vertebrates—animals with backbones

    c) vertebrates with legs

    d) hominids—the group of primates that only includes chimpanzees, gorillas, orangutan and humans

2. Are there any fossil-bearing rocks in the area where you live? What age are the rocks and what types of fossil have been found?

3. What evolutionary changes were needed for:

    a) fish to evolve into amphibians so that they could live on land;

    b) reptiles with legs to evolve into snakes;

    c) mammals living on land to evolve into whales living in water?

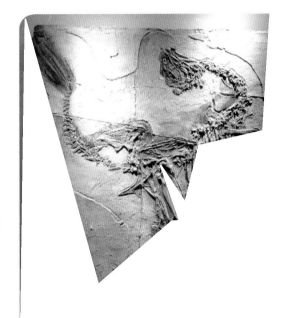

▲ Oviraptosaurs were flightless dinosaurs but they had feathered wing-like forelimbs and a feathered tail. The fossil seen here is *Caudipteryx zoui* and was found in early Cretaceous rocks at Liaoning in China. Imprints of the feathers appear black. Recent modeling experiments show that these feathers could have generated lift and increased running speed. They show that feathers and wing-like forelimbs evolved before true flight

4. For one of the transformations in question 3, or another transformation that interests you, find out what the fossil record tells us about how this change occurred.

## What causes a species to become extinct?

Every species depends on its environment and is adapted to it. On Earth, there are often changes in the environment. For example, there can be changes in sea level, temperature or amount of rainfall. There can also be changes in which other species live in the community and therefore in the predators, competitors or prey of a species.

When changes happen, there are several possible outcomes:

- Migration—move to a new location where the environment matches the adaptations of the species.

- Evolution—become adapted to the new environment.

- Extinction—disappear because the population fails to survive and reproduce.

◀ *Megatherium americanum* (giant ground sloth) of Central and South America had a body mass of up to 4 tonnes—extinction 10,500 years BP

A species that dies out in an area is locally extinct. As a result of local extinctions, a species that was once widespread may become restricted to fewer and fewer areas. If the last population dies, that species is extinct globally. Many species of plants and animals that once lived on Earth are no longer found anywhere, and are therefore extinct.

Fossil records tell us that very large numbers of species have died out during five brief periods in the Earth's history. These are called mass extinction events. In each case there was a major change to environments on Earth. One of the five mass extinctions was caused by an asteroid impact, but the other four were most likely due major changes in the volume of carbon dioxide or oxygen in the Earth's atmosphere.

We are currently living through the 6th mass extinction event. It started thousands of years ago, but has accelerated in recent decades. Currently species are becoming extinct at a faster rate than ever before in the history of our planet. What is the cause of this? What should we be doing about it?

◀ *Pongo abelii* (Sumatran orangutan) from rainforests on the island of Sumatra has a body mass of up to 80 kg— reduced to fewer than 7,000 individuals and now critically endangered

◀ *Mammuthus primigenius* (woolly mammoth) of tundra steppes in the Northern Hemisphere had a body mass of up to 6 tonnes—extinction 4,000 years BP

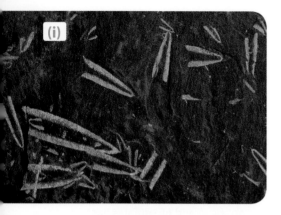

(i)

(ii)

(iii)

1. Photos (i) to (iv) on this page show fossils of four animal groups that are now entirely extinct:

   - **Ammonites:** a group of molluscs, related to octopus and squid
   - **Graptolites:** a group of colonial animals related to acorn worms
   - **Non-avian dinosaurs:** dinosaurs other than those that evolved into birds
   - **Trilobites:** a group of arthropods, related to sea spiders and horseshoe crabs.

   a) Match the description of each animal group above to the photos.

   b) Find out when each of the four groups of animals became extinct. Try to answer this question both in millions of years and according to geological periods.

2. When did these species become extinct and what were the causes?

   a) American mastodon (*Mammut americanum*)

   b) dodo (*Raphus cucullatus*)

   c) Carolina parakeet (*Conuropsis carolinensis*)

3. a) There are plans to carry out de-extinction of woolly mammoths and some other recently extinct species. What is de-extinction and how could it be done?

   b) What are the arguments for and against de-extinction?

4. Of all the species that have ever lived on Earth, are more species extinct or more alive today?

5. a) How are humans causing the 6th mass extinction event?

   b) What should we be doing to try to prevent it?

(iv)

# Summative assessment

## Understanding evolution

**1.** What causes evolution?

   **A.** Mutation

   **B.** Natural selection

   **C.** Overproduction of offspring

   **D.** People

**2.** When is evolution fastest?

   **A.** When a species is trying to adapt.

   **B.** When a species is in danger of extinction.

   **C.** When the fittest individuals survive.

   **D.** When the environment has changed.

**3.** Which species are currently evolving?

   **A.** No species

   **B.** Only humans

   **C.** All species apart from humans

   **D.** All species

**4.** What is the best description of evolution?

   **A.** Evolution happens by chance.

   **B.** Evolution happens because organisms are trying to improve themselves.

   **C.** Evolution happens in small steps that lead towards fully-formed organisms.

   **D.** Evolution makes organisms better adapted.

**5.** What is the quickest that evolution can happen?

   **A.** During a single lifespan

   **B.** Between one generation and the next

   **C.** Over a few hundred years

   **D.** Over millions of years

**6.** Which are the fittest organisms in a population, according to Darwin's definition?

   **A.** Those that are largest

   **B.** Those that are healthiest

   **C.** The best looking

   **D.** The best adapted

**7.** What is required for natural selection to change a population?

   **I** heritable variation

   **II** competition due to overproduction of offspring

   **III** differences in reproductive success between individuals

   **A.** I and II only

   **B.** II and III only

   **C.** I and III only

   **D.** I, II and III

**8.** Which traits of an organism are adaptations?

   **A.** Traits that have changed during the lifetime of the organism.

   **B.** All the heritable traits of an organism.

   **C.** Heritable traits that make an organism suited to its environment.

   **D.** Traits that can be changed by the environment.

Questions 9–10 refer to this evolutionary tree.

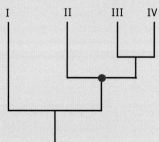

**9.** What does the red node represent?

   **A.** The time when I split from the other groups.

   **B.** The stage when II split from the other groups.

   **C.** The shared ancestor of II, III and IV.

   **D.** The time when half the evolution has happened.

**10.** What conclusion can be drawn?

   **A.** I is more closely related to II than to III and IV.

   **B.** II is more closely related to III than to IV.

   **C.** III is as closely related to I as to II.

   **D.** IV is more closely related to II than to I.

 **Spaghetti worms**

**11.** Model worms can be made by cooking spaghetti with food dye added to the water and then cutting the cooked spaghetti into 50 mm lengths. Single food dyes can be used to get pure colors such as green. Alternatively, dyes can be mixed, for example, mix red and black to make brown.

If placed on a bird table or other bird-only feeding area, local species of bird should feed on the spaghetti worms. If there are no birds to feed on the worms, you could use students to search for them in an area where you have distributed them.

**a)** Design a simulation of natural selection using spaghetti worms. Explain these aspects of your design:

   • the numbers and colors of spaghetti worm you will use as a first generation

   • where you will put the first generation of spaghetti worms and what the environment around them will be, including its color

   • how you will ensure that your simulation is a fair test

   • how you will assess the feeding of birds on the first generation of spaghetti worms

   • how you will simulate reproduction of the worms that are not eaten and the inheritance of color by the next generation

   • the number of generations of spaghetti worms you will include in your simulation. [8]

**b)** Formulate a hypothesis—a prediction of what you expect to find when you carry out your simulation. [2]

## Tawny owls

Tawny owls (*Strix aluco*) in Finland have either grey or brown plumage. This is a heritable trait that does not change during an owl's lifetime. Large numbers of tawny owls have been captured, marked and released and their survival and reproduction has been monitored since the 1960s. The graphs show the change in the frequency of the brown tawny owl in the population and survival rates according to the depth of snow in winter.

12. a) What is the proportion of brown tawny owls at the start and end of the study period? [2]

  b) Calculate the proportion of grey tawny owls at the start and end of the study period. [2]

13. a) What does the right-hand graph tell us about snow depth and survival of grey and brown tawny owls? [2]

  b) Suggest an explanation for the differences in survival between the two forms of tawny owl. [2]

  c) Suggest an explanation for the change in the proportions of grey and brown tawny owls during the study period.

▲ A tawny owl swoops to catch a mouse

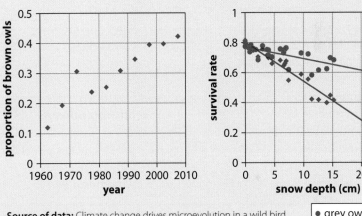

**Source of data:** Climate change drives microevolution in a wild bird, Patrik Karell, Kari Ahola, Teuvo Karstinen, Jari Valkama & Jon E. Brommer, *Nature Communications*, 2011, **2**, 208

● grey owls
◆ brown owls

## Responses to global warming

There is abundant scientific evidence showing that certain human activities cause global warming and other aspects of climate change. Despite this, some people still argue that there is no need for us to change our activities. For example, in 2018 Australian environment minister Melissa Price stated that it would be "irresponsible" to commit to phasing out coal burning.

One argument that some have put forward is that, in the event of a change caused by global warming, all species in natural ecosystems will be able to evolve the traits needed to survive.

14. Use scientific knowledge and understanding to explain:

  a) how natural selection could make a species adapt to warmer temperatures [4]

  b) reasons for doubting whether all species will successfully adapt if temperatures on Earth continue to rise rapidly [3]

  c) reasons for concern that changes to the Earth's atmosphere could lead to a mass extinction event. [3].

# Index

Index headings in **bold** indicate key terms; page numbers in *italics* indicate illustrations/caption text.